PEIRCE ON REALISM AND IDEALISM

This book offers a new interpretation of the metaphysics of Charles Peirce (1839–1914), the founder of pragmatism and one of America's greatest philosophers. Robert Lane begins by examining Peirce's basic realism, his belief in a world that is independent of how anyone believes it to be. Lane argues that this realism is the basis for Peirce's account of truth, according to which a true belief is one that would be settled by investigation and that also represents the real world. He then explores Peirce's application of his pragmatic maxim to clarify the idea of reality, his two forms of idealism, and his realism about generality and vagueness. This rich study will provide readers with a clear understanding of Peirce's thoughts on reality and truth and how they intersect, and of his views on the relation between the mind and the external world.

ROBERT LANE is Professor of Philosophy at the University of West Georgia. He is the editor of Peirce submissions for the *Transactions of the Charles S. Peirce Society* and has published numerous essays on Peirce.

T0384576

PEIRCE ON REALISM AND IDEALISM

ROBERT LANE

University of West Georgia

CAMBRIDGE
UNIVERSITY PRESS

CAMBRIDGE
UNIVERSITY PRESS

University Printing House, Cambridge CB2 8BS, United Kingdom

One Liberty Plaza, 20th Floor, New York, NY 10006, USA

477 Williamstown Road, Port Melbourne, VIC 3207, Australia

314–321, 3rd Floor, Plot 3, Splendor Forum, Jasola District Centre,
New Delhi – 110025, India

79 Anson Road, #06–04/06, Singapore 079906

Cambridge University Press is part of the University of Cambridge.

It furthers the University's mission by disseminating knowledge in the pursuit of
education, learning, and research at the highest international levels of excellence.

www.cambridge.org
Information on this title: www.cambridge.org/9781108415224
DOI: 10.1017/9781108231657

First published 2018

A catalogue record for this publication is available from the British Library.

ISBN 978-1-108-41522-4 Hardback

For

M.D. – borders, always.

Contents

Acknowledgments   *page* viii
List of Abbreviations   ix

Introduction: Basic Realism   1

1   The Dual-Aspect Account of Truth   13

2   The Pragmatic Clarification of the Idea of Reality   38

3   Basic Idealism and Objective Idealism   59

4   The Idealistic Theory of Reality: Idealism in the
    Cognition Series   84

5   Generals: Early Scholastic Realism   106

6   Generals and Vagues: Late Scholastic Realism   137

7   "A Lacuna in the Completeness of Reality": Deficit
    Indeterminacy   165

Bibliography   195
Index   201

vii

Acknowledgments

I have greatly benefited from discussions of Peirce's philosophy with many friends and colleagues, including Richard Atkins, Cornelis de Waal, Shannon Dea, Diana Heney, Christopher Hookway, Andrew Howat, Catherine Legg, Rosa Mayorga, Cheryl Misak, Matthew Moore, and Tom Short. My special thanks to Tom Short for extensive and extremely helpful comments on drafts of every chapter. Thanks also to Cornelis de Waal for assistance in dating several manuscripts, Diana Heney for comments on the introduction, Andrew Howat for comments on Chapters 1 and 2, and two anonymous reviewers for the Press for helpful criticisms and suggestions. Thanks to Hilary Gaskin for crucial advice about how to structure this book and for thinking it was a project worth pursuing in the first place. This is a better book because of all of you. Thanks especially to Susan Haack, who ignited my interest in Peirce and from whom I learned how to be a scholar and a philosopher (and to *always* double-check quotations!). I am grateful to the University of West Georgia College of Arts and Humanities and the Department of English and Philosophy for allowing me the research leave to complete several chapters. Finally, thanks to Murphy (now departed and sorely missed) and Milo, who both kept me company and demonstrated immeasurable patience – not to mention a fair amount of snoring and flatulence – while I worked on this book when I could have been taking them for longer walks, giving them belly rubs, or playing tug-of-war.

Abbreviations

Collected Papers of Charles Sanders Peirce, 8 vols. C. Hartshorne, P. Weiss, and A. Burks, eds. Cambridge, MA: Belknap Press of Harvard University Press, 1931–1960. References are in decimal notation by volume and paragraph number.Citations of other collections of Peirce's work employ the abbreviations shown here.

CD Peirce's contributions to *The Century Dictionary: An Encyclopedic Lexicon of the English Language.* W. D. Whitney, ed. New York: The Century Co., 1889–1891.

CN *Contributions to* The Nation, 4 vols. K. Ketner and J. Cook, eds. Lubbock: Texas Tech Press, 1975–1987. References are by volume and page number.

EP *The Essential Peirce: Selected Philosophical Writings,* 2 vols. N. Houser, C. Kloesel, and the Peirce Edition Project, eds. Bloomington: Indiana University Press, 1992–1998. References are by volume and page number.

HP *Historical Perspectives on Peirce's Philosophy of Science,* 2 vols. C. Eisele, ed. New York: Mouton, 1985. References are by volume and page number.

ILS *Illustrations of the Logic of Science.* C. de Waal, ed. Chicago: Open Court, 2014.

LI *The Logic of Interdisciplinarity: The Monist Series.* E. Bisanz, ed. Berlin and Boston: Walter de Gruyter, 2009.

NEM *The New Elements of Mathematics,* 4 vols. C. Eisele, ed. Atlantic Highlands, NJ: Humanities Press, 1976. References are by volume and page number.

PM *Philosophy of Mathematics: Selected Writings.* M. Moore, ed. Bloomington and Indianapolis: Indiana University Press, 2010.

R Peirce's manuscripts in the Houghton Library of Harvard University, as cataloged in Robin 1967 and 1971. These manuscripts are available in a microfilm edition, *The Charles S. Peirce Papers*, produced by Harvard University Library. References are by Robin's manuscript number and, when available, page number.

RLT   *Reasoning and the Logic of Things: The Cambridge Conferences Lectures of 1898.* K. Ketner, ed. Cambridge, MA: Harvard University Press, 1992.

SS   *Semiotics and Significs: The Correspondence between Charles S. Peirce and Victoria Lady Welby.* C. Hardwick, ed. Bloomington: Indiana University Press, 1977.

W   *Writings of Charles S. Peirce: A Chronological Edition*, 7 vols. M. Fisch, C. Kloesel, E. Moore et al., eds. Bloomington: Indiana University Press, 1982–. References are by volume and page number.

Frequently cited articles and manuscripts by Peirce are referenced as follows.

AT   "The Architecture of Theories" (1891)
DC   "Design and Chance" (1883–1884)
FOB   "The Fixation of Belief" (1877)
GAR   "A Guess at the Riddle" (1887–1888)
GVLL   "Grounds of Validity of the Laws of Logic" (1869)
HTM   "How to Make Our Ideas Clear" (1878)
IP   "Issues of Pragmaticism" (1905)
LM   "The Law of Mind" (1892)
LOR   "The Logic of Relatives" (1897)
MAN   "Multitude and Number" (R 25, 1897)
MGE   "Man's Glassy Essence" (1892)
OQ   "On Quantity" (R 14, 1896)
QCCF   "Questions Concerning Certain Faculties Claimed for Man" (1868)
RL   "The Regenerated Logic" (1896)
RR   Review of Josiah Royce, *The Religious Aspect of Philosophy* (1885)
SCFI   "Some Consequences of Four Incapacities" (1868)
WPI   "What Pragmatism Is" (1905)

Introduction: Basic Realism

According to Charles Peirce, "[t]he word 'reality' . . . is one of the words of whose meaning it is indispensible [*sic*] to have a perfectly distinct apprehension before drawing any conclusion, or forming any opinion, upon almost any philosophical subject" (R 852: 3 of alternative run of pages, 1911). Most philosophers have not realized this. Although many use the word "reality" and describe things as "real," they rarely stop to say how they understand those words to be defined. The phrase "independent of the mind" might initially appear to be a promising definition, and it seems to be the one that Michael Loux assumes in his statement of realism: "the world is a mind-independent structure: it consists of objects whose existence, character and relations are fixed independently of what we happen to say, believe, or desire" (2001: 49). But if the real is exactly that which is independent of minds, then minds themselves are not real. Realists about the mind would rightly object that defining "real" in this way begs the question against their view. A definition of "real" as "independent of us" or "independent of humans" would be even more problematic, since a realism that assumed that sort of definition would imply that not just minds, but also artifacts, things made by humans and thus not independent of us, are not real.

Happily, Peirce stated and relied upon explicit definitions of "real" and a number of related terms, and in so doing he avoided some of the problems that characterize the views of more recent thinkers, including the problem of inadvertent anti-realism about minds. According to Peirce's definition of "real," something is real exactly when it has the properties it has whether or not anyone believes that it has them or otherwise represents it as having them. The earth is real, since its properties, like being a certain size and traveling around the sun at a certain speed, do not depend on anyone thinking that it has them. The earth really does orbit the sun, since it does so whether or not anyone believes that it does. My dog is real, since he weighs seventy-five pounds whether or not I choose to believe what the veterinarian tells me. Peirce's earliest statement of his definition may have been in a lecture from 1867: "It is important to observe that the essential difference between a reality and a nonreality, is that the former has an existence entirely independent of what you or I or any number of men may think about it" (W 2: 104). He restated the definition repeatedly, in works published during his lifetime, e.g., "How to Make Our Ideas Clear" – "we may define the real as that whose characters are independent of what anybody may think them to be" (5.405, W 3: 271, 1878) – and in manuscripts that remain unpublished, e.g., "*being such as it is, no matter how you, or, I, or any man or definite collection of men may think it to be*" (R 681: 35, 1913). At one time he credited Duns Scotus with the "invention [of] the word *reality*" (4.28, 1893), but later he took a different view:

> The word "reality" . . . is used in ordinary parlance in its correct philosophical sense. It is curious that its legal meaning, in which we speak of "real estate," is the earliest, occurring early in the twelfth century. Albertus Magnus, who, as a high ecclesiastic, must have had to do with such matters, imported it into philosophy. But it did not become at all common until Duns Scotus, in the latter part of the thirteenth century[,] began to use it freely. (6.495, ca. 1906)[1]

A central thesis of this book is that Peirce held there to be real things and thus that he believed in a real world, a world that is the way it is regardless of whether you, or I, or anyone else believes that it is that way. I will call Peirce's view that there is a real world his *basic realism*. Christopher Hookway (2012: 65–66) uses the phrase "basic realism" in his discussion of Peirce's views about truth and reality, but he does not seem to mean by it quite what I do. The basic realism he describes "leaves open most of the different options that have been discussed by philosophers who have debated realism about mathematical objects, external things, values, causation, and the like," and this much it has in common with the view that I attribute to Peirce. But Hookway also suggests that "we can think of basic realism as a sort of logical doctrine rather than a metaphysical one." The view that I am attributing to Peirce is straightforwardly metaphysical: it is the idea that there are things that have the traits they do whether or not

---

[1] In R 200 (1908), portions of which are found in the *Collected Papers*, Peirce wrote: "Except in the legal sense, the vernacular word was derived from *realis*, which (except in the legal sense) was a vocable invented by medieval metaphysicians for their own purposes. Especially, it is a prominent word in the works of Duns Scotus, of which I have been an attentive and meditative student" (6.328). For other accounts of the history of "real" and its cognates, see R 641: 7–9, 1909; R 642: 9–12, 1909; R 659: 35, 1910; R 852: 8–9, 1911; R 681: 33–34, 1913; R 930: 22–23, late.

anyone thinks they have them or otherwise represents them as having them.[2]

Peirce contrasted real things with *figments*, the *fictional*, or, as he sometimes wrote, the *fictive*. Something is a figment exactly when it has the properties it has only because someone thinks of it as having those properties or otherwise represents it as having those properties. "A fiction is something whose character depends on what some mind imagines it to be" (W 3: 49, 1872); "[a] figment is a product of somebody's imagination; it has such characters as his thought impresses upon it" (5.405, W 3: 271, 1878). Atticus Finch is fictional, since being a lawyer, living in Alabama, being the father of Scout and Jem, etc. are properties that he has only because Harper Lee imagined him to have them in the course of writing *To Kill a Mockingbird*. But it is a real fact about Lee that she imagined Atticus Finch as having those properties; her having done so does not depend on whether anyone believes that she did. To say that something is a figment does not "in the least imply[] that it has been intentionally made up or knowingly fabricated" (R 683: 33, ca. 1913); someone might sincerely believe that there is a monster under the bed when there really isn't. Peirce's definitions imply that both the real and the fictional have properties: nothing is real that does not possess traits, and no fictional thing can be imagined without being imagined to be some way or other.

Peirce also distinguished between that which is independent of what anyone thinks *about it* – the real – and that which is independent of what anyone thinks *about anything at all*. The latter is, in his terminology, the *external*, that which is external to the mind (i.e., not within my mind or your mind or anyone else's mind) and so upon which "thinking has no effect" (5.384, W 3: 253, 1877). "That is external to the mind, which is what it is, whatever our thoughts may be on any subject" (7.339, W 3: 29, 1872). The earth is, in addition to being real, external, since it has the traits it has regardless of what anyone thinks, either about it or about anything else whatsoever. Peirce's distinction between the real and the external is crucial for a correct understanding of his views, but unfortunately even scholars of his work are sometimes not careful to keep them distinct. For example, after noting Peirce's

---

[2] Almeder (1980) attributes to Peirce what he calls "epistemological realism," by which he seems to mean the view that there is a world of external objects of which we are capable of having knowledge. As we will see, what I call Peirce's basic realism is consistent with the belief in both real external and real internal things and events. The question whether we can represent and thereby have knowledge of real things is covered by Peirce's pragmatic clarification of the idea of reality, on which see Chapter 2. T. L. Short rightly suggests that it would be a mistake to use "scientific realism" as the name of what I am calling Peirce's basic realism and prefers instead simply "realism" (2007a: 199).

verbal definition of "real," Hookway parses that definition as "independence of thought" and "independent of what any individual thinks" (2000: 46–47), which is what Peirce meant by "external." He then uses "mind-independent" in a way that leaves unclear whether he means the real or the external (ibid.: 76–79). In considering the sense in which truth might be "objective" on Peirce's account, Cheryl Misak correctly attributes to him the view that "believing a hypothesis to be true does not make it true," which implies that what the hypothesis says is either really true or really false. But she then restates this "objectivity requirement" as "whether a thing is real cannot be a matter of what someone thinks," thus inadvertently limiting the real to the external (1991/2004: 130), and she subsequently misstates his definition of "real" as "that which is independent of whatever 'you, I, or any number of men' think" rather than as what is independent of what anyone thinks about it (ibid.: 131).

On Peirce's view, the real is not exhausted by the external. Some real things are *internal*, items within, states of, or facts about the mind of someone or other. "Thus an emotion of the mind is real, in the sense that it exists in the[t] mind whether we are distinctly conscious of it or not. But it is not external because[,] although it does not depend upon what we think about it, it does depend upon the state of our thoughts" – that is, the state of *someone's* thoughts – "about something" (7.339, W 3: 29–30, 1872).[3] Whether I am angry at a given time depends on the state of my mind at that time, since being angry is, at least in part, a matter of one's mind being in a specific state. But whether I am angry does not depend on whether I or anyone else *believes* that I am angry, and as Peirce noted, anger can "exist[] in the mind," even if the angry person is not fully aware, and thus does not believe, that she is angry.[4]

---

[3] Here "exists in the mind" means "is in the mind." Peirce eventually began to use "exist" and its cognates to express a more specific idea, one that I will address in Chapter 5. On one occasion, he contrasted the external with the mental, implying that the mental is coextensive with the internal (6.327, 1908). He wrote several definitions of "external" for the *Century Dictionary*, one of which includes the following: "in *metaph.*, forming part of or pertaining to the world of things or phenomena in space, considered as outside of the perceiving mind" (CD 2094). And of the several definitions of "internal" he provided, one reads: "Inner; pertaining to the mind, or to the relations of the mind to itself. [In this sense the word *interior* is preferable]" (CD 3149). For other examples of Peirce's use of the external/internal distinction, see 5.405, W 3: 271, 1878; 4.157, ca. 1897; 5.45, EP 2: 151, 1903; 8.284, 1904; 5.474, 1907; 5.487, EP 2: 412–413, 1907; 5.493, 1907; 1.321, ca. 1910. Peirce used "internal world" and "external world" frequently, both early (e.g., 5.244, W 2: 206, 1868; 5.265–266, W 2: 213, 1868) and late (e.g., 1.37, W 8: 78, ca. 1890; 8.144, EP 2:62, 1901; 7.369, 1902; 5.539, ca. 1902; 6.96, 1903; 8.284, 1904; 1.321, EP 2: 369, 1905; 6.325, 329, 1908).

[4] Almeder seems to overlook the fact that Peirce recognized both external and internal reals when he writes that "[t]he difference between a fiction and an external fact (real fact) is that the former, and not the latter, is subject to control by our will" (1980: 168). But there are internal facts – facts about

Peirce was also careful to distinguish the real from the *genuine*: "A thing is Genuine or not according as it is or is not of the description it professes or is supposed to have: a false diamond may be genuine paste" (R 642: 14, 1909). Haack calls this the "humdrum" use of "real" (2013: 210, 216).[5] On the other hand, Peirce was not so careful to define two other terms that he sometimes used: "objective" and "subjective." He seems on many occasions to have meant by "subjective" something like "relative or specific to one or more perceivers" and to have meant by "objective" something like "not relative or specific to any perceiver."[6] At one point he followed Kant in taking the "objective validity of a judgment" to mean that "all the world will agree in it" (7.259, R 1123, 1901); but later, after noting that "[i]t is good economy for philosophy to provide itself with a vocabulary so outlandish that loose thinkers shall not be tempted to borrow its words," he wrote that "Kant's adjectives 'objective' and 'subjective' proved not to be barbarous enough, by half, long to retain their usefulness in philosophy, – even if there had been no other objection to them" (2.223, EP 2: 265, 1903).

In light of Peirce's distinctions, we can see that Loux's statement of realism – "the world is a mind-independent structure: it consists of objects whose existence, character and relations are fixed independently of what we happen to say, believe, or desire" – implies that the only reals (to use Peirce's convenient term) are external and thus that minds and mental states are not real. A statement of basic realism that draws upon Peirce's definition of "real" does not beg this question, since it allows for there to be both external and internal reals. It also allows for there to be real artifacts, unlike a realism that assumes the real to be only what is "independent of humans."[7] I am assuming, not that an adequate definition of "real" or an adequate statement of basic realism must imply that minds and artifacts are real, but only that such a definition or statement is faulty if it implies that *no* such things are real. A definition of "real" and a statement of basic realism should be narrowly focused, assuming the answers to as few philosophical questions as possible. Peirce's definition of "real" avoids this kind of error; it does not beg any questions about the reality of human creations, minds, or mental states.

---

the mind of a given person – that are not within the control of that person's will, e.g., whether he is angry at a given time.

[5] For a very different perspective on the word "real," see Austin 1962: 62ff.

[6] For examples, see 2.696, W 4: 410, 1883; 8.61, W 8: 234, 1891; 7.555, EP 2: 22, 1895; 2.153, 156, 1902; 5.86, 1903; 1.590, ca. 1903; 5.467, 1907. At least once he used "objective" as a synonym of "real" (1.16, 1903). On usages of "subjective" to describe a kind of modality, see Chapter 6.

[7] On the superiority of Peirce's definition of "real" to "independent of humans" and "independent of the mind," see Haack 2013: 211–212 and Haack 2016.

Peirce's basic realism also does not beg the question against the kind of *ontological idealism* according to which everything that there is, is mental or is mind. It is not contradictory to say that there are real things – things the traits of which do not depend on what anyone thinks about them – and that all real things are mental, either minds or mental states. A mind *m* can be real so long as its properties do not depend on any mind, including *m* itself, thinking that it has those properties, and there is nothing inconsistent in the view that the only things that are real in that way are minds. My point is not that an adequate definition of "real" or an adequate statement of basic realism must imply ontological idealism; it is that no such definition or statement should decide the question whether this kind of idealism is true. Peirce's basic realism avoids this error as well.

Not everyone is careful to maintain a clear distinction between things that are independent of what anyone thinks and things that are independent of what anyone thinks *about them.* For example, R. J. Hirst writes that:

> [i]n modern philosophy ... ["realism"] is used for the view that material objects exist externally to us and *independently of our sense experience.* Realism is thus opposed to idealism, which holds that no such material objects or external realities exist *apart from our knowledge or consciousness of them,* the whole universe thus being dependent on the mind or in some sense mental. (1967: 77, emphases added)

The first italicized phrase calls to mind Peirce's definition of "external," the second his definition of "real." (Note that as Hirst defines it, realism is a doctrine about only *material* objects, and is thus narrower than Peirce's basic realism.) Michael Devitt provides a characterization of realism that, he says, will be "along [the] lines" of Hirst's (1997: 13), and he then follows Hirst in slipping back and forth, apparently without realizing it, between describing what Peirce called the real and what he called the external:

> Key terms that feature in statements of ... realism are 'independent', 'external', and 'objective'. Hirst uses the first two, and when he says that material objects exist 'apart from our knowledge ... of them', he might just as well have used the third. For an object has objective existence, in some sense, if it exists and has its nature *whatever we believe, think, or can discover:* it is *independent of the cognitive activities of the mind.* (1997: 14–15, emphases added)

The quoted phrase from Hirst comes close to Peirce's definition of "real," while the emphasized phrases pretty well capture what Peirce meant by "external." Drew Khlentzos also slips back and forth between the real and the external:

> According to metaphysical realism, the world is as it is *independently of how humans or other inquiring agents take it to be*. The objects the world contains, together with their properties and the relations they enter into, fix the world's nature and these objects exist independently of our ability to discover they do. Unless this is so, metaphysical realists argue, none of our beliefs about our world could be objectively true since true beliefs tell us how things are and beliefs are objective when true or false *independently of what anyone might think*. (2016, emphases added)

Elsewhere Khlentzos defines "realism" in terms closer to Peirce's: "the thesis that the objects, properties, and relations the world contains exist independently of our *thoughts about them or our perceptions of them*" (2004: 2, emphasis added). But he continues:

> An obvious problem with [this] characterization of realism in terms of mind-independent existence is that it seems to make anti-realism about minds or experience obligatory, for the existence of minds is surely "mind-dependent." To be sure, but *the world's containing minds* is not. This is a mind-independent fact if there are minds at all, according to the metaphysical realist. (2004: 3)

However, his initial, Peircean definition of "realism" does *not* make anti-realism about minds or experience obligatory. That he thinks there is a problem here suggests that he does not recognize the importance of the phrases "about them" and "of them" in that definition and thus of the distinction between the real and the external. This is also suggested by a statement of (metaphysical) realism that Khlentzos gives later in the same work, a statement that lacks the Peircean flavor of his initial statement: "The objects and structures that comprise the furniture of the universe exist mind-independently" (2004: 25).

An understanding of Peirce's basic realism and of precisely how he used the terms "real," "external," and "internal" illuminates a number of other aspects of his philosophy, including his views on truth, his pragmatism, his idealism, and his so-called scholastic realism. The rest of this book proceeds as follows. In Chapter 1, I examine Peirce's account, in 1877's "The Fixation of Belief" (FOB), of the four methods of establishing belief and his view that "the method of science," i.e., investigation, is best at permanently settling beliefs. That material is familiar to Peirce scholars, but my treatment of it is, I hope, both interesting and surprising. I argue that woven into his account of the methods of "fixing" belief is a genealogy of the idea of truth, an account of how our best currently available idea of what it is for a belief to be true has developed from earlier, less adequate ideas. On my reading, that best idea has two aspects. On one hand, it has an *investigative* aspect: a true belief is one that would be permanently settled in the minds of inquirers who use investigation in their attempts to replace doubt with belief. On the other hand, there is a *representation-alist* aspect: a true belief is one that represents reality. What I call the investigative aspect of Peirce's account of truth is popularly known as his pragmatic theory of truth and is typically thought to result from his use of the pragmatic maxim to clarify the idea of truth. But as I will show, Peirce articulated the investigative aspect of his account in FOB, before stating the pragmatic maxim in that article's sequel, "How to Make Our Ideas Clear" (HTM). What he had to say about truth in HTM does not super-sede the staunchly realist account provided in FOB. This chapter con-cludes with an examination of Peirce's statements that seem to connect, or even to identify, the truth of a belief with either its capacity to help the believer achieve her goals or with a kind of psychological satisfaction. Properly understood, those statements turn out to be compatible with his view that true beliefs represent reality.

In Chapter 2, I consider the philosophical work to which Peirce actually did put the pragmatic maxim in HTM. It was to clarify, not the idea of truth, but that of reality: "*The opinion which is fated to be ultimately agreed to by all who investigate, is what we mean by the truth*" – this is the investigative aspect of his account of truth, which he had already estab-lished in FOB – "and the object represented in this opinion is the real" (HTM, 5.407, W 3: 273). Peirce's pragmatic clarification of the idea of reality amounts to this: the real is exactly what is represented in beliefs that would be permanently settled if inquirers were to use investigation in an attempt to settle their beliefs. This clarification relies on the investigative aspect of the account of truth that he had already given in FOB; he did not derive the investigative aspect by way of the pragmatic maxim. After defending this interpretation, I consider whether Peirce's idea of true belief *can* be pragmatically clarified. I conclude that it can, and I argue that, contra Misak, a pragmatic clarification of that idea must presuppose that a true belief represents reality. I then consider Peirce's responses to two objections that he anticipated against his pragmatic clarification of reality. One is that it is inconsistent with his verbal definition of "real"; the other is that it fails to take account of "buried secrets" about the past that are now forever beyond the reach of investigation. I show that in order to defend against these objections, Peirce altered – perhaps unwittingly – the nature of the pragmatic clarifications he had advocated up to that point, and he did so in a way that foreshadowed a major shift in his views about modality that occurred two decades later.

One possible threat to my interpretation of Peirce's views on reality and truth is that, beginning in the 1860s and continuing into the last decade of his life, he described himself as an idealist and defended views that he called "idealism." These views might be thought to be incompatible with the basic realism that I attribute to him. But the doctrines that Peirce called "idealism" are in fact consistent with his basic realism. In Chapter 3, I argue that one of those doctrines was that every aspect of reality is capable of being represented by the cognitive processes of inquirers. I call this view *basic idealism*, and I show not only that it is consistent with both his basic realism and his realism about the external but also that it follows from the pragmatic clarification of the idea of reality that he articulated in HTM. I will also consider his *objective idealism*, which he defended in the "cosmological series" of articles published in *The Monist* in the early 1890s. According to objective idealism, "matter is effete mind, inveterate habits becoming physical laws" (6.25, W 8: 106, 1891). This is a peculiar doctrine, but as I will argue, it, like basic idealism, is consistent with both basic realism and realism about the external. To buttress the arguments of Chapter 3, it is necessary to consider several seemingly anti-realistic claims that Peirce made, most prominently in his so-called cognition series of articles published in 1868–1869, e.g., that "[t]he real ... is that which, sooner or later, information and reasoning would finally result in" (5.311, W 2: 239). This could be read as implying that reality will eventually be brought about by "information and reasoning," that it will be, not discovered, but *created*, by investigation. If this is the case, then, for any *x* and any property *F*, whether *x* is *F* will depend on what is thought about *x* at the end of investigation, and so basic realism is not true. Some scholars have been led by such statements to think that the idealism of Peirce's early works was anti-realistic. But as I argue in Chapter 4, the "idealistic theory of reality" (5.353, W 2: 270, 1869) that he defended in the cognition series is consistent with both basic realism and realism about the external world.

Chapters 5 and 6 employ some of the lessons of earlier chapters to clarify another doctrine familiar to scholars of Peirce's thought, viz. his scholastic realism. This is his realism about what he called *generals*, by which he meant what have more frequently been called *universals*: kinds and laws of which particular things and events are instances. I begin Chapter 5 by explaining the fundamentals of this theory, including the view that generals are external rather than internal to the mind and his view that, although they are real, generals do not "exist," i.e., they cannot respond or react to other things. Peirce defended scholastic realism both early on and later, but those defenses are quite different. Chapter 5 continues with an explanation of the argument for scholastic realism that he gave in the late 1860s and early 1870s. This argument assumes what Peirce, in his 1871 review of Alexander Campbell Fraser's edition of the works of Berkeley, called the *realist conception of reality*: reality is what is represented in a true proposition. This conception anticipated the pragmatic clarification of reality that he would state a few years later in HTM, and, paired with his view that all true propositions contain at least one general sign, it implies that there are real generals. To get clear on just what sense of "general" is relevant to this argument, I explain Peirce's early views on individuality and semiotic indeterminacy. The chapter concludes with an examination of the kinds of abstraction by which we arrive at general concepts. As we will see, the abstractive process by which we first arrive at a general concept need not occur within the natural sciences in order for that concept to represent a real general. Concepts corresponding to real generals can originate within any area of investigation, including the social sciences, history, economics, and philosophy.

The focus of Chapter 6 is Peirce's later scholastic realism. In the 1900s, that theory expanded to become realism about two kinds of indeterminacy: generality and *vagueness*. But by "vague" he did not mean exactly what is exemplified by terms having borderline cases or "fuzzy" boundaries, like "bald" and "heap." On his late view, real vagueness is associated with an "Aristotelian . . . real *possibility*" (R 288: 129, ca. 1905), and real generality is associated with real necessity and lawfulness. After describing his later conceptions of generality and vagueness, I analyze his late argument in support of his revised scholastic realism. As mentioned previously in this introduction, his earlier argument relied on an anticipation of his pragmatic clarification of the idea of reality. His later argument depends on that clarification itself as well as on another aspect of his pragmatism. The pragmatic maxim directs us to clarify a general idea by articulating conditionals that describe the experiential consequences that would follow were we to perform some action involving objects of that idea. Since generals are applicable, not only to actual individual things and events, but also to merely possible things and events, those conditionals must be able to cover merely possible circumstances. And since those conditionals are capable of being true, merely possible circumstances – *vagues* – are real. Following an examination of that argument, I further elucidate his position on modality by describing his transition, in the mid-1890s, from a weak form of modal realism, according to which all senses of the modal terms can be defined in terms of states of information, to a strong form, on which some senses of those terms cannot be defined in that way. Peirce's adoption of a strong modal realism affected his scholastic realism, but not in a straightforward fashion. That change in his views about possibility was intertwined with his changing views on continuity, which, beginning in the early 1890s, he identified with generality. On his eventual view, unactualized possibility of a sort that cannot be explained in epistemic terms is a necessary condition of generality; the reality of generals thus implies the reality of vagues.

In the final chapter, I argue that beginning in the 1880s, Peirce acknowledged a sort of metaphysical indeterminacy different from generality and vagueness: "there is an assumption involved in speaking of *the* actual state of things . . . namely, the assumption that reality is so determinate as to verify or falsify every possible proposition . . . I do not believe it is strictly true" (NEM 3: 759–760). His view was that some propositions about real things are such that neither they nor their denials will ever be permanently believed as a result of investigation and that this implies that there are no real facts for those propositions to represent. He did not name this sort of indeterminacy, but because it amounts to there being deficiencies, gaps, or, as he put it, "*lacuna*[*e*] in the completeness of reality" (8.156, ca. 1900), I call it *deficit indeterminacy*. That there is deficit indeterminacy implies that the principle of bivalence, according to which each proposition is either true or else false, is mistaken: if there is no fact of the matter about whether S is P, then neither "S is P" nor "S is not P" is either true or false. After arguing against Hookway's (2012) view that Peirce distanced his conception of truth from his conception of reality in order to maintain that there are real facts even where there are no truths, I present evidence that from the mid-1880s until the early 1900s Peirce held that where investigation will not lead to a permanently settled belief – i.e., where there is no truth – there is no reality. But as we will see, during this period he also maintained that investigators must continue to hope that any course of inquiry they actually embark upon will eventuate in permanently settled belief. After the early 1900s, Peirce continued to think that there is deficit indeterminacy, but his reason for thinking this changed, and he stopped drawing a connection between deficit indeterminacy and failed investigation. My conjectural explanation for this is that that connection made sense to Peirce only before he came to believe, in 1903, that the pragmatic clarification of the idea of reality must cover what is represented, not just in beliefs actually fixed by investigation, but also what is represented in permanently settled beliefs that inquirers *would* have as a result of investigation. Having gotten clear on Peirce's views regarding deficit indeterminacy and the hope that must guide investigation, I address Misak's views on some of these matters. In particular, I will argue against her view that the hope that, according to Peirce, governs actual cases of inquiry is best expressed as follows: "*if H* is true *then* if inquiry relevant to *H* were pursued as far as it could fruitfully go, *H* would be believed" (1991/2004: 43). Finally, I will consider Peirce's reasons for continuing to believe that there is deficit indeterminacy after he severed its connection with investigative failure. This will involve an examination of the reasons that led him to develop a set of operators for a three-valued system of propositional logic. The motivation for this work was his desire to accommodate within formal logic propositions about merely possible individuals, things that are real but that nonetheless have "a lower mode of being such that [they] can neither be determinately P, nor determinately not-P, but [are] at the limit between P and not P" (R 339: 344 r, 1909).

The Dual-Aspect Account of Truth

1.1

"The Fixation of Belief" (FOB) and "How to Make Our Ideas Clear" (HTM) are the first and second of a series of six articles by Peirce collectively titled *Illustrations of the Logic of Science*, published in *Popular Science Monthly* from 1877 to 1878. In FOB, he described four methods of eliminating doubt and permanently settling or "fixing" belief – the method of tenacity, the method of authority, the a priori method, and the method of science – and he argued that the method of science is more successful than the others in establishing beliefs that will not be uprooted by further inquiry.[1] In this chapter, I show that there is *a genealogy of the idea of truth*, an account of how that idea has developed over the course of human inquiry, intertwined with Peirce's account of the four methods of fixing belief.[2] Each of the four methods is accompanied by an idea that is a forerunner of the eventual idea of truth. As each of the first three methods fails, we learn something new about what a belief must be like in order for it to become fixed, and so the idea that accompanies each method improves upon the one that had accompanied the previous method. The idea that accompanies the fourth method – the idea of a belief that is *true* – is *dual-aspect*: it has a *representationalist* aspect, on which a true belief is one that represents the real world, and an *investigative* aspect, on which a true belief is one that would be permanently settled in the minds of those who use the method of science.

---

[1] As Short notes, Peirce's descriptions of the four methods in FOB "are an ahistorical idealization and are meant to be such" (2007a: 331). In "History of Science," a manuscript of ca. 1896, Peirce said the following about the transition from the method of tenacity to that of authority: "The next step which is to be expected in a logical development not interrupted by accidental occurrences will consist in the recognition that a central authority ought to determine the beliefs of the entire community" (1.60). This suggests that he viewed the progression from one method to another, not as historical, but as, in some sense, logical.

[2] This interpretation of Peirce's account of the four methods, as having embedded within it an account of the development of the idea of truth, is also defended by Haack (1997: 246–248) and Short (2000).

If I am right that there is a representationalist aspect to Peirce's account of truth, then he must have believed that there is an important connection between truth and reality. Some scholars downplay the idea that he saw such a connection. For example, Hookway argues that "the Peircean idea of truth is metaphysically neutral" between realism and anti-realism and that it "does not require a uniform account of the metaphysical character of all truths" and is instead "compatible with being a realist about some truths and an anti-realist about others" (2000: 45, 80).[3] Another example is Misak, who holds that Peirce was "happy to let [some form of correspondence theory] stand as a 'nominal' or 'formal' definition" of truth, but that he thought such "definitions fail to meet the pragmatic standard; they cannot be made the centre-piece of a substantial account of truth" (1991/2004: 37–38). My interpretation is very different. I will argue that, according to Peirce, a true belief is one that would be permanently established by the method of science, and the success of that method is due in part to the fact that it attempts to arrive at beliefs that represent how the world is apart from how it is believed to be, i.e., it attempts to arrive at beliefs that represent the real. When it succeeds – when it permanently dispels doubt and establishes belief – that belief represents reality.

Misak's reference to "the pragmatic standard" is a symptom of the fact that she assumes, as do Hookway and other Peirce scholars, that Peirce, in HTM, intended to provide a "pragmatic theory of truth," a theory of truth that results from applying his pragmatic maxim to the idea of truth. But as I will show in the next chapter, this is not the case. What has been understood as Peirce's pragmatic account of truth – that a true belief is one that we will have at "the end of inquiry" – is simply the investigative aspect of his account of truth and is already present in FOB. The investigative aspect of his account of truth plays a crucial role in HTM, but it is in support of the application of the pragmatic maxim to the idea, not of truth, but of reality.

I.2

Peirce held that we naturally "cling tenaciously, not merely to believing, but to believing just what we do believe" (FOB, 5.372, W 3: 247). So it is natural that he began his account of the four methods with the method of *tenacity*. This method amounts to "taking any answer to a question which

---

[3] In Chapter 7, I argue against Hookway's claim that "truth and reality were less intimately connected [in Peirce's writings] after 1880" (2012: 63).

we may fancy, and constantly reiterating it to ourselves, dwelling on all which may conduce to that belief, and learning to turn with contempt and hatred from anything which might disturb it" (FOB, W 3: 248–249).[4] The tenacious believer sticks to a belief simply because he "fancies" it, even going to extreme lengths to avoid anyone and anything that might cause him to change his mind. For this believer, "[t]he truth . . . is that for which he fights" (1.59, ca. 1896). It "is simply his particular stronghold," and he "can use the word truth only to emphasize the expression of his determination to hold on to" what he believes (HTM, 5.406, W 3: 272). It is not that the tenacious believer has anything like an idea of what Peirce calls truth; it is that the closest he can come to such an idea is just the idea of *what he currently believes.*

The method of tenacity is *private*, in that the contents of the tenacious individual's beliefs are up to him and no one else. Given that different individuals, even those living together in the same society and sharing the same culture, will prefer different beliefs, wide variations in what is believed will be inevitable if all of those individuals are tenacious believers. On Peirce's view, this is the source of the method's inevitable failure. Despite its "strength, simplicity, and directness" (FOB, 5.386, W 3: 256), it cannot "hold its ground in practice," and this is because "[t]he social impulse is against it" (FOB, 5.378, W 3: 250).[5] We are naturally inclined to be influenced by others when we form our own beliefs, and the fact that others disagree with us about a given matter has a tendency to weaken our beliefs. I might start the day believing that the baseball game starts at 7:00 PM, but if it emerges in conversation that all of my friends think it starts at 7:30 PM, I will be less inclined to continue in my original belief. So given that one's goal is to establish a belief that will not be shaken by the natural human tendency to take seriously that others disagree with them, "the problem becomes how to fix belief, not in the individual merely, but in the community" (FOB, 5.378, W 3: 250). So a permanently settled belief

---

[4] Here I quote from the original published version of FOB, which is reprinted in W 3. The version included in the *Collected Papers* contains numerous revisions Peirce made in later years. He revised the quoted passage as follows: "taking *as* answer to a question *any* we may fancy, and constantly reiterating it to ourselves, dwelling on all which may conduce to that belief, and learning to turn with contempt and hatred from anything *that* might disturb it" (5.377, emphases added). For more on the method of tenacity, see 7.324, W 3: 15, 1872; 7.317–318, W 3: 17, 1872; W 3: 18, 1872. Peirce sometimes called it "the method of obstinacy"; see 7.317, W 3: 17, 1872; W 3: 25, 1872; W 3: 28, 1872.

[5] I am less interested in Peirce's argument that the method of tenacity will not always work for everyone than I am in the way in which its alleged failure gives rise to a new way of thinking about what is required to settle belief permanently. On the question whether Peirce even intended this as an argument, see Short 2000.

will have to be *public*; a successful method will be capable of establishing exactly the same beliefs for large numbers of people, perhaps even for every member of a given population.[6]

The method that comes next in Peirce's story is one that aims at causing everyone who is subject to it to have the same belief. The method of *authority* relies on "the will of the state" to impose the same beliefs on the masses by whatever means necessary (FOB, 5.379, W 2: 250).[7] If what people are to believe is determined by a single source and imposed upon all or nearly all of them, then there will be much greater agreement among different people's beliefs. As idealized as Peirce's history may be, it is not a complete fiction; this method "has, from the earliest times, been one of the chief means of upholding correct theological and political doctrines, and of preserving their universal or catholic character" (FOB, 5.379, W 2: 250–251). For those who are subjected to this method, the closest that they can come to an idea of true belief is the idea of *what the authority tells them to believe*.

> When the method of authority prevailed, the truth meant little more than the Catholic faith. All the efforts of the scholastic doctors are directed toward harmonizing their faith in Aristotle and their faith in the Church . . . [W]here different faiths flourish side by side, renegades are looked upon with contempt even by the party whose belief they adopt; so completely has the idea of loyalty replaced that of truth-seeking. (HTM, 5.406, W 3: 272)

While in the method of tenacity "the conception of truth as something public is not yet developed," the method of authority at least incorporates the idea that a permanently settled belief will be based on "something public . . . something which affects, or might affect, every man" (FOB, 5.384, W 3: 253).

On Peirce's view, the method of authority "will always govern the mass of mankind" (FOB, 5.386, W 3: 255), whose "highest impulse [is] to be intellectual slaves" (FOB, 5.380, W 3: 251) – and, he added in a note from 1893, "[i]f slavery of opinion is natural and wholesome for men, then slaves they ought to remain" (5.380, n. 1). But this method will not succeed in settling every belief of every person, since "no institution can undertake to regulate opinions upon every subject," and even "in the most priestridden

---

[6] On the public nature of truth, see also SS 73, 1908.

[7] See also 7.324, W 3: 15, 1872; 7.317, W 3: 17, 1872 (where Peirce referred to the method of authority as "the method of persecution"); W 3: 18–19, 1872; W 3: 25–28, 1872 (where he called it "the method of despotism"); W 4: 476, 1883; 1.60, ca. 1896.

states some individuals will be found who" can "put two and two together" (FOB, 5.381, W 3: 251). Although it aims at public belief, this method will also fail to establish universally held beliefs about all subjects, and as before, this failure is due to the social impulse. Doubt will be sown as some people reflect upon the fact that those in other societies and at other times have held beliefs very different than their own and "that it is the mere accident of their having been taught as they have, and of their having been surrounded with the manners and associations they have, that has caused them to believe as they do and not far differently" (FOB, 5.381, W 3: 252). Beliefs that are imposed publicly, upon a great number of people, may still be arbitrary and accidental, and it is for that reason that they may be dislodged and replaced by doubt.

What is needed is a method that is capable of establishing beliefs in a non-arbitrary, non-accidental way, a method that "shall not only produce an impulse to believe, but shall also decide what proposition it is which is to be believed" (FOB, 5.382, W 3: 252), and "except so far as rulers are likely to adopt views of a certain cast[, the method of authority] does not determine at all what opinions shall become settled" (7.317, W 3: 17, 1872). A successful method must be able to fix beliefs the contents of which are determined impersonally – what is believed will be a result of applying the method, not decided in advance by one or more individuals before the method is applied. We have taken another important step toward the idea of truth: to be permanently settled, a belief must be, not just public, but also *impersonal*, not decided upon by any person or group.

The a priori method purports to yield beliefs having just this character:

> Let the action of natural preferences be unimpeded . . . and under their influence let men, conversing together and regarding matters in different lights, gradually develop beliefs in harmony with natural causes . . . [and that are] "agreeable to reason." This is an apt expression; it does not mean that which agrees with experience, but that which we find ourselves inclined to believe. (FOB, 5.382, W 3: 252)

The "inclination to believe" is not a matter of "fancy" or personal preference, nor is it a matter of reasoning deductively from first principles in order to ascertain how things must be of necessity. "Conversing together" with others is required by the more developed form of this method. At one point Peirce called it the "method of public opinion" and emphasized its

> tend[ency] to develope a particular body of doctrine in every community. Some more widely spread and deeply rooted conviction will gradually drive out the opposing opinions, becoming itself in the strife somewhat modified

by these. But different communities, removed from mutual influence, will develope very different bodies of doctrine, and in the same community there will be a constant tendency to sporting which may at any time carry the whole public. (7.317, W 3: 17, 1872; see also W 3:19, 1872)

Think of the various isolated "bubbles" or "echo chambers" of contemporary political and cultural discourse – partisans of a given view forming communities of the like-minded who read websites and blogs written by, watch television news networks featuring, and engage in discussions with only those who share similar beliefs. The a priori method "makes of inquiry something similar to the development of taste," which "is always more or less a matter of fashion" (FOB, 5.383, W 3: 253).[8]

Still, there are limits, other than just the content of the opinions of the like-minded, on what at least some practitioners of this method will believe:

> [T]he philosophers have been less intent on finding out what the facts are, than on inquiring what belief is most in harmony with their system. It is hard to convince a follower of the *a priori* method by adducing facts; but show him that an opinion he is defending is inconsistent with what he has laid down elsewhere, and he will be very apt to retract it. (HTM, 5.406, W 3: 273)

Logical relationships among beliefs, i.e., among the propositions that are the contents of beliefs, provide a constraint that may enable this method to be not just public, but also impersonal. Whether p and q are logically consistent is not determined by what anyone thinks about them or how anyone feels about them.[9] Still, the closest that an inquirer who uses this method can come to an idea of true belief is the idea of *what seems reasonable after conversation with the like-minded and after eliminating any inconsistencies with other beliefs.*

Factors other than the requirement of logical consistency help to determine what people believe, and one of them – sentiment – also helps prevent the a priori method from establishing the same beliefs in all of its practitioners. Because sentiments differ from community to community, and even from person to person, and because they "will be very greatly determined by accidental causes" such as the culture and period in which one resides, this method fails to avoid the arbitrary element of the method

---

[8] Elsewhere Peirce referred to this method as that of "Natural Inclination" (W 4: 476, 1883).
[9] Wiggins overlooks this constraint on the a priori method, which he describes as "only a resumption of protorational ways of information gathering" like the methods of tenacity and authority (2004: 94).

of authority and thus "does not differ in a very essential way from that" method (FOB, 5.383, W 3: 253). While it might fix beliefs that are impersonal, in that their content is not decided upon by anyone in advance of the method's being put to use, those beliefs are not public – they will not be the same for everyone who uses the method – and so the social impulse will again result in doubt.

What now arises is the idea that in order for one's beliefs to be permanently settled, and thus for them to be both impersonal and public, they must result from interaction with something external to anyone's mind.[10] A method will result in beliefs that better resist the social impulse if it requires "input" from something outside the mind of any individual believer and thus from outside the minds of *all* individual believers.[11] To be sure, each adherent of the more developed form of the a priori method receives input from outside her own mind; but that input has to do only with the contents of others' beliefs. Only the method of science transcends the personal, and therefore the "accidental and capricious" element, that infects beliefs formed via any other method. In introducing this fourth method, Peirce wrote that "there are some people . . . who, when they see that any belief of theirs is determined by any circumstance extraneous to the facts, will from that moment not merely admit in words that that belief is doubtful, but will experience a real doubt of it, so that it ceases to be a belief" (FOB, W 3: 253).[12] Peirce's reference to "the facts" is striking, and it is echoed in the comments in HTM quoted earlier ("finding out what the facts are," "adducing facts"). What might succeed where the first three methods failed is "a method . . . by which our beliefs may be caused by

---

[10] Short (2000) describes how the goal of inquiry shifts as we move from one method to the next: it begins as the fixation of one's own beliefs, then becomes the fixation of belief in a community, then fixing communal belief in a way that depends on no one's will. My account is largely consistent with his, but differs in emphasis by showing what it is that, according to Peirce, the method of authority, the a priori method, and the method of science each add to the eventual idea of truth: respectively, that true belief is public, that it is impersonal, and that it requires input from external reality. N.b., I mean something different by "impersonal" than Short, who writes that it is "[n]ot until we adopt [the method of science that] we conceive of truth as impersonal, as independent of what anyone actually believes" (2007a: 332; see also 2000: 11).

[11] This does not imply that impersonal and public beliefs can be about only the physical world. First, the fact that a belief is the result of interaction with the external does not mean that the belief itself must be *about* only external things. In his 1868–1869 cognition series (on which see Chapter 4), Peirce argued that humans lack the faculty of introspection and thus that an individual's knowledge of her own mind is always indirect, a result of reasoning from what is known about the world outside of her mind. Second, and as we will see in Chapters 5 and 6, the external is not limited to physical objects, but includes what Peirce called *generals*, including kinds, laws, and *would be's*.

[12] In 1909–1910, Peirce revised this to read: "so that it ceases *in some degree at least* to be a belief" (5.383, emphasis added). He wrote this change on an offprint of FOB, which offprint is R 334; see EP 1: 377, n. 24.

nothing human, but by some external permanency – by something upon which our thinking has no effect" (FOB, W 3: 253).[13,14] And since it is external, it must be real – it must be such that our thinking *about it* has no effect on it. He made this point explicitly in a 1903 revision of FOB: "by something upon which our thinking has no effect. But which, on the other hand, unceasingly tends to influence thought; or in other words, by something Real" (5.384 and n. 1).[15] So it is at this point in Peirce's genealogy of the idea of truth that he introduced his basic realism, according to which there is a world that is the way it is regardless of whether you, or I, or anyone else, believes that it is that way.

Basic realism is not the only important idea introduced at this point. As we have just seen, the method of science is accompanied by the assumption that our beliefs can be determined – causally and perhaps otherwise – by the world external to the mind. This causal influence comes by way of sense experience, and it is the addition of sense experience (more specifically, sense experience regarding matters other than the contents of others' beliefs) as a determining factor of the content of an inquirer's beliefs that makes the crucial difference between the a priori method and the method of science. By requiring that the evidence of the senses contribute to the shaping of our beliefs, the method of science makes beliefs sensitive to external reality. This is why the method of science is the one most likely to yield beliefs that "coincide with the fact" and why "there is no reason why the results of [the other] three methods should do so. To bring about this effect is the

---

[13] Peirce (R 334, 1909–1910) eventually replaced the word "caused" with "determined," so that the relevant passage reads: "a method ... by which our beliefs may be determined by nothing human" (5.384; see EP 1: 377, n. 24). Wiggins notes that this emendation "suggests that [Peirce] wanted to construe '[beliefs or opinions] determined by circumstances not extraneous to the facts' in a way that *allowed but did not require* such determination to be simple causal determination" (2004: 105–106). This seems right, since Peirce's realism was not limited to physical items capable of causal interaction.

[14] My reading of this passage differs from that of Paul Forster, who writes that "[i]n using the term 'external permanency' Peirce is not invoking an ontological contrast between the inner realm of the mind and an extra-mental world. Rather he is making the purely logical point that from the fact that a symbol represents an object as having a certain characteristic it does not follow that the object really has that characteristic" (2011: 161–162). Peirce first made the distinction between the external and the internal no later than 1872 (7.339, W 3: 29), and he relied on it in many different works across several decades (see Introduction, Note 3), including – albeit without using the word "internal" – in HTM (5.405, W 3: 271). There is nothing in FOB or HTM that suggests Peirce did not mean by "external," in his phrase "external permanency," what he had defined the term to mean and what he used it to mean on so many other occasions, viz. that which is independent of what anyone thinks, i.e., the nonmental.

[15] Peirce's 1903 description of reality as that which tends to influence thought echoes an idea from the original version of HTM, viz. that what all real things have in common *qua* real things is that they cause belief. See Chapter 2.

prerogative of the method of science" (FOB, 5.387, W 3: 256), i.e., *investigation*, which "necessarily consists of observation and inference" (W 3: 48, 1872).[16]

With the method of science we have finally arrived at the idea of truth, and the passage quoted previously reveals one aspect of it: a true belief is one that "coincide[s] with the fact" (FOB, 5.387, W 3: 256), that "conform[s]" to "*one* thing" (FOB, W 3: 254), viz., reality.[17] As vague as that is, it makes clear at least this much: a true belief is one that stands in a relation ("coincides with," "conforms to") with reality; i.e., truth requires a relation between that which is true and a world that is independent of what anyone thinks about it. In my view, this is enough to qualify it as a *correspondence* account of truth.[18]

Peirce did not say much about the nature of that relation in FOB, but in HTM he was explicit that it is one of *representation*: "the object *represented* in [a true belief] is the real" (HTM, 5.407, W 3: 273, emphasis added). In various works both early and late, he maintained that truth and falsity are properties of representations, i.e., *signs*, and specifically of *propositions*:

> *True* is an adjective applicable solely to representations and things considered as representations. (W 1: 79, 1861)

> The reference of a Symbol to its object is its *truth*. This kind of symbol is therefore one which is intended merely to Embody a truth. So that it is a *proposition*. (W 1: 477, 1866)

> Truth belongs to signs, particularly, and to thoughts as signs. (W 2: 439, 1870)

---

[16] See also W 3: 55, 1872. Peirce frequently referred to the method of science as "investigation" (7.316–320, W 3: 16–19, 1872; W 3: 34, 1872; 7.326, W 3: 35–36, 1872; 7.327ff., W 3: 40ff., 1872–1873; FOB, 5.384–385, W 3: 254, 255; HTM, 5.407–409, W 3: 273–274). He sometimes referred to it as "the method of scientific investigation" or "scientific investigation" (FOB, 5.385–386, W 3: 254–256; W 4: 476, 1883). He also called it "the scientific method" (W 3: 27–28, 1872; FOB, 5.386, W 3: 255). At least once, he referred to it as "the method of reasoning" (7.325, W 3: 15, 1872). In a later revision of HTM, he referred to it as "the experiential method" (5.406). In a late manuscript, he equated "inquiry" with "experience and reflexion" (R 289: 17, LI 304, ca. 1905). Haack calls the method of science "the method of experience and reasoning" (2003: 125), echoing Peirce's statement that "what would be the result of sufficient experience and reasoning" is what "is meant by the final settled opinion" (W 3: 79, 1873).

[17] In a later revision of FOB, Peirce replaced "there is some *one* thing to which a proposition should conform" with "there is some *one* thing which a proposition should represent" (5.384).

[18] As Marian David notes, the term "Correspondence Theory of Truth" "is usually applied . . . to any view explicitly embracing the idea that truth consists in a relation to reality, i.e., that truth is a relational property involving a characteristic relation (to be specified) to some portion of reality (to be specified)" (2016).

> Truth is a character which attaches to an abstract proposition, such as a person might utter ... Truth and falsity are characters confined to propositions. (5.565, 569, 1902)

> [I]t is propositions alone that are either true or false. (EP 2: 224, 1903)

> Truth belongs exclusively to propositions. (5.553, EP 2: 379, 1906)

And he maintained that true beliefs – more specifically, the propositions that are the contents of true beliefs – represent reality or "facts":

> Truth is the agreement of a meaning with a reality. (W 2: 439, 1870)

> Truth consists in the existence of a real fact corresponding to the true proposition. (2.652, W 3: 282, 1878)

> If a proposition is true, that which it represents is a *fact*. (6.67, RLT 198, 1898)

> That which [a] truth represents is a reality. (8.153, ca. 1900)

> [T]he fact that I *know* that this stone will fall to the floor when I let it go ... is the proof that the formula, or uniformity, as furnishing a safe basis for prediction, is, or if you like it better, *corresponds to*, a reality. (5.96, EP 2: 182, 1903)

> There would not be any such thing as truth unless there were something which is as it is independently of how we may think it to be. (7.659, 1903)

> That which any true proposition asserts is *real*, in the sense of being as it is regardless of what you or I may think about it. (5.432, EP 2: 343, 1905)

> [T]ruth ... is obviously the character of a representation of the real as it really is. (R 655: 30, 1910)

Notably, Peirce took Aristotle's well-known dictum – "To say of what is that it is not, or of what is not that it is, is false, while to say of what is that it is, and of what is not that it is not, is true" (*Metaphysics* 1011b25) – to mean that truth is a relationship of representation between a proposition and reality: "to Aristotle's mind, truth consists in the accordance, falsity in the discordance, between the representation made in a proposition and the real fact ... to which that proposition refers" (R 870: 18½–18¾, ca. 1901).

But an important qualification needs to be made here. Peirce maintained that no proposition can represent the world with complete accuracy. One of his most explicit statements of this caveat occurred in the article titled "Truth and Falsity and Error" in Baldwin's *Dictionary of Philosophy and Psychology*:

> Truth is a character which attaches to an abstract proposition, such as a person might utter. It essentially depends upon that proposition's not professing to be exactly true. But we hope that in the progress of science its error will indefinitely diminish, just as the error of 3.14159, the value given for π, will indefinitely diminish as the calculation is carried to more and more places of decimals. What we call π is an ideal limit to which no numerical expression can be perfectly true ... Truth is that concordance of an abstract statement with the ideal limit towards which endless investigation would tend to bring scientific belief, which concordance the abstract statement may possess by virtue of the confession of its inaccuracy and one-sidedness, and this confession is an essential ingredient of truth. (5.565, 1902)

What Peirce said here is implied by a position he had taken about representation in the 1860s – whether or not he recognized the implication at that time[19] – namely, that no representation is completely determinate in its meaning and that every representation, and therefore every cognition, is *in*determinate (or, as he wrote during that period, *general*) to at least some degree (e.g., 5.312, W 2: 239, 1868). Just as there is no maximum degree of precision or specificity that could ever be reached in the calculation of π, there is no actual limit to the determinacy, precision, specificity with which a given truth can be expressed. Absolute accuracy of propositional representation – exact or absolute truth – is practically impossible; "no real proposition is exactly true" (W 4: 490, 1883). "But ... it must be admitted that there is a pretty close approximation to absolute truth" (R 329: 10 alternative run of pages, ca. 1904), that is, to a hypothetical, ideal, but practically impossible proposition the meaning of which could not be made any more precise. The impossibility of completely determinate representation does not imply that propositions never do accurately represent the world – it implies that any true proposition could be made to represent the world even *more* accurately.[20]

Peirce's claim that the method of science is best at fixing belief is consistent, I think, with his notorious claim, made during his 1898 Cambridge Conferences lectures, that "what is properly and usually called

---

[19] He seems not yet to have come to believe it by the time he reviewed Venn's *The Logic of Chance*: "propositions are either absolutely true or absolutely false" (8.2, W 2: 99, 1867).

[20] There is much more to be said about Peirce's views on semiotic indeterminacy, and I will cover some of that ground in Chapters 5 and 6. For very different readings of 5.565, see Skagestad 1981: 78 and Hookway 2000: 64–66.

belief . . . has no place in science at all" (1.635, EP 2: 33, RLT 112).[21] A correct understanding of his views on these matters requires that we distinguish between (i) what he called the "method of science," a.k.a. investigation or the method of experience and reasoning, which, on his view, is best at permanently fixing belief and which "[e]verybody uses . . . about a great many things" (FOB, 5.384, W 3: 254) and (ii) the professional activities of physicists, chemists, biologists, psychologists, etc., which, as he insisted in the Cambridge lectures, should not be directed toward the permanent settlement of belief. It is consistent to say that if one's aim *is* to settle one's beliefs permanently, then investigation is the best means to that end, but that *qua* scientists, working physicists, etc. should not pursue permanently fixed beliefs in the course of their work.

So the idea with which Peirce's genealogy ends – the idea of truth – is representationalist: a true belief represents reality. This is far from all that Peirce had to say about truth, and I have more to say on the subject in what follows. But for now, the points on which I wish to insist are, first, that his genealogy concludes with the idea of a true belief as one that represents reality, and second, that this representationalist aspect of his account of true belief is present in both his early and late writings.[22]

Peirce's statements in various other works confirm that he intended FOB's account of the four methods to serve as a genealogy of the idea of truth. In HTM, he recounted the first three methods, described each as lacking an adequate understanding of truth, and asserted that it is only with the advent of the method of science that the idea of truth has reached

---

[21] Hookway notes that "if application of the scientific method cannot (or should not) produce *belief* at all, it is hard to see how we can view the method of science as a method for the fixation of *belief*" (2000: 23). Scheffler issues a related criticism: "In holding all its claims to be provisional and subject to the test of continuing experience, [science] places them all in jeopardy and makes them all vulnerable to unsettlement . . . Science might thus be persuasively presented as a systematic method for unfixing belief and unsettling opinion" ([1974] 2011: 71).

[22] I am not alone in recognizing a representationalist element – or more generally, a correspondence element – in Peirce's account of truth. See, for example, Haack 1976: 232ff., Skagestad 1981: 76, Almeder 1985: 79, Cooke 2007: 163, n. 16, Forster 2011: 161ff., and Glanzberg 2014. George Englebretsen rightly notes that of the theories of truth offered by the early pragmatists, "Peirce's version most resembled standard correspondence theory," but he misinterprets Peirce as having maintained that "it is agreement among ourselves rather than agreement between our beliefs and the facts that accounts for truth" and so mistakenly concludes that Peirce's view "seems to have ended in utter nonsense" (2006: 45–46). In interpreting Peirce's genealogy of truth as introducing a representationalist element into the idea of truth only at the point at which the method of science has been reached, I read FOB very differently than Migotti, who suggests that "the tenacious believer might well have an adequate grasp of the concept 'truth' at the second grade of clearness" (1998: 85), which, on his interpretation, means an adequate grasp of the idea of truth as correspondence of a representation with what it represents (ibid.: 82).

its "full development" (5.406, W 3: 272).[23] In his 1903 Harvard lectures on pragmatism, he described the view he had taken in FOB and HTM as that "[t]he conception of truth ... was *developed* out of an original impulse to act consistently, to have a definite intention" (5.28, EP 2: 140, emphasis added). And in a manuscript of ca. 1906, he wrote that in FOB he had tried to show how the attempt to settle belief eventually "create[d] the conception of real truth" (5.563, R 330: 10):

> My paper of November 1877, setting out from the proposition that the agitation of a question ceases when satisfaction is attained with the settlement of belief, and then only, goes on to consider how *the conception of truth gradually develops* from that principle under the action of experience; beginning with willful belief, or self-mendacity, the most degraded of all intellectual conditions; thence rising to the imposition of beliefs by the authority of organized society; then to the idea of a settlement of opinion as the result of a fermentation of ideas; and finally reaching the idea of truth as overwhelmingly forced upon the mind in experience as the effect of an independent reality. (5.564, R 330: 10–11, emphasis added)[24]

As this later characterization makes explicit, Peirce held that a true belief is one that will be "forced upon" the mind after sufficient experience of the real world and reasoning about that experience. As he put it in FOB, "any man, if he have sufficient experience and reason enough about it, will be led to the one true conclusion" (W 3: 254).[25]

So the genealogy of FOB concluded with a dual-aspect account of truth, one with a representationalist aspect, according to which a true belief is one that represents reality, and an investigative aspect, according to which a true belief is one that would be permanently settled in the minds of those

[23] Short (2000: 22, n. 12) and (2007a: 332) cites this passage in support of the genealogy interpretation of FOB. N.b. the following, from 1873: "there [is no] matter of fact involved in saying that the truth is the object aimed at in investigation; for investigation implies that the conception of truth is *developed*" (W 3: 79, emphasis added).

[24] Both Haack (1997: 246) and Short (2000: 9) cite 5.564 to support their respective interpretations of FOB as containing a genealogy of the idea of truth. Wiggins cites this passage as well, noting that "[i]t might be questioned how exactly and faithfully, dating from 1906, [5.564] reflects Peirce's intentions of 1877" (2004: 91). But the passage from HTM cited previously (5.406, W 3: 272) establishes that Peirce's intention in writing FOB and HTM was to give an account of the development of the idea of truth. According to the *Collected Papers*, 5.555–564 were taken from "Reflexions upon Pluralistic Pragmatism and upon Cenopythagorean Pragmaticism," a manuscript dated ca. 1906. EP 2 says that this manuscript "seems to have disappeared from the Harvard collection of Peirce's papers" (EP 2: 543, n. 14). Although it is not mentioned in Robin 1967, 5.555–556 are obviously a different draft of the first two paragraphs of R 330: 6, and 5.557–564 is a nearly verbatim reproduction of the content of R 330: 6ff.

[25] A later revision reads as follows: "any man, if he have sufficient experience and *he* reason enough about it, will be led to the one *True* conclusion" (5.384, emphases added).

who use the method of science, i.e., in the minds of those who investigate.[26] Peirce's contribution to the article "Truth and Falsity and Error" in Baldwin's *Dictionary* shows that both aspects survived in his thinking about truth into the twentieth century. His portion of the article is a definition of "logical" truth, which he described as "the concordance of a proposition with reality" (5.570, 1902).[27] What manner of concordance? "Truth and falsity are characters confined to propositions," and "[a] proposition is a sign which separately indicates its object" (5.569). This implies that truth is a property possessed only by a specific kind of sign, i.e., by a specific kind of representation; the representationalist aspect of his earlier account remains. So does the investigative aspect: "Truth is that concordance of an abstract statement with the ideal limit towards which endless investigation would tend to bring scientific belief" (5.565).

1.3

By the time of his 1903 lectures on pragmatism, Peirce had come to believe that there was an important flaw in the FOB/HTM genealogy. He had woven that genealogy into his account of the attempt to eliminate doubt and replace it with belief, and he had construed belief as "consist[ing] mainly in being deliberately prepared to adopt the formula believed in as the guide to action" (5.27, EP 2: 139). Given that view of belief, the "impulse to act consistently" amounts to the impulse to move beyond the chaotic, irregular behavior associated with doubt and to adopt a single principle upon which one might act given some specific set of circumstances, i.e., to establish a

---

[26] This differs from the interpretation Migotti defended in "Peirce's Double-Aspect Theory of Truth." Migotti reads Peirce as having applied the pragmatic maxim to the idea of truth in HTM and as thereby arriving at the view that truth is both *independent* and *accessible*: "the *independence* of truth *from* thought is captured in the claim that if something is true, then 'it is SO, whether you or I or anybody think it is so or not . . . [and] no matter if there be an overwhelming vote against it' (2.135); and the *accessibility* of truth *to* thought is captured in the claim that honest inquiry, carried out sufficiently far, is fated to arrive at the truth" (1998: 90). On my view, the first part of this formulation gives insufficient weight to the role of representation in Peirce's view of truth. I prefer to say that reality is (by Peirce's definition) independent of what anyone thinks about it and that a true belief accurately represents that independent reality. On Migotti's view, the representationalist aspect of Peirce's view of truth is relegated to the merely verbal definition that provides a second grade of clearness with regard to the idea of truth.

[27] Peirce's long contribution to the entry is followed by a portion dedicated to "psychological truth" and authored by James Mark Baldwin and Christine Ladd-Franklin. This portion of the entry is dedicated primarily to criticizing correspondence accounts and to explaining how they have arisen. More relevant for present purposes is the fact that Baldwin and Ladd-Franklin took Peirce's account of logical truth to be just the sort of correspondence account they were criticizing: they wrote that the account given in Peirce's definition of "Logical" truth "goes by the term 'correspondence'" (Baldwin and Ladd-Franklin 1902: 720).

belief. In the 1903 lectures, Peirce complained that all of this "was not very clearly made out" in the earlier articles. But his more important criticism was that it is not

> satisfactory to reduce such fundamental things to facts of psychology. For man could alter his nature, or his environment would alter it if he did not voluntarily do so, if the impulse were not what was advantageous or fitting. Why has evolution made man's mind to be so constructed? That is the question we must nowadays ask, and all attempts to ground the fundamentals of logic on psychology are seen to be essentially shallow. (5.28, EP 2: 140; see also 8.255–257, 1902)

Whether or not Peirce's criticism – that the genealogy of truth provided in FOB was objectionably psychologistic – was justified, he did not change his attitude toward the culmination of that genealogy.

Peirce's statement that "all attempts to ground the fundamentals of logic on psychology are . . . essentially shallow" suggests that he came to view his FOB genealogy as objectionably psychologistic because it made the mistake of deriving results belonging to a *coenoscopic* (or *cenoscopic*) science from those of an *idioscopic* science. The former kind of science "deals with positive truth, indeed, yet contents itself with observations such as come within the range of every man's normal experience, and for the most part in every waking hour of his life" (1.241, 1902). Philosophy, which includes logic, is a coenoscopic science. But psychology is an idioscopic science, or special science, one that "depend[s] upon special observation, which travel or other exploration, or some assistance to the senses, either instrumental or given by training, together with unusual diligence, has put within the power of its students" (1.242, 1902). Peirce wrote in 1896's "The Regenerated Logic" that

> the only sound psychology being a special science, which ought itself to be based upon a wellgrounded logic, it is indeed a vicious circle to make logic rest upon a theory of cognition so understood. But there is a much more general doctrine to which the name theory of cognition might be applied. Namely, it is that speculative grammar, or analysis of the nature of assertion, which rests upon observations, indeed, but upon observations of the rudest kind, open to the eye of every attentive person who is familiar with the use of language, and which, we may be sure, no rational being, able to converse at all with his fellows, and so to express a doubt of anything, will ever have any doubt. (3.432)

This suggests that theorizing about truth, which is within the purview of philosophy, cannot legitimately be grounded upon the results of psychology, including results having to do with doubt and belief. But the assumptions Peirce made about doubt and belief in FOB and that helped to initiate his genealogy of truth are not results of the special science of psychology – they are the sort of basic claims that readers might be expected to agree with based on their own general experiences: that belief and doubt feel different, that they are accompanied by different sorts of behavior, and that belief is satisfactory and doubt unpleasant (5.370–373, W 3: 247). So a better explanation will point to the specific claim that he made in the passage just quoted, that "man could alter his nature, or his environment would alter it if he did not voluntarily do so, if the impulse were not what was advantageous or fitting." This suggests that he understood true belief to be something not unique to our species and thus that it is best explained without reference to *human* psychological states, even those of which we can have knowledge apart from the work of the special sciences. This explanation is in harmony with those passages in which he suggested that inquiry might be conducted by members of species other than our own that are capable of establishing belief (e.g., HTM 5.408, W 3: 274).

Toward the end of the final 1903 Harvard lecture, Peirce reaffirmed his view that truth requires a relationship with reality: "Every man is fully satisfied that there is such a thing as truth, or he would not ask any question. *That* truth consists in a conformity to something *independent of his thinking it to be so*, or of any man's opinion on that subject" (5.211, EP 2: 240). Paired with the view, also affirmed in the Harvard lectures, that only propositions can be true or false (EP 2: 224), this amounts to a restatement of the representationalist aspect of his account of truth. Further, Peirce continued to characterize truth as that which would result from continuing investigation until belief is permanently settled, sometimes obliquely (e.g., truth is "that to a belief in which belief would tend if it were to tend indefinitely toward absolute fixity" (5.416, 1905)), sometimes explicitly (e.g., truth is "the predestinate opinion ... that which *would* ultimately prevail if investigation were carried sufficiently far in that particular direction" (EP 2: 457, 1911)). So his later criticisms of FOB and HTM as having been too psychologistic in their arguments are not evidence that he gave up the views about truth that he had endorsed in those articles.[28] And this makes sense. Given that Peirce did not intend the genealogy to be a strictly literal account of the history of inquiry, it is not clear that it is relevant to the assessment of its final stage that its starting

---

[28] N.b., Peirce did eventually criticize his FOB/HTM account of reality, which depends on the investigative aspect of his account of truth, for having been grounded on an insufficiently realistic view of possibility. I will return to this issue in Chapters 2, 6, and 7.

point was a psychological claim rather than a logical one. What is more important is the greater understanding of the idea of truth gleaned from contrasting that final stage with its predecessors.

1.4

Why is it that beliefs that would be permanently settled by the method of science represent reality? More fundamentally, how is it possible for a proposition – or anything else – to represent *anything*? Peirce put the question pointedly in an early set of lecture notes: "Truth belongs to signs, particularly, and to thoughts as signs. Truth is the agreement of a meaning with a reality . . . [I]n what sense can two things as incommensurable as a meaning and a reality be said to agree[?]" (W 2: 439, 1870).

Some of Peirce's work in *semiotic* or the theory of signs is directed at answering the more basic question about representation and the more specific one about propositions. For example, he eventually required that a proposition have a certain structure and that its component parts have their own semiotic relations with objects in the real world: "A proposition has a subject (or set of subjects) and a predicate. The subject is a sign; the predicate is a sign; and the proposition is a sign that the predicate is a sign of that of which the subject is a sign. If it be so, it is true" (5.553, EP 2: 379, 1906). Neither the more specific nor the more general semiotic question is addressed in FOB or HTM. But in FOB he did provide a broad framework within which an understanding of human thought and its sensitivity to the "external permanency" might be worked out. He called this framework the "fundamental hypothesis" of the method of science:

> There are real things, whose characters are entirely independent of our opinions about them [this is Peirce's basic realism]; those realities affect our senses according to regular laws, and, though our sensations are as different as our relations to the objects, yet, by taking advantage of the laws of perception, we can ascertain by reasoning how things really are, and any man, if he have sufficient experience and reason enough about it, will be led to the one true conclusion [this reflects the investigative aspect of his account of truth]. (W 3: 254)[29]

---

[29] See also W 3: 27, 1872. Peirce later revised this passage in FOB to read as follows: "There are Real things, whose characters are entirely independent of our opinions about them; those *Reals* affect our senses according to regular laws, and, though our sensations are as different as are our relations to the objects, yet, by taking advantage of the laws of perception, we can ascertain by reasoning how things really *and truly* are; and any man, if he have sufficient experience and *he* reason enough about it, will be led to the one *True* conclusion" (5.384, emphases added). As we will see in Chapter 7, from the

For our beliefs – more specifically, for the propositions that are the contents of our beliefs – to accurately represent some aspect of the real world, that world must impinge on us so as to cause us to have sensations, and it must do so in regular, lawful ways.[30] Even though our respective experiences of the world differ – even though "[t]wo men cannot . . . make the same observation any more than one man can repeat an observation" (W 3: 55, 1872) – we are capable of coming to understand the laws governing those experiences and thus of arriving at the same beliefs. The method of science yields results that are public and impersonal because it requires that the process of belief formation involve experiential input from the external world.[31] The representation relation required for truth is not established in ways having nothing to do with human activity or sensory experience – it is nothing like what Hilary Putnam calls "noetic rays" that magically connect human thought to the external world.[32] A true belief is not simply one that accurately represents reality; it is also one that will be brought about as a result of *experiential interaction with* reality. One might stumble upon a true belief while using some other method of fixation. The person who thinks, because it was revealed to her in a dream, that there will soon be enough rain to avert a drought and save the crops, may in fact be right. But she would have that true belief only accidentally. On Peirce's telling, a true belief is one that will be *forced* upon the minds of those who investigate. The inquirer who self-consciously employs the method of science assumes that there are real things, that those real things behave in regular ways, that at least some of those real things are external, and that by employing both reasoning and sense experience she will eventually arrive at beliefs that accurately represent the world. In this way, the method of science presupposes basic realism. In a sense, the a priori method also presupposes basic realism, since whether or not one belief is logically consistent with another does not depend on whether anyone *thinks* it is, and whether a member of your community of interlocutors believes that *p*

---

mid-1880s until the early 1900s, Peirce took a somewhat different attitude toward the relationship between basic realism and investigation.

[30] Those lawful regularities must themselves be independent of any representation of them as being one way rather than another, i.e., they must be real. This is one aspect of Peirce's *scholastic realism*, which I discuss in Chapters 5 and 6.

[31] Anticipating his later characterization of the method of science as yielding (what I am calling) impersonal beliefs, Peirce wrote in 1872 that "investigation . . . tends . . . to confirm a certain opinion which depends only on the nature of investigation itself" (7.317, W 3: 16–17).

[32] In his argument that we cannot be brains-in-vats, Putnam writes: "Suppose we assume a 'magical theory of reference'. For example, we might assume that some occult rays – call them 'noetic rays' – connect words and thought signs to their referents" (1981: 51).

does not depend on whether anyone believes that she believes that *p*. Still, basic realism plays a very different role for "followers of science" than it does for partisans of the other methods. Of the four methods, only the method of science *self-consciously assumes* that there is a real world, and only its followers seek to have their beliefs fixed by way of experiential interactions with external (nonmental) portions of it.

But why assume that investigation pushed sufficiently far would ever settle on a *single* belief about a given subject? Peirce's view that there is one real world that all investigators inhabit is also presupposed by this assumption.[33] In an earlier work that anticipated his statement of "the fundamental hypothesis" in FOB, he wrote:

> [W]e seem fated to come to the final conclusion. For whatever be the circumstances under which the observations are made & by which they are modified they will inevitably carry us at last to this belief. The strangeness of this fact disappears entirely when we adopt the conception of external realities. We say that the observations are the result of the action upon the mind of outward things, and that their diversity is due to the diversity of our relations to these things; while *the identity of the conclusion to which the mind is led by them is owing to the identity of the things observed*, the reasoning process serving to separate among the many different observations that we make of the same thing the constant element which depends upon the thing itself from the differing and variable elements which depend on our varying relations to the thing. (7: 334–335, W 3: 44, 1872, emphasis added)

You and I may have very different sensory experiences of some aspect of the world. But so long as those experiences are of the same thing – so long as there is *one aspect of the world* with which we are both interacting – then it is possible for us to reach agreement about how that thing must be by communicating with each other about our respective experiences and then reasoning toward an account of the world that would explain why each of us experiences it in his own unique way. Given that it is a fact that *p*, neither my sincere belief that not-*p* nor your skeptical doubts about whether it is the case that *p* will have any effect whatsoever on whether or not it is the case that *p*. It is a real world that we investigate, and so it is the fact that *p* that influences our various experiences and the beliefs that result from them when we investigate.

But why should we believe that there is a real world at all? How can we simply assume that there are things the properties of which do not depend

---

[33] On this point I agree with Migotti (1998: 92–93).

on what anyone thinks about them? An anti-realist – someone who denies basic realism – might say that any claims that we make at this point in support of that doctrine are themselves subject to the same sort of challenge: why believe that those claims say how things really are? If we have arrived at those claims via the method of science itself – i.e., through the use of experience and reasoning – then our use of them in support of basic realism begs the question. As Peirce put the objection, "If [basic realism] is the sole support of my method of inquiry, my method of inquiry must not be used to support my hypothesis" (FOB, 5.384, W 3: 254). He offered four responses to this objection. None of the first three is a straightforward argument in defense of basic realism; instead, they constitute an argument that no one ever actually doubts that view. I will take these out of order, since the first and third are better explained in conjunction.

Peirce's first response was that the method of science does not itself give rise to doubts about basic realism. No one who uses the method will be led by its use to doubt that there are things whose characters are independent of what anyone thinks about them (FOB, 5.384, W 3: 254), and so no one who uses the method will be led to doubt its efficacy – at least, he will not be led to have doubts about the efficacy of investigation by any doubts about its fundamental hypothesis. Peirce's third response was that everyone already uses the method of science with regard to many subjects. People fail to use it only when they do not know how to apply it to a given subject. Presumably, he meant to suggest that, since everyone uses the method, everyone already believes its "fundamental hypothesis," including basic realism. It is only with regard to some topics – he may have had in mind religion or theology – that people cease to use it. And again, the use of the method does not engender doubts about either the method itself or about basic realism, and since everyone already uses the method, no one will be caused by its use to doubt the method itself or its assumption that there is a real world.

Peirce's second response was that anyone who seeks to dispel doubt and fix belief is motivated by a feeling of "dissatisfaction at two repugnant [i.e., logically inconsistent] propositions" and therefore must already believe "that there is some *one* thing to which a proposition should conform" (FOB, W 3: 254)[34], some single reality about which not both p and not-p

---

[34] Peirce later revised the quoted passage to read: "there is some *one* thing *which a proposition should represent*" (5.384, latter emphasis added). That there is a single reality about which not both p and not-p are true calls to mind the principle of contradiction, that for any p, it is not the case both that p and not-p. I examine Peirce's commitment to the principle of contradiction, and his attitude toward the principles of excluded middle and of bivalence, in Chapters 6 and 7.

are true. When you have doubts about the claim that *p*, this involves a feeling of dissatisfaction resulting from your recognition that it cannot be the case both that *p* and that not-*p*. For example, if you are unsure what time the baseball game begins, you experience a feeling of discomfort, and this stems from your recognition that "The game begins at 7:00 PM" and "The game does not begin at 7:00 PM" are not both true. But if you were not assuming that there is only *one* way things are, then the inconsistency of these propositions would not bother you. So you cannot consistently deny that there is a single reality *and* at the same time be bothered by doubt. But since each of us experiences doubt and is bothered by it, everyone does in fact believe that there is a single way that the world is.

Peirce's fourth and final response to the anti-realist challenge began with a reiteration of a point he made in his first response: "Experience of the method has not led me to doubt it" (FOB, W 3: 254).[35] He then proceeded to give what seems like an argument, not that everyone already believes basic realism, but that that theory is in fact true: "on the contrary, scientific investigation has had the most wonderful triumphs in the way of settling opinion" (FOB, 5.384, W 3: 254). This is not to say that investigation has settled opinions about everything, or even about most things, among all people, or even among most people. Peirce's point, I think, was that among those who use the method of science to settle beliefs about topic *x*, there is a remarkable amount of agreement about *x* – a much more stable and widely spread consensus about *x* than among those who would use one of the other three methods to try to settle beliefs about *x*. There is, for example, a greater consensus among those who use investigation to settle questions about the earliest stages of the universe, or the earliest stages of life on earth, than there is among those who use the method of authority to settle opinions on those issues. The wider consensus among the followers of science is best explained by positing a single real world that they all inhabit and with which they are all interacting in their investigative activities.

Peirce concluded his defense of basic realism as follows:

> These [four responses] afford the explanation of my not doubting the method or the hypothesis which it supposes; and not having any doubt, nor believing that anybody else whom I could influence has, it would be the merest babble for me to say more about it. If there be anybody with a living doubt upon the subject, let him consider it. (FOB, 5.384, W 3: 254)

---

[35] He later revised this to read: "Experience of the method has not led *us* to doubt it" (5.384, emphasis added).

The message is clearly anti-Cartesian. If you are *really* in doubt about whether there are real things external to the mind, you are free to expend your energy attempting to dispel that doubt. But Peirce had no such doubts, and so he was not compelled to spend further time on the matter.

1.5

So again, Peirce's view was that a true belief is one that accurately represents reality and that would be permanently settled if the method of science, i.e., investigation, were used in an attempt to dispel doubt and settle belief; that method is better than its competitors at permanently settling beliefs because it requires experiential interaction with a law-governed world of real things, some of which are external to the mind. But how does this interpretation square with Peirce's statements connecting – and sometimes even seeming to identify – truth with the capacity of a belief to help one achieve one's goals, or with a psychological state of satisfaction? For example, toward the end of FOB, Peirce wrote:

> The person who confesses that there is such a thing as truth, which is distinguished from falsehood simply by this, that if acted on it will carry us to the point we aim at and not astray, and then, though convinced of this, dares not know the truth and seeks to avoid it, is in a sorry state of mind indeed. (W 3:257)[36]

His claim here seems to have been that the only difference between true beliefs and false ones is that true beliefs guide behavior in ways that enable us to attain our goals while false beliefs do not. In later works, he apparently identified the truth of a belief with its capacity to help us satisfy our desires and purposes:

> [T]ruth is neither more nor less than that character of a proposition which consists in this, that belief in the proposition would, with sufficient experience and reflection, lead us to such conduct as would tend to satisfy the desires we should then have. To say that truth means more than this is to say that it has no meaning at all (5.375, n. 2, 1903).

> To be angry with sceptics ... is a manifest sign that the angry person is himself infected with skepticism – not, however, of the innocent and wholesome kind that tries to bring truth to light, but of the mendacious, clandestine, disguised, and conservative variety that is afraid of truth, although truth merely means the way to attain one's purposes ... I say to

---

[36] Peirce later revised this to read: "that if acted on it *should, on full consideration*, carry us to the point we aim at and not astray" (5.387, emphasis added).

them, "Gentlemen, your strongest sentiment, to which I subscribe with all my heart, is that a man worthy of that name will not allow petty intellectual predilections to blind him to truth, which consists in the conformity of his thoughts to his purposes." (1.344, 1903)

These passages suggest that Peirce held that a sufficient condition of a belief's being true is that it conduce the achievement of the goals of she who believes it. That view is inconsistent with the dual-aspect account of truth that he defended on so many other occasions.

But I think that these passages are in fact consistent with his dual-aspect account. A charitable reading of the claim Peirce made at the end of FOB – "truth, which is distinguished from falsehood simply by this, that if acted on it will carry us to the point we aim at and not astray" – will take the "point we aim at" to be the goal of inquiry – permanently settled belief – which he had spent so much of that article discussing. And it will take the action that he mentioned to be inquiry itself – the attempt to dispel doubt and fix belief. On this reading the claim becomes simply this: the difference between a true belief and a false belief is that in the process of investigation, a true belief will eventually become fixed so as not to be dislodged by the social impulse. I suspect that the desire to which he referred in the fragment of ca. 1903 (5.375, n. 2) was not just any desire at all, but the desire to replace doubt with belief.[37] If these interpretations are plausible, it seems fitting to understand the purposes mentioned at 1.344 as the settlement of our respective beliefs, as well.[38]

It is easier, I think, to see how his assertion that "a state of *satisfaction*, is all that Truth, or the aim of inquiry, consists in" (6.485, EP 2: 449, 1908) is consistent with his dual-aspect account. "[B]elief is essentially satisfactory" (R 842: 19, ca. 1905), and a true belief is the satisfying state of mind that practitioners of the method of science will experience if they apply that method until no further application will cause any change in what they

---

[37] Wiggins cites 5.375, n. 2 as "the kind of statement that has given pragmatism such a bad name" (2004: 110). It was added as a footnote to FOB in the *Collected Papers*; the date is 1903, according to that edition's editors, but they do not indicate its origin. In his recent edition of the *Illustrations* series, de Waal indicates that the *Collected Papers*' editors added as footnotes to the version of FOB that appears in that collection several notes taken from Peirce's later revisions of that article; but this seems unlikely to be one of those notes, as de Waal comments that it is from "a non-identified manuscript" (ILS 55). I have not been able to find this passage among the manuscripts cataloged by Robin.

[38] One later statement of the purpose of inquiry was a bit different but still involved as an intermediate goal the establishment of belief: "the principal end of inquiry, as regards human life . . . the chief end of man . . . [is t]o actualize ideas of the immortal, ceaselessly prolific kind. To that end it is needful to get beliefs that the believer will take satisfaction in acting upon, not mere rules set down on paper" (2.763, ca. 1905).

believe.[39] Peirce did not identify truth with satisfaction *simpliciter*, and on his view, it would not make much sense to do so: "Mr. Ferdinand C.S. Schiller informs us that he and James have made up their minds that the true is simply the satisfactory. No doubt; but to say 'satisfactory' is not to complete any predicate whatever. Satisfactory to what end?" (5.552, EP 2: 379, 1906). A true belief is one that satisfies the end of she who seeks to dispel doubt and permanently fix her beliefs. It is no surprise, then, that the apparent identification of truth and satisfaction quoted at the beginning of this paragraph was no such thing:

> My original essay [viz., FOB and HTM] ... assumes ... that "a settlement of Belief," or, in other words, a state of *satisfaction*, is all that Truth, or the aim of inquiry, consists in ... The first part of the essay [viz., FOB], however, is occupied with showing that, if Truth consists in satisfaction, it cannot be any *actual* satisfaction, but must be the satisfaction which *would* ultimately be found if the inquiry were pushed to its ultimate and indefeasible issue. (6.485, EP 2: 449–450, 1908)[40]

This characterization of truth is echoed in another manuscript of the same year: "the truth is of the nature of satisfaction, ... not that it consists in the satisfaction of any individual, but in that ultimate satisfaction which nothing would shake" (R 844s, 1908). Finally, Peirce affirmed in an undated fragment that the satisfaction associated with true belief requires the sort of connection between the believer and the external world described earlier:

> We must never forget ... that to say that a thing is true is only a compact expression whose only iconical meaning is that at last every scientific intelligence will be bound to admit it, that is, to rest in the idea as satisfactory. This is not a Berkleyan conception of truth; but quite the contrary. It is the compulsion that makes the truth; and compulsion is essentially extrinsic. (R 817: 4)

---

[39] My reading of Peirce on truth and satisfaction is in line with Haack's: "[S]ince truth is the opinion on which the scientific method will eventually settle, and since the scientific method is constrained by reality, truth is correspondence with reality. It also follows that truth is satisfactory to believe, in the sense that it is stable, safe from the disturbance of doubt" (1978: 97).

[40] Peirce thought of FOB and HTM as together constituting a single essay; see his ca. 1910 letter to Paul Carus in which Peirce referred to FOB and HTM as "the first Essay consisting of the first two articles" of the *Illustrations* series (8.216). See also LI 44–45n, which includes a quotation from R 619 (1909) in which Peirce describes FOB and HTM as "two chapters" composing a single "Essay" (the same material is quoted at *Collected Papers* v.5, 223n, but there it is incorrectly dated 1903). And since nothing in the first section of HTM meets the description Peirce gives at 6.485 / EP 2:449–450, it stands to reason that "[t]he first part of the essay" to which he there refers is in fact FOB.

So the relationship Peirce saw between a belief's being true and its being satisfactory is no threat to the realist account of truth that he defended in FOB. According to that account, a true belief is one that represents the real world *and* that would be permanently settled by investigation. As we will see in the next chapter, Peirce employed the investigative aspect of this account of truth when he applied his pragmatic maxim to clarify the idea of reality.

CHAPTER 2

The Pragmatic Clarification of the Idea of Reality

2.1

In "How to Make Our Ideas Clear" (HTM) Peirce publicly stated his pragmatic maxim for the first time, although without using the terms "pragmatic maxim" or "pragmatism," and he used it to clarify the idea of reality: "The opinion which is fated to be ultimately agreed to by all who investigate, is what we mean by the truth, and the object represented in this opinion is the real. That is the way I would explain reality" (5.407, W 3: 273). Because he employed the idea of true belief in this pragmatic clarification, one might be tempted to think that the genealogy that began in "The Fixation of Belief" (FOB) continues into HTM and concludes there with a further development of the idea of truth, one that supersedes FOB's dual-aspect account of truth. Indeed, Peirce's so-called pragmatic theory of truth and pragmatism about truth in general are sometimes taken to be competitors of a realist theory of the sort embodied in the representationalist aspect of the FOB account.[1]

But this would be a mistake. The idea of truth that Peirce employed in HTM is exactly that with which his FOB genealogy concludes. Nowhere in HTM did he apply the pragmatic maxim to the idea of truth; the sole philosophical use of the maxim in that article was its application to the idea of reality. His later statements confirm this: "We have hitherto applied the rule of clearness to ordinary conceptions and have found our advantage in it. In a paper in the *Popular Science Monthly* I have analyzed in a similar way the notion of reality" (W 4: 7, 1879); "[the pragmatic] maxim was first proposed by C.S. Peirce in the *Popular Science Monthly* for January, 1878 [in HTM] . . . and he explained how it was to

---

[1] For example, J. J. C. Smart lumps Peirce together with later anti-realists and attributes to him the view that truth is "warranted assertability in the limit. That is, a proposition would be true if it occurred in an ideal theory, and for a theory to be ideal is the same as for it to be maximally coherent and comprehensive" (1986: 301).

be applied to the doctrine of reality" (5.3, 1902). A syllabus for a series of lectures on logic that Peirce drafted in 1883 describes the third and fourth of those lectures as covering much of the same ground as FOB and HTM, and therein is treated the "[*n*]*ature of reality*," not that of truth (W 4: 476–477). Looking back on the *Illustrations of the Logic of Science*, he wrote that in it he had treated his account of truth, not as following from pragmatism, but rather as being a support to it:

> The next application I shall make of pragmaticism[2] is to support a principle which might very well be regarded on the contrary, as a support of pragmaticism, and was in fact originally so treated by me, being proved independently in my article of Nov. 1877 [viz., FOB]. At any rate, it is most intimately bound up with pragmaticism and if this latter is ever to find a refutation it is as likely to come from the criticism of the principle to which I refer as anywhere. The principle is that whatever is true would be logically inferred from sufficient experience by sufficient thought. (R 289: 13, LI 303, ca. 1905)

So far as I have been able to discover, this passage is the earliest in which Peirce treated the investigative aspect of his account of truth as a result of applying the pragmatic maxim to clarify the idea of truth.[3] But regardless of the exact time at which he began thinking of that aspect as resulting from the maxim, it is clear that he did not think of it that way at the time he wrote FOB and HTM and that he did not intend HTM to advance FOB's genealogy of truth: "as we have seen in the former paper [viz., FOB], the ideas of truth and falsehood, *in their full development*, appertain exclusively to the scientific method of settling opinion" (HTM, W 3: 272, emphasis added).[4] He took the dual-aspect account of truth provided in FOB, the account which he then employed in HTM as part of his pragmatic clarification of the idea of reality, to be fully developed; the account given in HTM is not a further development of it.[5]

---

[2] In "What Pragmatism Is," Peirce renamed his view "pragmaticism" in order to distinguish it from those of other pragmatists, like James and Schiller (5.414, EP 2: 334–335, 1905; see also R 329, ca. 1904).

[3] Other passages in which Peirce seems to have treated the investigative aspect in this way are 5.494, EP 2: 419, 1907; R 322: 20–21, 1907; R 844s, 1908.

[4] Peirce later revised this passage to read: "exclusively to the *experiential* method of settling opinion" (5.406, emphasis added).

[5] Migotti is puzzled by HTM's reference to FOB's account of truth: "This talk of 'the ideas of truth and falsehood, in their full development' is puzzling. Is 'in their full development' supposed to be equivalent to 'at the third grade of clearness'? If so, why does the idea of truth not, officially anyway, get put to the pragmatic test for another two pages? Indeed, if the pragmatic clarification of truth has already been carried out by the end of 'Fixation,' then why repeat the exercise in 'How to Make Our Ideas Clear'? But if 'full development' here does *not* mean 'full pragmatic clarification,' then what does it mean?" (1998: 84). Migotti argues that "full development" – or, as he suggests is better,

So how did Peirce attempt to clarify the idea of reality, and what role did his dual-aspect account of truth play in that clarification?

2.2

Over the years, Peirce gave various statements of the pragmatic maxim, and in the 1900s he criticized the psychological arguments he had provided for it in the 1870s, replacing them with other arguments involving his newly developed ideas about what he called the "normative sciences": logic, ethics, and esthetics. Here my focus will be on the 1878 statement of the maxim in HTM: "Consider what effects, which might conceivably have practical bearings, we conceive the object of our conception to have. Then, our conception of these effects is the whole of our conception of the object" (W 3: 266).[6] The purpose of the maxim, so stated, is to clarify a given idea by translating or explaining it in terms of the "practical bearings" of the object(s) to which the idea is thought to apply. Peirce's illustrations of the maxim show that these "practical bearings" include both *action* and *experience*. Consider the proposition that an object x has property F. The pragmatic maxim tells us to translate this proposition in terms of actions that we can perform that are relevant to x and in terms of experiences associated with those actions. In doing this, our idea of F will attain a greater degree of clarity than that required by the earlier standard of "clear and distinct ideas."

"Clear" and "distinct" are technical terms. A clear idea "is so apprehended that it will be recognized wherever it is met with, and so that no other will be mistaken for it" (HTM, 5.389, W 3: 258). Clearness "consists in the connexion of the word with familiar experience" (3.457, 1897), and one's idea is clear if it "contain[s] no element which perfect familiarity does not enable [him] to use with entire confidence" (7.284, R 254, ca. 1895).[7] This does not require that he have an infallible power always "to recognize

---

"sufficient development" – is something that happens "*in between* the second and third grades of clearness" (1998: 85), that "a tension between verbal and epistemic commitments or practices" (1998: 87) exists for tenacious, authoritarian, and a priori inquirers, and that it is the elimination of that tension "that constitutes the full development of the ideas of truth and falsity and renders them suitable for being raised to the third grade of clearness promised by the Pragmatic Maxim" (1998: 86–87). I favor a much simpler solution to this apparent puzzle. Peirce did not "repeat the exercise" of pragmatically clarifying the idea of truth in HTM, nor did he go through that exercise a first time in FOB. By "full development," Peirce meant simply the outcome of the genealogy that I described in Chapter 1.

[6] Peirce later revised this to read: "Consider what effects, *that* might conceivably have practical bearings" (5.402, emphasis added).

[7] I take the date of R 254 from ILS 102, n. 2.

an idea, and under no circumstances to mistake another for it," but something more modest, merely "hav[ing] such an acquaintance with the idea as
to have become familiar with it, and to have lost all hesitancy in recognizing it in ordinary cases," and this is nothing more than "a subjective feeling
of mastery which may be entirely mistaken" (HTM, 5.389, W 3: 258). A
distinct idea possesses a "second grade" of clearness, one that "is far more
important" than the first (8.218, ILS 274, 1910).

> A distinct idea is defined as one which contains nothing which is not
> clear ... [B]y the *contents* of an idea logicians understand whatever is
> contained in its definition. So that an idea is *distinctly* apprehended, accord-
> ing to them, when we can give a precise definition of it, in abstract terms.
> (HTM, 5.390, W 3: 258)

A distinct idea "consists in the abstract definition, depending upon an
analysis of just what it is that makes the word applicable" (3.457, 1897); it is
"that which results from analytic definition" (8.214, ILS 273, 1910). Peirce
urged that we aspire to a higher degree of clearness of ideas, one that
"consists in such a representation of the idea that fruitful reasoning can be
made to turn upon it, and that it can be applied to the resolution of
difficult practical problems" (3.457, 1897).

Again, the sole philosophical use to which Peirce put the pragmatic
maxim in HTM was to clarify the idea of reality. He began by considering
that idea in its first grade of clarity, saying that none "could be clearer than
this. Every child uses it with perfect confidence, never dreaming that he
does not understand it" (5.405, W 3: 271). Ask a seven-year-old whether
Santa Claus is real and she might say either "yes" or "no," but she will
certainly understand the question. Having an idea of reality that is clear to
the first degree requires only that one understand the idea well enough to
feel confident in her judgments about whether specific things are real, not
that she be infallible in such judgments. One's idea of reality is clear to the
second degree when she can provide a verbal definition of "reality," which,
as we have already seen, Peirce took to be "that whose characters are
independent of what anybody may think them to be" (HTM, 5.405,
W 3: 271).

To apply the pragmatic maxim to the idea of reality, Peirce first
considered what "peculiar sensible effects" that real things have in virtue
of their being real, and he concluded that the only such effect that they
"have is to cause belief, for all the sensations which they excite emerge into
consciousness in the form of beliefs" (HTM, 5.406, W 3: 271–272). In other
words, the only sensible effect that a real thing has *qua* real thing – the only

sensible effect that is common to *all* real things – is that it causes sensations and thereby results in beliefs. But in what way is having a belief a sensible effect? In FOB, Peirce had asserted that belief *feels* different than doubt (5.370, W 3: 247). I suspect that he made this point in anticipation of the claim made in HTM, that believing is a "sensible effect." Furthermore, Peirce, inspired by Alexander Bain (5.12, EP 2: 399, 1907), maintained that genuine belief is in part a disposition to behave in specific ways in specific situations, and you can be aware, by way of the senses, that others, as well as you yourself, have a disposition to behave in certain ways. So the fact that one believes a given proposition has at least these sensible aspects: it feels a specific way to believe that *p* rather than to have doubts about whether *p*, and it can give rise to observable behavior.

If "the only effect which real things have is to cause belief," then we are led to the question "how ... true belief (or belief in the real) [is] distinguished from false belief (or belief in fiction)" (HTM, 5.406, W 3: 272). Thus does the pragmatic clarification of the idea of reality depend on an account of true belief. So what are we saying when we say that a belief is true rather than false? Peirce had already answered that question in FOB: a true belief is one that represents reality and that will result from sufficient investigation. But only one aspect of this dual-aspect account of truth would prove useful in this context. The question that Peirce asked at this point presupposed that a true belief is "belief in the real," i.e., it presupposed the representationalist aspect of his account, which itself relies on the idea of reality. Since he was here concerned to clarify the idea of reality, the representationalist aspect was of no use – to use it would make that clarification dependent on an idea of reality that itself was clear only to the second degree. So it stands to reason that Peirce would rely only on the investigative aspect of his account of truth:

> [A]ll the followers of science are fully persuaded that the processes of investigation, if only pushed far enough, will give one certain solution to every question to which they can be applied ... Different minds may set out with the most antagonistic views, but the progress of investigation carries them by a force outside of themselves to one and the same conclusion. This activity of thought by which we are carried, not where we wish, but to a foreordained goal, is like the operation of destiny. No modification of the point of view taken, no selection of other facts for study, no natural bent of mind even, can enable a man to escape the predestinate opinion. This great law is embodied in the conception of truth and reality. The opinion which is fated to be ultimately agreed to by all who investigate [i.e., by all who employ the method of science in order to dispel doubt and fix belief], is what

we mean by the truth, and the object represented in this opinion is the real. (W 3:273)[8]

So what was new in HTM was a clarification of the idea, not of truth, but of reality: something real is the object of a belief that will be "forced upon the mind" given sufficient experience and reasoning, or, as he put it in "The Probability of Induction" (the fourth paper in the *Illustrations* series), "reality is only the object of the final opinion to which sufficient investigation would lead" (2.693, W 3: 305, 1878).

New in HTM, but not without antecedents in earlier works. Peirce anticipated his pragmatic clarification of reality in the "cognition series" of papers published in the *Journal of Speculative Philosophy* in 1868–1869. There he wrote that the real is

> that which, sooner or later, information and reasoning would finally result in, and which is therefore independent of the vagaries of me and you.[9] . . . [A] proposition whose falsity can never be discovered, and the error of which therefore is absolutely incognizable, contains, upon our principle, absolutely no error. Consequently, that which is thought in these cognitions is the real, as it really is. (5.311, W 2: 239, 1868)

Earlier, in a draft of the cognition series, he wrote that the real is "the object of an absolutely true proposition" (W 2: 175). And a few years later, in his review of Fraser's edition of the works of Berkeley, he defended what he called the *realist conception* of reality: "Everything . . . which will be thought to exist in the final opinion is real, and nothing else" (8.12, W 2: 468–469, 1871).[10] I hesitate to say that these relatively early pronouncements are statements of the pragmatic clarification itself rather than antecedents of it, for two reasons. First, at the time of these statements Peirce had not yet formulated the pragmatic maxim, so characterizing them as pragmatic clarifications would be misleading.[11] Second, the version of the pragmatic clarification given in HTM depends on the dual-aspect account of truth that he defended in FOB. According to the investigative aspect of that account, a belief is true exactly when it would result from continuing investigation (inquiry that relies on experience and reasoning) until beliefs are

---

[8] Peirce revised HTM in 1893 and changed portions of this passage (5.407). I quote the revised passage and discuss the reason for his revisions in Chapter 7.

[9] One might be tempted to read this passage as committing Peirce to an anti-realist view according to which investigation somehow gives rise to reality itself; I argue against this reading in Chapter 4.

[10] He called this the "realist conception" because he believed that it implies scholastic realism, i.e., realism about "generals" or universals. See Chapter 5.

[11] I am grateful to T. L. Short for pushing me on this point.

permanently settled. When he made these early statements about reality, he had not yet formulated the investigative aspect of his account of truth.[12] At any rate, by the time he wrote HTM, he felt sufficiently confident about the pragmatic clarification of reality that he stated:

> [W]e have, by the application of [the pragmatic maxim], reached so clear an apprehension of what we mean by reality, and of the fact which the idea rests on, that we should not, perhaps, be making a pretension so presumptuous as it would be singular, if we were to offer a metaphysical theory of existence for universal acceptance among those who employ the scientific method of fixing belief. (5.410, W 3: 275)

Peirce did not intend the pragmatic clarification of the idea of reality to invalidate or undermine the verbal definition of "real."[13] It is supposed to clarify, but not replace, the verbal definition by making clear what reality, so defined, has to do with purposeful behavior and its experiential consequences. If HTM gives the impression that an idea clarified to the third grade of clearness supersedes first- or second-grade clarifications of that idea, then, by Peirce's own admission, he is to blame. But this was not his considered view: "I ought to say that my three grades of clearness are *not*, as I seemed then [i.e., at the time he authored HTM] to think, such that

---

[12] However, Peirce did say some things about truth in 1868 draft manuscripts leading up to the cognition series that foreshadowed the investigative aspect of his eventual account: "Does truth consist in anything but agreement with a conclusion logically inferable from the sum of all information? No" (W 2: 162); "if a proposition is logically inferable ... from the sum of all possible information, past, present, and to come, then it is absolutely true, for it is true in the whole of its meaning" (W 2: 175); "I may define a true proposition as one which is determined by the sum of all information and which denies no particular of all information" (W 2: 182); "a proposition ... is *true*, when it is affirmatively determined by the sum of information" (W 2: 183). And although he did not mention truth in the following passages from SCFI, they are strongly suggestive of the investigative aspect of his eventual account of truth: there is a series of cognitions "which, at a time sufficiently future, the community will always continue to re-affirm ... [T]hat which is thought in these cognitions is the real, as it really is" (5.311, W 2: 239); "what anything really is, is what it may finally come to be known to be in the ideal state of complete information" (5.316, W 2: 241).

[13] I agree with Wiggins that Peirce's intention in formulating a pragmatic account of reality was not to undermine anything he had said in FOB about reality, but rather to "explicate [that] notion[] – in the spirit of 'look[ing] to the upshot of our concepts in order rightly to apprehend them'" (2004: 110); Wiggins quotes from 5.3, 1901. Almeder (1980: 153) fails to see that Peirce's account of reality in terms of the outcome of investigation is not an alternative *definition* of "real." Mayorga also seems to overlook the fact that Peirce's pragmatic clarification of the idea of reality is not a *definition* of "real," and this leads her to worry that that clarification may imply some unpalatable views: "if the final opinion (albeit the result of investigation) is what defines reality, what keeps Peirce's theory from slipping into a sort of relativism (or even nihilism)?" (2007: 142). She proceeds to argue that Peirce's synechism is a bulwark against that danger. On my view there is no such danger, since Peirce's clarification of the idea of reality augments rather than supplants his definition of "real" as that which is independent of what anyone actually thinks about it.

either the first or the second are superseded by the third although we may say that they are acquired, – *mostly*, – in the order of those numbers" (8.218, ILS 273, 1910). Even if the verbal definition of "reality" conveys an idea that is clear to the second degree and the pragmatic clarification of the idea of reality conveys one that is clear to the third, the latter does not supplant the former. In fact, Peirce held that "there is no reason why all three [grades of clearness of a given concept] should not be symmetrically developed" (8.218, ILS 274, 1910).[14] That the verbal definition is pragmatically insufficient does not mean that it is illegitimate. This point is crucial for my interpretation of FOB and HTM, since my formulation of Peirce's basic realism relies on the verbal definition of "real." The word "real" *just means* that which is independent of what anyone thinks about it, and the fact that that verbal definition does not meet the pragmatic maxim's standard of clarity is no reason to abandon it. In fact, we could not abandon it without *changing the subject* to something *other than* reality. Compare a verbal definition of "lithium" – e.g., "the element whose atomic weight is 6.941 ± 0.002u" – mastery of which counts as the possession of the idea of lithium clarified to the second degree. Once one can explain what lithium is in terms of purposeful behavior and its experiential consequences (see 2.330, EP 2: 286, 1903), her concept is clear to the third degree, but that in no way invalidates the verbal definition. Analogously, the fact that the verbal definition of "real" is not pragmatically clear does not imply that "real" means something besides what that verbal definition provides, nor does it call into question theories, like basic realism, that are stated in terms of that definition.

2.3

Again, the idea of truth was not among those to which Peirce applied the pragmatic maxim in HTM. However, given that he chose to base his pragmatic clarification of the idea of reality on what he had said about true belief in FOB, it is fair to ask whether that account of true belief is itself pragmatically clear. Peirce did not address this question explicitly, but he said enough about both truth and belief to suggest the sort of answer he might have given. We saw previously that one difference between believing that p and doubting whether or not p is that one will be disposed to behave differently in various situations if one believes that p rather than doubting

---

[14] This calls into question Misak's reading, on which the project of providing a pragmatic account of a given concept "overshadows" the further development of the first- and second-grade understandings of that concept (1991/2004: 36).

whether *p*. So "*S* believes that *x* is ice cream" might get pragmatically clarified by propositions like "if you point out to *S* that *x* is melting, and if *S* wants to eat *x* later, then *S* will put *x* in the freezer" – propositions that describe how one might interact with someone who has specific beliefs (and desires) and the experimental consequences of such interactions.

The question whether the idea of *truth* that Peirce employed is pragmatically clear warrants a more detailed examination, one that considers what that idea looks like when clarified only to the first and second degrees. To possess the idea of truth to the first grade of clearness is to be sufficiently familiar with it to use it with confidence. Even young children can meet this standard. I ask my six-year-old niece whether she brushed her teeth, and she says that she did. Suspicious, I respond, "Really?" Her reply: "Yes, I'm telling the truth!" But such confidence does not guarantee that one's idea of truth is clear to the second degree, not even if one happens to be a logician:

> The problem of the logician is to determine the general conditions of the attainment of truth. This problem as it first comes before him, may be clothed in various forms of words, all of which are used by every man every day of his life, so that he feels himself to be a perfect master of their meaning [i.e., he possesses the relevant concepts to at least the first grade of clearness]. Yet the first thing that the logician's studies disclose to him is that he does not know what it is that they mean. What is truth? An assertion is said to be an expression which is either true or false; but what is it that makes an expression either true or false? The logician at the outset is met by a multitude of such needs of definitions, and finds that his science must be all guesswork until they are answered. (R 693, NEM 4: 196, 1904)

There is strong textual evidence that Peirce took the verbal definition of "truth" to be given in terms of representation of reality.[15] He provided a definition in terms of "conformity" of a representation with reality in his entry for "truth" in the *Century Dictionary*: "Conformity of thought with fact; conformity of a judgment, statement, or belief with the reality" (CD 6514). In a 1906 manuscript, he wrote: "That truth is the correspondence of a representation with its object is, as Kant says, merely the nominal definition of it" (5.553, EP 2:379).[16] And in a 1910 manuscript, he asserted that "a

---

[15] Among those who think that Peirce believed that a representationalist – or more generally, a correspondence – account of truth provides a verbal definition of "truth" are Migotti (1998: 83), Bergman (2011: 25), and Legg (2014: 205).

[16] The relevant passage is *Critique of Pure Reason* A58/B82. Compare the passage from Peirce just quoted to an alternative draft of the same work: "So what is truth? Kant is sometimes accused of saying that it is correspondence of a predicate with its object. The great analyst was guilty of no such puerility. He calls it a nominal definition, that is to say, a suitable explanation to give to a person who

definition of the *real* amounts to a definition of *truth*, which is obviously the character of a representation of the real as it really is" (R 655: 30).

Earlier I made the point that any pragmatic clarification of the idea of reality assumes the verbal definition of "reality" and cannot abandon it without changing the topic of the clarification from reality to something else. The same point applies to the verbal definition of "truth." Any purported theory of truth – be it a coherence theory, a deflationist theory, Huw Price's (2003) truth-as-norm-of-assertoric-discourse theory, or some other sort of theory – that does not incorporate a representationalist element *is not a theory of truth at all*. Misak rightly notes that we should "avoid taking [Peirce's] thoughts on truth to be in direct competition with accounts of truth which focus on one of the first two aspects of understanding," i.e., clarifications of the idea of truth to the first and second grades of clearness, the latter of which Peirce would be "happy to let . . . stand as a 'nominal' or 'formal' definition"; after all, "he holds that definition retains all of its importance" even once an idea has been pragmatically clarified (1991/2004: 37). But she also says that he "would argue that a theory which does not go beyond [Tarski's] adequacy condition is not up to much and a theory which elaborates the adequacy condition in terms of correspondence is up to too much" (1991/2004: 128). More recently, she has written that

> [w]hen Peirce turns his pragmatic maxim on the concept of truth, the upshot is an aversion to "transcendental" accounts of truth, such as the correspondence theory, on which a true belief is one that corresponds to, or gets right, or mirrors the believer-independent world (*CP* 5. 572; 1901). Such accounts . . . make truth the subject of empty metaphysics. For the very idea of the believer-independent world, and the items within it to which beliefs or sentences might correspond, seems graspable only if we could somehow step outside our corpus of belief, our practices, or that with which we have dealings. (2013: 35)

The phrase "believer-independent" is similar to "mind-independent," which, as we saw in the Introduction, is ambiguous between the real (independent of what anyone thinks about it) and the external (independent of what anyone thinks about anything); Peirce believed that there is a

---

has never before seen the word 'Wahrheit'" (R 283: 39 of assorted pages, 1906; quoted in Misak 1991/ 2004: 38, 128). Peirce also referenced this view of Kant's in *Minute Logic*: "'Truth is the conformity of a representation to its object,' says Kant. One might make this statement more explicit; but for our present purpose it may pass. It is nearly correct, so far as it is intelligible" (1.578, 1902). I disagree with Misak's assessment that "[i]t is this sort of definition that [Peirce] is especially set against" (1991/ 2004: 36); see later in this chapter.

mind-independent world in the first sense and that some reals are mind-independent in the second sense. But Misak's use of "believer-independent" suggestions a third meaning, one on which the claim that the world is believer-independent means that there are aspects of the world that we can never know, things about the world that we would never understand, no matter how far we were to push our investigations. Peirce did indeed deny that the world is believer-independent in that sense, and Misak is right that he would reject a correspondence account of truth according to which truth is a relation with objects that are inaccessible to our cognitive activities. But he did not reject correspondence and representationalist theories altogether. As we saw in the previous chapter, he repeatedly asserted that a true proposition is one that represents reality. Misak continues:

> That is, the correspondence concept of truth is missing the dimension that makes it suitable for inquiry. It fails to make "readily comprehensible" the fact that we aim at the truth or at getting things right (*CP* 1. 578; 1902). How could anyone aim for a truth that goes beyond what we can experience or beyond the best that inquiry could do? How could an inquirer adopt a methodology that might achieve that aim? The correspondence theory makes truth "a useless word" and "having no use for this meaning of the word 'truth', we had better use the word in another sense." (*CP* 5. 553; [1906])
>
> Peirce, that is, is set against representationalist theories of truth – theories that take truth to be a matter of words representing, mirroring, or copying reality. (2013: 35)

But as I have shown, Peirce's account of truth was dual-aspect: a true belief is one that both represents a world that is independent of how anyone thinks about it and that would be fixed in the mind of a believer via sensory and cognitive interaction with that real world. This sort of belief does not "go[] beyond what we can experience or beyond the best that inquiry could do"; indeed, it is *the result of* what we experience when conducting investigation to the best of our abilities.

One of the passages that Misak cites to support her interpretation is 5.553, from which she quotes in the passage just cited. But to see what Peirce was really up to in that passage, consider the context of that claim:

> That truth is the correspondence of a representation with its object is, as Kant says, merely the nominal definition of it. Truth belongs exclusively to propositions. A proposition has a subject (or set of subjects) and a predicate.

The subject is a sign; the predicate is a sign; and the proposition is a sign that the predicate is a sign of that of which the subject is a sign. If it be so, it is true. But what does this correspondence, or reference of the sign to its object, consist in? The pragmaticist answers this question as follows. Suppose, he says, that the angel Gabriel were to descend and communicate to me the answer to this riddle from the breast of omniscience. Is this supposable; or does it involve an essential absurdity to suppose the answer to be brought to human intelligence? In the latter case, "truth," in this sense, is a useless word, which never can express a human thought. It is real, if you will; it belongs to that universe entirely disconnected from human intelligence which we know as the world of utter nonsense. Having no use for this meaning of the word "truth," we had better use the word in another sense presently to be described. (5.553, EP 2: 379–380, 1906)

After characterizing the statement that "truth is the correspondence of a representation with its object" as the "nominal" definition of "truth," Peirce considered a disjunction: either (i) the correspondence relation that amounts to truth *is* something that we can understand, something that can be "disclosed to human intelligence," or (ii) the correspondence relation that amounts to truth is something that humans cannot understand. It is only on disjunct (ii) that "truth" is "a useless word." He proceeded to flesh out disjunct (i) by describing ideas to which he had already committed himself decades before:

But if, on the other hand, it be conceivable that the secret should be disclosed to human intelligence, it will be something that thought can compass. Now thought is of the nature of a sign. In that case, then, if we can find out the right method of thinking and can follow it out, – the right method of transforming signs, – then truth can be nothing more nor less than the last result to which the following out of this method would ultimately carry us. In that case, that to which the representation should conform is itself something in the nature of a representation, or sign, – something noumenal, intelligible, conceivable, and utterly unlike a thing-in-itself. (5.553, EP 2: 380, 1906)

His reference to "the angel Gabriel . . . descend[ing] and communicat-[ing] . . . the answer to th[e] riddle [of correspondence] from the breast of omniscience" is obviously not literal; it is a humorous flourish he used to poke fun at those who thought that the correspondence of a representation with reality, i.e., *truth*, could not be understood by us mere mortals. Peirce was not rejecting the idea that truth involves correspondence with reality; he was denying that the correspondence relation is something outside of possible human understanding. So Misak is right to say that a pragmatic clarification – or as she prefers, a "pragmatic elucidation"

(1991/2004: 42) – of truth should illuminate that idea "by considering its linkages with inquiry, assertion, and acquisition of belief," but the idea to be illuminated in that way has an ineliminable representationalist aspect. Again, any account of truth that denies that truth amounts to representation of the real world is guilty of changing the subject, of providing an account of something *other than* truth. Just as a pragmatic clarification of the idea of reality must be an account, in terms of action and experience, of what it means to say that something has the traits it has whether or not anyone believes it to have them, a pragmatic clarification of the idea of truth must be an account, in terms of action and experience, of what it means to say that something *accurately represents reality*.[17]

Peirce may have thought that a representationalist definition of "truth" is correct but not very illuminating, and that in particular it does not show how the idea of truth is tied to action and to experience.[18] If we are to understand the idea of reality in terms of actions and their experiential consequences, what we say about true belief cannot be limited to this merely verbal definition. In a later work, Peirce argued this point:

> "Truth is the conformity of a representation to its object" . . . [But] what is that "object" which serves to define truth? Why it is the *reality*: it is of such a nature as to be independent of representations of it, so that, taking any individual sign or any individual collection of signs (such, for example, as all the ideas that ever enter into a given man's head) there is some character which that thing possesses, whether that sign or any of the signs of that collection represents the thing as possessing that character or not. Very good: now only tell me what it means to say that an object possesses a character, and I shall be satisfied. But . . . we can only reach a conception of the less known through the more known, and . . . consequently the only meaning which we can attach to the phrase that a thing "has a character" is that something is *true* of it. So there we are, after threading the passages of this labyrinth, already thrown out at that very conception of truth at which we entered it. Indeed, when one comes to consider it, how futile it was to

---

[17] Misak assumes that a thing meets the criterion of reality given by Peirce's "pragmatic view" if it is "believed, at the end of inquiry, to be real," e.g., "[e]xternal entities would be believed to be real at the end of inquiry" (1991/2004: 135, 134). But on my view, Peirce's pragmatic view should not be stated in that way. Misak's statement implies that whether something is real *does* depend on what someone thinks about it – it depends on whether someone thinks it is real! – and thus implies that real things are, in Peirce's sense, fictional; but that's absurd. The correct statement of the clarification of the idea of reality *does* refer to belief; more specifically, it refers to what is *represented* in belief: that is real which would be represented in beliefs permanently fixed by investigation. It may be that Misak avoids this kind of formulation because she downplays the correspondence element – what I have called the representationalist aspect – of his account of truth.

[18] Peter Skagestad writes that "[i]n Peirce's view, it is not *wrong* to speak of truth as correspondence with facts; it just is not very informative" (1981: 76).

imagine that we were to clear up the idea of *truth* by the more occult idea of *reality*! (1.578, 1902; see also R 432: 7–8, ca. 1902)

A pragmatic clarification of the idea of truth cannot rely on the idea of reality if the latter idea is clear only to the second degree. This is because the verbal definition of "reality" assumes something that is itself in need of pragmatic clarification: the notion of a thing having a character or property. And a verbal definition of the phrase "having a character" employs the notion of truth.

So how might we explain the meaning of the claim that p is true in terms of activity and its experiential consequences? We could say, as Peirce did in FOB, that a true belief is one that we will eventually have if we attempt to settle our beliefs by way of investigation. The activity is the attempt to replace doubt with belief by way of experience and reasoning, and the experiential consequences are that beliefs actually get settled (and a settled belief does make an experiential difference, as described previously). The pragmatic difference made by the idea of truth has to do with our attempts to dispel doubt and the experiential consequences of those attempts. This is one way in which the investigative aspect of Peirce's dual-aspect account might be clarified so as to meet Peirce's standard of pragmatic clarity, and this is a reason for thinking that Peirce's employment of that account in his pragmatic clarification of the idea of reality does not ipso facto render that account any less clear.

2.4

I now need to address one further aspect of what Peirce had to say about investigation, truth, and reality. It is the question whether the pragmatic clarification of reality should be understood in terms of what *will* eventually be permanently believed as a result of investigation or in terms of what *would* be permanently believed if some condition were fulfilled, whether or not it is actually ever fulfilled.

My point of entry into this discussion is the "buried secrets" objection that Peirce anticipated against his pragmatic clarification of reality: "I may be asked what I have to say to all the minute facts of history, forgotten never to be recovered, to the lost books of the ancients, to the buried secrets . . . Do these things not really exist because they are hopelessly beyond the reach of our knowledge?" (HTM, 5.409, W 3: 274). The pragmatic clarification seems to imply that investigation will eventually reveal every aspect of reality, every fact that there is or ever has been. But it seems like there are facts about the past that will never be discovered, no matter how far investigation is ever actually carried out. Exactly how many people set foot in Placentia Palace on Sept. 7, 1533, the day of Queen Elizabeth I's birth? Common sense tells us that there is a determinate fact of the matter about this. But it is unlikely that someone will ever actually discover what that number is. In fact, it is unlikely that anyone will ever even *try* to discover it. These considerations suggest two problems for Peirce's pragmatic clarification of reality. The first is that there will be investigations that will fail to settle belief about whether or not x is F, despite the fact that x is F. The second problem is that there are facts that will never be investigated at all, matters about which no one cares enough to investigate. That there are meaningful questions that either will be investigated but never settled or will never be investigated at all implies that there are facts – realities – that will never be represented in the settled beliefs of investigators, contrary to Peirce's account.

The buried secrets objection poses the following dilemma. On the one hand, Peirce could say that there is, despite what common sense tells us, no real fact of the matter about how many people visited Placentia Palace on that day. On the other hand, he could insist that investigation *will* at some point permanently settle the belief that exactly n people visited Placentia Palace on that day, for some specific value of n. But this is an implausible position to take, as it makes extraordinarily optimistic assumptions about our capacities for discovery (how could we possibly settle this question now?) and about the range of questions that will eventually be investigated (why would anyone ever bother trying to settle it?).

In HTM Peirce grasped neither horn. Instead, he switched without comment, and I suspect without being aware of it, to a subtly different way of clarifying the idea of reality, one that involves, not the beliefs that investigation will eventually settle, but those that it *would* settle were it carried out until beliefs are permanently fixed:

> [T]hough in no possible state of knowledge can any number be great enough to express the relation between the amount of what rests unknown to the amount of the known, yet it is unphilosophical to suppose that, with regard to any given question (which has any clear meaning), investigation would not bring forth a solution of it, if it were carried far enough. Who would have said, a few years ago, that we could ever know of what substances stars are made whose light may have been longer in reaching us than the human race has existed? Who can be sure of what we shall not know in a few hundred years? Who can guess what would be the result of continuing the pursuit of science for ten thousand years, with the activity of the last hundred? And if it were to go on for a million, or a billion, or any number

of years you please, how is it possible to say that there is any question which might not ultimately be solved? (HTM, 5.409, W 3: 274–275)[19]

Here Peirce shifted from describing reality in the indicative mood – what *will be* represented in the beliefs of those who investigate – to describing it in the subjunctive mood – what *would be* represented in such beliefs in the hypothetical situation in which investigation were to settle those beliefs permanently. In HTM, Peirce provided indicative-mood clarifications of the ideas of hardness (5.403, W 3: 266), weight (5.404, W 3: 267), force (5.404, W 3: 270), and reality (5.407, W 3: 273). But when the time came to defend his clarification of the idea of reality against the buried secrets objection, he made use of the subjunctive mood, and he did so without drawing attention to the change. Peirce eventually adopted a strong modal realism that recognized the reality of what he called *would be's*, and he came to believe that the reality of *would be's* was a necessary condition of the truth of subjunctive-mood pragmatic clarifications. But that was much later. In the 1870s he was neither an avowed realist about *would be's* nor clear on the importance of the choice between indicative and subjunctive conditionals. I will examine his realism about *would be's* in detail in Chapter 6. For now, I will consider his use of the subjunctive mood to respond to the buried secrets objection in HTM.[20]

If it is a necessary condition of the hardness of a diamond (to use Peirce's well-known example; see HTM, 5.403, W 3: 266) that it actually be pressed and resist that pressure, then a diamond that is never pressed is not hard. Analogously, if a necessary condition of the reality of *x* is that *x* actually be represented in beliefs permanently settled in the minds of those who use the method of science, then *x* is real only if the method of science (i.e., investigation) does eventually fix beliefs in which *x* is represented. On the other hand, if it is a necessary condition of the hardness of a diamond only that it would resist pressure if it were pressed, then a diamond can be hard even if it is never actually pressed; if a necessary condition of the reality of *x* is only that it would be represented in beliefs permanently fixed by investigation, then *x* can be real even if investigation never does

---

[19] Peirce again used the example of the composition of the stars in 1887 (6.556, W 6: 64) and 1898 (1.138, EP 2: 49, RLT 179). As T. L. Short reminded me, it was the invention of the spectroscope that made it possible to answer the question of the stars' composition and Peirce was one the first American scientists to use the new device extensively (EP 2: 553, n. 21).

[20] Other, earlier works illustrate Peirce's ambivalence about the choice between indicative- and subjunctive-mood conditionals in pragmatic clarifications, e.g., W 3: 59, 1872. Mayorga (2007: 170, n. 300) notes this early ambivalence.

permanently settle beliefs in which *x* is represented. Adopting the subjunctive-mood clarification of reality allows us to say, e.g., that there is a fact of the matter about the number of occupants of Placentia Palace on a given day in the sixteenth century even if no one ever bothers looking into the question. What matters is whether investigation *would* eventually settle beliefs about this.

This might get around the problem of matters never investigated. But what about matters actually investigated but without success? It seems likely that a future team of historians who dedicate themselves to the question of the population of Placentia Palace will quickly exhaust the available evidence without arriving at a permanently settled consensus.[21] Regardless of how long their studies were to continue, they would never reach a settled belief. If this is right, then explaining reality as that which *would* be represented in the beliefs of scientific investigators is no solution to the problem.

There are at least three responses open to Peirce, and he gave each one of them at different times. The first is simply to say, *contra* the objection, that for any past fact, investigation carried far enough *would* fix relevant beliefs about that fact, so that there are no permanently buried secrets. This is the view that Peirce seems to have taken in HTM and elsewhere during the 1870s: investigation can settle any meaningful question, even if we cannot now imagine the specific means by which a question – such as that about Placentia Palace – might be answered. For example, in the 1871 Berkeley review he maintained that "there is a definite opinion to which the mind of man is, on the whole and in the long run, tending. On many questions the final agreement is already reached, on all it will be reached if time enough is given" (8.12, W 2: 469).[22] Over the next two years, he reiterated that optimism about investigation, writing that "we seem fated to come to the final conclusion" (W 3: 44, 1872). During this time he sometimes

---

[21] If I am wrong about this example, others are easy to find, and without even reaching into the distant past. How many rubber bands were in the junk drawer of my kitchen exactly one year ago today?

[22] This could be read as implying that there will be a future time at which all possible questions have been answered. But other comments during this period support a more charitable interpretation: the final agreement on *any specific question* will be reached if time enough is given for investigation on that question. In 1869, he wrote that "information may increase beyond any assignable point" and that there will never be a point in the future at which "everything will be known"; the claim that there will be such a point in time is something that "no one can maintain" (5.330, W 2: 250–251). Later he wrote that "we shall never know the true answer to every question" (W 3: 57, 1872). And in HTM he maintained that "in no possible state of knowledge can any number be great enough to express the relation between the amount of what rests unknown to the amount of the known" (5.409, W 3: 274). So he did not entertain the possibility of a future time at which every single question will have been answered.

presented his optimism not as a doctrine asserted but as an assumption made by investigators with regard to any question they actually pursue. For example:

> Disputes undoubtedly occur among those who pursue a proper method of investigation. But these disputes come to an end. At least that is the assumption upon which we go in entering into the discussion at all, for unless investigation is to lead to settled opinion it is of no service to us whatever. We do believe then in regard to every question which we try to investigate that the observations though they may be as varied and as unlike in themselves as possible, yet have some power of bringing about in our minds a predetermined state of belief. (7.334, W 3: 43–44, 1872; see also W 3: 57, 1872)

The second response is to alter the pragmatic clarification of reality even further than what is suggested by his shift into the subjunctive mood, so that reality includes both what *would be* represented in the permanently settled beliefs of investigators and what *would have been* represented in those beliefs had investigation been pursued at a time before the relevant evidence disappeared. Some determinate number of people occupied the palace on the day of Elizabeth's birth, and had our intrepid historians staked out the place on that day and counted the folks coming and going, they would have agreed on what that number was. This is analogous to saying, about a diamond that was destroyed before it was ever subjected to pressure, that it would have resisted had pressure been applied to it and therefore that it was really hard. Peirce did eventually embrace realism, not just about *would be's*, as mentioned earlier, but also about *would have been's* (see Chapter 6), and so he was eventually able to make this move. But so far as I am aware, he endorsed it only once, in 1911:

> In [HTM], I call "truth" the predestinate opinion, by which I ought to have meant that which *would* ultimately prevail if investigation were carried sufficiently far in that particular direction . . . I nevertheless talked, – except perhaps in a single sentence, – as if, for example, it was at least questionable whether any Real flower was ever "born to blush unseen, and waste its sweetness on the desert air."[23] But beyond question, such there are, which would have been found if inquiry could have been, and had been, sufficiently pushed in the right direction, although, in fact, it was not; and of things in which we rightly but vaguely believe, the immense majority are similarly unknown; and this majority grows relatively (and not merely numerically) larger the further inquiry is pushed. (EP 2: 457)

---

[23] The quotation is from Thomas Gray's "Elegy Written in a Country Churchyard" (1751).

I will examine the modal realism that made this response possible in Chapter 6. But at this point we should note how surprising it is that he eventually took this position. Any hypothetical past group of investigators would have been limited in the time and the technological means that they could devote to investigation, and thus it is incorrect to think of the beliefs they would have established as necessarily sharing the contents of the beliefs that would be fixed if investigation were carried as far as it could possibly go. The investigative aspect of Peirce's account of truth imposes no constraints on the time or technology available to investigators, and any hypothetical investigators operating during some finite span of time in the past would necessarily face such constraints.[24]

The third possible response to the buried secrets objection is to concede the point of the objection and say that if there is "a question that no amount of research can ever answer," then "there is a *lacuna* in the completeness of reality" (8.156, ca. 1900). This seems to be the response Peirce favored from the mid-1880s until the early 1900s. During that time, he treated the investigative optimism that he had evinced during the 1870s only as an assumption – a "hope" – that governs actual investigative practices, not also as a doctrine universally true of all meaningful questions, and he acknowledged that there are meaningful questions that investigation will never settle and to which there are, therefore, no true answers. Paired with the indicative-mood pragmatic clarification of the idea of reality, this implies that there is no reality corresponding to such questions – that reality has gaps, or lacunae. In Chapter 7, I examine Peirce's acceptance of this position and how it might have been impacted by his eventual view that pragmatic clarifications must cover *would be's*.

Peirce also shifted from the indicative to the subjunctive mood in response to another anticipated objection, viz. that his pragmatic clarification of reality "makes the characters of the real to depend on what is ultimately thought about them" and is thus "directly opposed to the abstract definition ... of reality" as that which is independent of what anyone thinks about it (HTM, 5.408, W 3: 273–274). His response began

---

[24] I owe this point to Misak (1991/2004). She borrows Jardine's (1986) phrase "counterfactual bravado" to describe this response to the buried secrets problem, and she argues that it is "against the spirit of [Peirce's] account of truth" because it implies that whether a belief is true depends on whether "those who had been around at the right time would have believed it ... Peirce found this view repugnant ... [On his account,] the truth of a hypothesis cannot be a matter of what some inquirer or group of inquirers think" (1991/2004: 150–151). I agree with Misak about this. But note that she understands the buried secrets objection as targeting, not Peirce's pragmatic clarification of reality, but what she takes to be his pragmatism about truth.

with the insistence that "reality is independent . . . of what you or I or any finite number of men may think about it," but "not necessarily [independent] of thought in general." How are these two claims to be reconciled?[25]

If how the world is is independent of how "any finite number" of people think it is, then it is that way independent of how any actual number of people think it is. Even if in the entire history of the universe, the total number of investigators – beings who use experience and reasoning to settle beliefs – totals 10^{100}, and even if every one of them eventually comes to believe that x is F, still, their collective belief that x is F is not what makes it the case that x is F, if x really is F. How the world is is not *causally* dependent on any actual investigators believing that it is that way. The fact that x is F is causally independent of any actual investigators' representations of x as being F.

> [T]he final opinion . . . does not depend on what you or I or any man thinks. Our perversity and that of others may indefinitely postpone the settlement of opinion; it might even conceivably cause an arbitrary proposition to be universally accepted as long as the human race should last. Yet even that would not change the nature of the belief, which alone could be the result of investigation carried sufficiently far; and if, after the extinction of our race, another should arise with faculties and disposition for investigation, that true opinion must be the one which they would ultimately come to . . . [T]he opinion which would finally result from investigation does not depend on how anybody may actually think. (HTM, 5.408, W 3: 274)

Responding to a similar objection in 1873, Peirce put the point as follows:

> The perversity or ignorance of mankind may make this thing or that to be held for true, for any number of generations, but it can not affect what would be the result of sufficient experience and reasoning. And this it is which is meant by the final settled opinion. This therefore is no particular opinion but is entirely independent of what you, I, or any number of men may think about it; and therefore it directly satisfies the definition of reality. (W 3: 79)

Still, "the object of the final opinion depends on what that opinion is." Given the pragmatic clarification of reality, the claim that x is F – that is, that x *really is* F – is *logically* dependent on the claim that investigation would lead to a consensus that x is F. How the world is is "not necessarily [independent] of thought in general," since the idea of reality, pragmatically clarified, incorporates the idea of how investigators would represent

---

[25] For a very different interpretation of Peirce's response to this objection, see Hausman 1993: 45–46, 159–160.

the world to themselves under certain conditions.[26] The notion of representation – and in particular of how investigators represent the world in
their beliefs – is part of the clearest idea of reality, or at least, it is part of the
clearest idea of reality that is currently available to us. The way that reality
most directly bears on our actions and experiences is that it is what is
represented by a certain class of our beliefs, viz. those that would be forced
upon us if we were to push investigation so far as to settle our beliefs
permanently. Anything that is represented in such a belief is *not* "independent of all relation to the mind's conception of it" (8.13, W 2: 469, 1871), so
nothing real is independent of all relation to the mind's conception of it. In
sum, Peirce's basic realism was tempered by the view that everything real is
capable of being cognized, ergo of being thought about, ergo of being
represented in thought. The view that anything real can be represented in
thought is implied by his pragmatic clarification of the idea of reality, and
as I will show in Chapter 3, it is one of the theories that he called "idealism."

Again, in HTM Peirce shifted from an indicative- to a subjunctive-mood
statement of his pragmatic clarification to defend it against anticipated
objections. Briefly returning to the topic of reality in a later article in the
Illustrations series, he shifted once again into subjunctive talk: "reality is only
the object of the final opinion to which sufficient investigation would lead"
(2.693, W 3: 305, 1878). But he was not consistent. After responding to one of
the objections in HTM he shifted in that same article back into the
indicative mood: "the reality of that which is real does depend on the real
fact that investigation *is* destined to lead, at last, if continued long enough, to
a belief in it" (5.408, W 3: 274, emphasis added). Again, Peirce himself did
not seem aware of this vacillation. As we will see in Chapter 6, in later years
he came to view the use of the subjunctive mood in stating pragmatic
clarifications to be all important.

---

[26] Compare Peirce's assertion that reality is "not necessarily [independent] of thought in general" to his
claim of a few years earlier, about, not reality, but the final opinion: "The objective final opinion is
independent of the thoughts of any particular men, but is not independent of thought *in general*.
That is to say, if there were no thought, there would be no opinion, and therefore, no final opinion"
(7.336, W 3: 29, 1872). Peirce was not contradicting himself here. To see this, note his distinction
between the *thinking* of individual human beings and *thought* in general, which does not mean
"what takes place in the brain but . . . [rather] the object which is brought before us when the act of
cerebration takes place" (W 3: 58, 1872). "I do not say that any thinking process is the reality; but I
say that that thought to which we struggle to have our thoughts coincide, is the reality" (W 3: 47,
1872).

CHAPTER 3

Basic Idealism and Objective Idealism

3.1

In a still unpublished manuscript, Peirce wrote that

> [t]he main position of idealism[,] which is that being an object of thought –
> actual or possible – is an essential part of existence[,] seems to me entirely
> sound and has often been set forth with great force. The gist of the matter
> seems to me to be that it is a part of the very conception of a thing existing
> that it is an object of thought, – a part of what we mean by the word thing.
> (R 935: 3, 1872)[1]

Peirce took "the main position of idealism" to be that anything real is a
possible, if not also an actual, object of thought. If something is real, then it
can be represented in a mental state; it can be thought about, understood,
cognized. The quoted passage echoes and clarifies what he had written four
years earlier: "Our principle . . . is simply that realities, all realities, are nominal,
significative, cognitive. This is simply the pure doctrine of idealism, not of this
or that modification of idealism, but the constitutive mark of idealism in
general" (W 2: 181, 1868). And it is echoed in what he wrote in the following
decades: "I am myself . . . idealist . . . [T]he whole motive to idealism is to make
the world cognizable" (letter to F. E. Abbott, W 5: 280–281, 1886)[2]; "the totality
of things [is] thinkable . . . This is what is called Idealism" (7.563–564, ca. 1893).
In order to distinguish this view – that anything real can be represented in

---

[1] In the Peirce Edition Project's numbering of manuscripts, R 935 is MS 201, dated fall 1872; see
W 3: 548.

[2] He continued: "Being an idealist, of course, I cannot yet accept the objectivity of relations in the sense
in which you [Abbot] mean it. But that relations are as real as anything in the world, – much *more* real,
according to my notion, than being dead things-in-themselves would make them, – to this, I fully
subscribe" (W 5: 281, 1886). Peirce took his idealism to be incompatible with Abbot's view that relations
are "objective," by which Peirce understood him to mean, not that they are real (as Peirce defined that
term), but that they are "dead things-in-themselves." This is reflected in Peirce's review of Abbot's 1885
book, *Scientific Theism*, in which he wrote that in Abbot's system, "[t]he appearance and the thing are
sundered by an impassable gulf" (W 5: 286) and that "Dr. Abbot holds that things . . . possess absolute
existence in themselves, not relative to or dependent upon thought of any kind" (W 5: 287).

ideas, thoughts, cognitions, etc. – from others that have been labeled "idealism," I will refer to it as *basic idealism*.[3]

Basic idealism was not the only sort of idealism that Peirce accepted. As part of the evolutionary cosmology that he described in a series of papers published in the *Monist* in the early 1890s, he defended a view that he called *objective idealism*. This is the doctrine that "matter is effete mind, inveterate habits becoming physical laws" (6.25, W 8: 106, 1891); "matter [is] mere specialized and partially deadened mind" (6.102, W 8: 135, 1892).

That Peirce was an avowed idealist might be taken to undermine the views about reality and truth that I have attributed to him so far. On my reading, those views are staunchly realist, in that they assume what I have called basic realism. But idealism (in some senses) has frequently been thought to be opposed to realism (in some senses). For example, Hirst defines realism as "[t]he view that material objects exist externally to us and independently of our sense experience" and then asserts that "[r]ealism is ... opposed to idealism, which holds that no such material objects or external realities exist apart from our knowledge or consciousness of them, the whole universe thus being dependent on the mind or in some sense mental" (1967: 77). But as I argue in this chapter, there is no inconsistency between Peirce's basic realism and either of the forms of idealism he accepted.

Many earlier commentators have addressed the matter of Peirce's idealism, but I believe that the reading I offer here is unique. It differs from those of, e.g., Altshuler (1980: 118): "the final theory [is] reality itself and ... this ideal entity [is] the 'final cause' of the progress of inquiry"; Savan (1995: 315): "no proposition is true or false unless there is, or will be, some cognitive event from which the truth or falsehood of that proposition can be inferred"; Sfendoni-Mentzou (1995: 336): "'reality consists,' not in thought, but 'in the future'"; and Mayorga (2007: 108): "[W]hat is it about idealism that Peirce thinks is right? I believe it is the idea that reality has a mental component, since all we understand is by definition thought-related, and therefore all description of reality has a mental component."

---

[3] The term "idealism" was used in an extraordinary variety of ways beginning in the eighteenth century and down through Peirce's time. In the introduction to his 1874 edition of Berkeley's *Treatise Concerning the Principles of Human Knowledge*, Charles Krauth quoted no fewer than fourteen distinct definitions of "idealism" before commenting: "The diversity in these definitions arises very much from their confounding in various ways the *essential principle* of Idealism and the *processes* by which it is reached, or with the *inferences* which are deduced from it. Conflicting modes of arguing it may exist, and conflicting inferences be drawn from it" ([1710] 1874: 69–70). He then went on to offer a definition that was far removed from what Peirce took to be idealism's "main position": "the essential and common feature of idealism is that it holds that the final cognitions, the only cognitions, in the *absolute* or philosophical sense, are those which the mind has of its own states" ([1710] 1874: 70).

Almeder (1980: 153) writes that "when [Peirce] espoused what is apparently epistemological idealism he was simply espousing the view that the real is knowable," and with this I agree; but he goes on to gloss the claim that the real is knowable as "the real is dependent for its being known (or knowable) upon the minds of the community," and I do not think Peirce would have accepted that formulation. Boler (1963: 11–12) distinguishes what he calls Peirce's epistemological and metaphysical uses of the term "idealism" and says that the former refer to the view that "since an idea can resemble or represent only another idea, reality itself must be 'thoughtlike' or of the nature of an idea" while the latter refer to a view "which is most simply expressed in Peirce's avowed panpsychism"; Peirce's objective idealism is in my view similar to panpsychism, but not so similar as to warrant that label. Murphey (1968: 12; see also Murphey 1961: 353) reads Peirce's idealism as including the doctrine that "[a]ll individual minds are . . . but subsystems of the universal mind or world mind, and the aggregate of all such systems, which is the world mind, is the community to which Peirce appeals" in his accounts of reality and truth. Peirce did use the phrase "Universal mind," in his 1865 Harvard lectures:

> We have . . . considered . . . experience as a determination of the modifying object and of the modified soul; now, I say, it may be and is naturally regarded as also a determination of an idea of the Universal mind; a preëxistent, archetypal Idea. Arithmetic, the law of number, *was* before anything to be numbered or any mind to number had been created. (W 1: 168–169)

> [Locke's] opinion that the individuality of the mind which has the idea corresponding to a word is of no account, shows that the idea is regarded as belonging to mind in general, to the universal mind, and that words are considered, however obscurely, as determinations of the pure idea. (W 1:172)

But these passages do not suggest that there is a universal mind in the sense of something that is composed of the conscious minds of all humans. They are better read as anticipating his distinction between *thinking*, which is a mental process in which each individual engages on her own, and *thought*, which is, at least in part, a content that can be shared by multiple thinkers but the character of which does not depend on their thinking.[4] Although Peirce did, in the *Monist* cosmological papers, suggest that a community of human beings can come to possess something like a group consciousness (6.271, W 8: 182–183, 1892; on this issue see Lane 2009: 12ff.), and although

---

[4] For example, see W 3: 46–47, 1872; W 3: 58, 1873; 2.53, 1902; 8.256, 1902; 4.6, LI 353–354, 1906; R 683: 26–27 variant, ca. 1913; R 735:3–4, no date.

in his 1903 Harvard lectures on pragmatism he considered the view that natural laws are "ideas or resolutions in the mind of some vast consciousness, who, whether supreme or subordinate, is a Deity relatively to us" (5.17, EP 2: 184–185), so far as I am aware he never asserted that the minds of all humans are parts of a single, unified mind, nor did he identify the community of investigators in terms of which he explained truth and reality with such a mind.

The remainder of this chapter further clarifies Peirce's idealisms and their relationships with his basic realism. As I will argue, basic idealism and objective idealism are logically independent of each other, and each is compatible with both basic realism and realism about the external world.

3.2

As Peirce recognized, basic idealism is implied by his pragmatic clarification of the idea of reality. The view that reality is that which will – or on Peirce's considered view, *would* – be represented in beliefs permanently settled by the method of science "is instantly fatal to the idea of a thing in itself, – a thing existing independent of all relation to the mind's conception of it" (8.13, W 2: 469, 1871). If x is real exactly when it is the object of a belief that would eventually be fixed by investigation, then it is possible for anything that is real to be the object of a belief, and therefore it is possible for x to be represented in thought.[5]

To deny basic idealism – to assert that there is something real that cannot be represented in thought – is to imply that there are Kantian *Dinge an sich*. Peirce's basic idealism is thus very different from Kant's *transcendental*

---

[5] In the Introduction I insisted that philosophical terms like "real" should not be defined in ways that assume the answers to important philosophical questions. An anonymous reviewer suggested that an analogous point could be made against my claim that the pragmatic clarification of the idea of reality implies basic idealism: that clarification is objectionable because it begs the question in support of basic idealism. But I do not think this sort of objection works against pragmatic clarifications. Generally speaking, verbal definitions do not make substantive claims about the world, and so they should not imply any such claims or imply the answers to substantive questions. A verbal definition can capture the way in which a word is actually used, but it does not say anything about the extralinguistic world. The same is not the case for a pragmatic clarification, which is an attempt to deepen our understanding of an idea by translating it in terms of intentional behavior and the experiential consequences of that behavior. Those translations are in the form of conditional statements that can be true or false of the extralinguistic world. So it is a very different thing for a pragmatic clarification to imply an answer to an important philosophical question than it is for a definition to do the same. My point is not that it is necessarily acceptable for a given pragmatic clarification to imply the answer to such a question; it is rather that the reason it is objectionable for verbal definitions to do so is not a reason for thinking that it is objectionable for pragmatic clarifications to do so.

idealism, which assumes that we can meaningfully distinguish between, on the one hand, the world as it is apart from humans' possible experiences of it, and on the other, the world as we experience it.[6] On Kant's view, we must sense the world as being in space and time, the two "forms of sensible intuition." And our judgments about the world must involve certain a priori concepts of the understanding, including, e.g., the concepts of unity, reality, substance, and possibility. Those forms and concepts are built into the way that humans must experience the one real world; there is no way that we can have sensations of, or make judgments about, the world without employing those forms and those concepts. Our sensations and our judgments *can* disclose reality to us, but what is disclosed is reality *as it appears to us*, not *as it is in itself.* The realm of *Dinge an sich* is not a world separate and apart from the one that we experience. It is one and the same world – just considered as separate from how we do and how we ever can experience it. Kant wrote that the fact that his transcendental idealism acknowledges the reality of the world as it is in itself, apart from how it appears to us, sets it apart from "actual idealism":

> Idealism consists in the assertion that there are none other than thinking beings; the other things which we believe to perceive in intuition are only representations in the thinking beings, to which in fact no object outside the latter corresponds. I say on the contrary: things are given to us as objects of our senses situated outside us, but of what they may be in themselves we know nothing; we only know their appearances, i.e., the representations which they bring about in us when they affect our senses. Consequently I do indeed admit that there are bodies outside us, i.e. things which, although wholly unknown to us, i.e. as to what they may be in themselves, we know through the representations which their influence on our sensibility provides for us, and to which we give the name of bodies. This word therefore merely means the appearance of that for us unknown but nonetheless actual object. Can this be called idealism? It is the very opposite of it.
> ... Now someone who will not allow colours to be attached to the object in itself as properties, but only to the sense of sight as modifications, cannot be called an idealist for that; equally little can my doctrine be called idealist

---

6 Kant called his view *transcendental idealism* (*transzendental Idealismus*) in 1781's A edition of the *Critique of Pure Reason* (CPR) (A491/B519; Kant [1787] 1998: 511). But in 1873's *Prolegomena to any Future Metaphysics*, he suggested that it might be more aptly named *critical idealism* (*kritischer Idealismus*; 4: 294, 375; Kant [1783] 2004: 99, 175). Why "transcendental" idealism? "[T]he word 'transcendental' ... for me never means a reference of our cognition to things, but only to our *faculty of cognition*" (*Prolegomena* 4: 293, Kant [1783] 2004: 99). In CPR, he wrote that "appearances in general are nothing outside our representations, which is just what we mean by their transcendental ideality" (A507/B535; Kant [1787] 1998: 519). In one of the *Century Dictionary's* three definitions of "transcendental" in its philosophical sense, Peirce defined it as follows: "Pertaining to the existence in experience of a priori elements; a priori. This is chiefly a Kantian term" (CD 6427).

merely because I find that more of, *indeed all, the properties that make up the intuition of a body* belong merely to its appearance; for the existence of the thing that appears is not thereby cancelled, as with actual idealism, but it is only shown that we cannot know it at all through the senses as it is in itself. (*Prolegomena* 4: 289; Kant [1783] 2004: 95)

But on Peirce's view, the concept of *eine Welt an sich* – a world considered apart from how it could ever be experienced or cognized – is empty. Peirce's basic idealism implies that the world as we must cognize it – as our eventual investigation-fixed beliefs would eventually represent it to be – *is reality*, and it makes no sense to speak of something that resides behind or apart from our experiences, something that causes those experiences and subsequent thoughts but that can never be represented by them: "there is a general *drift* in the history of human thought which will lead it to one general agreement, one catholic consent. And any truth more perfect than this destined conclusion, any reality more absolute than what is thought in it, is a fiction of metaphysics" (8.12, W 2: 469, 1871). Peirce described Kant as "nothing but a somewhat confused pragmatist" (5.525, 1905) and wrote that it is from pragmatism that "the general views of Kant derive such clearness as they have" (5.11, EP 2: 399, 1907). He thought of his own Critical Common-Sensism as subjecting Kant's views to critical evaluation and as just "a modification of Kantism ... The Kantist has only to abjure from the bottom of his heart the proposition that a thing-in-itself can, however indirectly, be conceived, and then correct the details of Kant's doctrine, and he will find himself to have become a Critical Common-Sensist" (EP 2: 353–354, 1905).[7] In ca. 1905, Peirce distinguished between two different kinds of "unknowable" in Kant's work: *Dinge an sich*, and transcendent ideas such as those of God, freedom, and immortality. Pragmatism rejects the former completely, and regarding the latter, either "indefinite research" would eventually settle questions about them, in which case those things are knowable, or it would not, in which case questions about them are meaningless (R 289: 13–16, LI 303–304).[8]

How might someone come to believe in such metaphysical fictions as *Dinge an sich*?

A real is anything that is not affected by men's cognitions *about it*; which is a verbal definition, not a doctrine. An external object is anything that is not

---

[7] The *Collected Papers* inserts "accordingly," which is absent from EP 2: "and then correct the details of Kant's doctrine accordingly, and he will find himself to have become a Critical Common-sensist" (5.452).

[8] For further criticism of Kant on these matters, see R 930: 23ff., late.

affected by any cognitions, whether about it or not, of the man to whom it is external. Exaggerate this, in the usual philosopher fashion, and you have the conception of what is not affected by any cognitions at all. Take the converse of this definition and you have the notion of what does not affect cognition, and in this indirect manner you get a hypostatically abstract notion of what the *Ding an sich* would be (5.525, 1905).[9]

But there are no *Dinge an sich*, no things that cannot be represented as they really are in the thoughts of investigators. Peirce was the sort of "idealist metaphysician" who held that "the whole *reality* behind [a true] proposition" "consists in the fact that the further we push our . . . studies, the more strongly will that conclusion force itself on our minds forever – or would do so, if study were to go on forever" (5.565, 1902). He rejected "ghost-like hypotheses about things-in-themselves which anybody can set up but nobody can refute" (7.370, 1902).[10]

But as Peirce also recognized, none of this threatens his basic realism, according to which there are real things, i.e., things that are the way they are regardless of how they are believed to be:

> That which [a] truth represents is a reality. This reality being cognizable and comprehensible, is of the nature of thought. Wherein, then, does its reality consist? In the fact that, though it has no being out of thought, yet it is as it is, whether you or I or any group of men think it to be so or not. (8.153, ca. 1900)

Reality "is of the nature of thought" in the sense that it can be thought *about*.[11] "[I]t has no being out of thought" – i.e., it is not a *Ding an sich* but is instead a possible object of thought – but it has the traits it has whether or not it is ever actually thought to have them. Nor does basic idealism threaten his realism about external things – things the properties of which do not depend on what anyone thinks (about those things themselves or anything

---

[9] Hypostatic abstraction is the operation by which something initially conceived as the predicate of a subject is thought of as a subject in its own right, e.g., "the abstraction which transforms 'it is light' into 'there is light here'" (4.235, 1902). I consider its relevance to scholastic realism in Chapter 5.

[10] Misak (1991/2004) correctly notes that Peirce would reject any theory of truth according to which truth is correspondence with things-in-themselves, things considered as they are apart from our possible experience of them. Hookway (2012: 54–55) notes that Peirce would reject anything like what Bernard Williams called the absolute conception of reality, which Williams described as "a conception of reality as it is independently of our thought, and to which all representations of reality can be related" (1990: 196). But if there is something here that is objectionable from Peirce's point of view, it is not the latter clause – Peirce held that all true representations are related to the real world. The former clause in Williams' description is ambiguous. If it means *logically* independent of the concept of *thought*, then Peirce would reject what he calls the absolute conception. But if it means independent of what anyone happens to think *about it*, then Peirce would not object to that clause.

[11] Here I agree with Friedman (1997: 266). Peirce also used the phrase "of the nature of thought" in his *Century Dictionary* definition of "idealism": "The metaphysical doctrine that the real is of the nature of thought; the doctrine that all reality is in its nature psychical" (CD 2974).

else). An external object, like the earth, can be represented in our thoughts without itself being dependent on the thoughts of any individual or group of individuals.[12] That something is capable of being represented in cognition does not imply that it is internal rather than external. "Even the idealists, if their doctrines are rightly understood[,] have not usually denied the existence of real external things" (7.335, W 3: 44–45, 1872).[13] No wonder, then, that Peirce described himself as accepting "realism and realistic idealism" (R 400: 43, 1893). It is in light of these claims that we should read Peirce's statements in his 1901 review of Karl Pearson's *Grammar of Science* that an inkstand, although it is "real and external," is "a purely psychical product, a generalized percept, like everything of which I can take any sort of cognizance" (8.144, EP 2: 62). An inkstand is "psychical," not in the sense that it exists in someone's mind (it is, after all, external) or has a given set of traits only because it is thought to have them (it is, after all, real), but only in the sense that it is a possible object of thought. "[R]eality being cognizable and comprehensible, is of the nature of thought" (8.153).[14]

The external can be represented in our thoughts without being part of some "Absolute" mind, à la Hegel or Royce. Peirce admired Hegel, but his basic idealism is nothing like Hegel's absolute idealism, which Peirce defined as follows: "things derive their reality from their being made by thought, which has an objective existence as a part of the divine absolute idea (this being the organic unity of all thought), and . . . things are not merely phenomena to us, but are of their inner nature phenomena or thoughts" (CD 2974). Peirce criticized Hegel's "idea that the Absolute is One" and what that idea implies, "that the three categories" – Firstness, Secondness, and Thirdness – "have not their several independent and irrefutable standings in thought" (5.91, EP 2: 177, 1903). And in his 1902 review of Josiah Royce's *The World and the Individual*, Peirce contrasted his basic realism with Royce's absolute idealism:

> The realist simply says that [a real thing *x*] is not constituted by its being represented in [an idea of *x*]; that is, he says that the fact that [*x*] is as it is, would

---

[12] Peirce distinguished between the external (that which does not depend on what anyone thinks) and that which is "entirely independent of thought," i.e., "that of which there is no idea," affirming the former and denying that the idea of the latter even makes sense (W 3: 31–32, 1872). For a different interpretation of this passage, one that takes Peirce to mean the same thing by "external" and "entirely independent of thought," see Mayorga (2007: 113–114).

[13] Almeder asserts that this claim is explained by appealing to Peirce's objective idealism and that "Peirce's endorsement of objective idealism late in life accounts for all those texts in which he claims to be an idealist" (1980: 156). But there is no textual evidence that Peirce adopted objective idealism until the 1890s, and as I discuss in Chapter 4, he defended an "idealistic theory of reality" decades earlier.

[14] 8.153–156 are from a partial draft of the Pearson review and are published in the *Collected Papers* but not in EP.

be logically consistent with [the idea] representing it to be otherwise ...
Professor Royce is blind to [the] fact ... that the essence of the realist's opinion
is that it is one thing to *be* and another thing to *be represented*; and the cause of
this cecity is that the Professor is completely immersed in his absolute idealism,
which precisely consists in denying that distinction. (8.129)[15]

That basic idealism follows from Peirce's pragmatic clarification of the
idea of reality explains why he sometimes described his views about reality
and truth as "idealistic." For example, in an 1872 manuscript, after stating his
verbal definition of "reality" – "if [an object's] characters are independent of
what you or I or any number of men think about it, it is a *reality*" (W 3: 58) –
he proceeded to advocate an "Idealistic theory of metaphysics": "observation
and reasoning are perpetually leading us towards certain opinions and ...
the fact of such a perpetual tendency is otherwise expressed by saying that
the objects of those final opinions have a real existence" (W 3: 59).[16] This was
an anticipation of his pragmatic clarification of the idea of reality, which was
also foreshadowed in lecture notes written in spring 1870: "We must mean
by how things are, how we are affected by them," i.e., "how [we] would be
affected after sufficient experience, discussion, and reasoning"; he described
this as "an idealistic doctrine concerning truth" (W 2: 440). In around 1907,
Peirce applied the term "conditional idealism" to his view that "truth's
independence of individual opinions is due (so far as there is any 'truth')
to its being the predestined result to which sufficient inquiry *would* ultimately lead" (5.494, EP 2: 419). In another manuscript of the same period, he
wrote:

> Among all the doctrines of metaphysics, there is none that seems to me to be
> more obviously favored by [pragmatism] than what may be called *condi-
> tional idealism* ... [T]he pragmatistic doctrine [is] that the immediate object
> of that conception of things in which minds would ultimately concur, if
> inquiry were to be pushed far enough, is the very reality itself. (R 322: 20–21,
> 1907)

So what he called "conditional idealism" was not basic idealism, but the
pragmatic clarification of the idea of reality, which implies basic idealism,

---

[15] But Peirce seems not to have intended a wholesale rejection of Royce's concept of the Absolute; a few
years later he wrote that he "acknowledge[d], not indeed the Existence, but yet the Reality, of the
Absolute, nearly as it has been set forth, for example, by Royce in his *The World and the Individual*"
(5.385n; this was dated 1903 in the *Collected Papers*, but, according to de Waal (ILS 44–45n), it is from
R 619 and dated March 26, 1909).

[16] At this early date, Peirce used "existence" in a loose, nontechnical sense. But by ca. 1896 (1.457), he
had begun to use it more strictly, to refer to "the mode of being of that which reacts with other
things" (8.330, 1904). For more on this later usage of "existence," see Chapter 5.

and which relies on the investigative aspect of his account of truth – and, as noted in Chapter 2, it was in around 1905 that he came to think of the latter as resulting from an application of the pragmatic maxim to the idea of truth (R 289: 13, LI 303).[17]

In another of its philosophical senses, "idealism" denotes the view that everything that there is is mind or is mental. This is what Kant meant by "actual idealism," and an example of it is Berkeley's doctrine that all that there are are minds and the ideas that they contain. In this sense, idealism is a claim, not about whether what is real can be represented by the mind, but about the basic nature of reality itself. This view, which I will call *ontological idealism*,[18] is logically independent of Peirce's basic idealism. That x can be represented in thought does not imply that x is itself mental, and that x is a mind or mental state does not imply that it can be represented in thought.[19] On the other hand, ontological idealism is compatible with basic realism. It is consistent to say both that there are real things and that all real things are either minds or mental states. A mind m can be real so long as its properties do not depend on any mind, including m itself, thinking that it has those properties, and there is nothing inconsistent in the view that the only things that are real in that way are minds. Sometimes ontological idealism is contrasted with *materialism*, understood as the view

---

[17] Note also that in a 1904 letter to William James, Peirce wrote that "the true idealism, the pragmatistic idealism, is that reality consists in the *future*," i.e., in "the public world of the indefinite future as against our past opinions of what it was to be" (8.284).

[18] Guyer and Horstmann use "ontological idealism" to mean the view that "something mental (the mind, spirit, reason, will) is the ultimate foundation of all reality, or even exhaustive of reality" (2015). In his *Dictionary of Philosophy*, Anthony Flew describes a number of varieties of idealism and says that what unites them is "the view that what would normally be called 'the external world' is somehow created by the mind" (1984: 160). But whether this qualifies as a form of ontological idealism depends on whether what is created by or dependent on the mind *is itself mind*. Consider the following theory: everything real is created by or otherwise dependent on some mind or other; but not everything that is so created or dependent is itself mind; some real things are themselves nonmental (e.g., they are material, physical, even though they are (somehow) brought into being by a mind, or even though their continuing existence is (somehow) dependent on a mind. This doctrine is *not* a form of ontological idealism. It does, however, resemble what Peirce called *objective idealism*, which I discuss later in this chapter.

[19] Peirce wrote that his conditional idealism "is Berkeleyanism with some corrections" (R 322: 20, 1907). One of those corrections is of the mistake of confusing actually being perceived with the possibility of being perceived; see R 663: 10ff, 1910. Unlike Peirce, Berkeley required that something actually be perceived as a condition of its being real. "For as to what is said of the absolute existence of unthinking things without any relation to their being perceived, that seems perfectly unintelligible. Their *esse* is *percipi*, nor is it possible they should have any existence, out of the minds of thinking things which perceive them" (*Principles of Human Knowledge* §3; [1710] 1998: n. 104). Something is real only when it is actually being perceived, either by a finite mind or God: "all those bodies which compose the mighty frame of the world[,] . . . so long as they are not actually perceived by me, or do not exist in my mind or that of any other created spirit, . . . must either have no existence at all, or else subsist in the mind of some Eternal Spirit" (*Principles* §6; [1710] 1998: 105).

that everything that there is is matter, physical. But whether these views are incompatible depends on the conceptions of mind and matter that they respectively assume. On a view like Descartes', according to which every instance of matter is extended in space and no instance of mind is extended in space, ontological idealism and materialism are indeed incompatible. But if one conceives of mind and matter as having compatible properties, then there is no logical inconsistency between the two views and so it is consistent to maintain that everything is *both* mind and matter. This was the view of Spinoza, who maintained that everything is mind, and matter, and an infinite number of other sorts of thing. But ontological idealism is not consistent with realism about a world that is external in Peirce's sense, viz. independent of the thinking of all individual minds. If everything there is is a mind or its mental states, then there is nothing that has its properties regardless of what anyone thinks – everything real will depend on the thinking of some mind or other.

Once we see that Peirce took basic idealism to be "the main position of idealism," it becomes clear why he wrote the following:

> That upon Cartesian principles the very realities of things can never be known in the least, most competent persons must long ago have been convinced. Hence the breaking forth of idealism, which is essentially anti-Cartesian, in every direction ... The principle now brought under discussion [viz., that "the absolutely incognizable is absolutely inconceivable"] is directly idealistic; for, since the meaning of a word is the conception it conveys, the absolutely incognizable has no meaning because no conception attaches to it. It is, therefore, a meaningless word; and, consequently, whatever is meant by any term as "the real" is cognizable in some degree, and so is of the nature of a cognition, in the objective sense of that term. (5.310, W 2: 238, 1868)[20]

That is, everything real "is of the nature of a cognition, in the objective sense of" the term "cognition," i.e., in the sense in which it refers to *objects* of cognition, things that can be cognized: "Every cognition involves something represented, or that of which we are conscious, and some action or passion of the self whereby it becomes represented. The former shall be termed the objective, the latter the subjective, element of the cognition" (5.238, W 2: 204, 1868).

---

[20] The quoted passage is from the "cognition series" of 1868–1869 and is part of his explanation of his "idealistic theory of reality" (5.353, W 2: 270, 1869). In explaining that theory, both in the cognition series and afterwards, Peirce made several comments that seem to be at odds with his basic realism and thus with the reading that I am defending here. I argue in Chapter 4 that those comments are in fact consistent with both basic realism and realism about the external.

So Peirce's basic idealism is the view that anything real is a possible object of cognition. It is thus implied by his pragmatic clarification of the idea of reality, according to which the real is what is represented in a belief that would be permanently settled by investigation, the method of science. It is compatible with both basic realism and realism about the external, but it is very different from Kant's transcendental idealism, which denies that our thoughts can represent reality as it is in itself, from Hegel's and Royce's forms of absolute idealism, which posit the reality of an absolute mind, and from Berkeley's ontological idealism, which denies that there are real external things.

3.3

In his review of John Watson's *Comte, Mill, and Spencer: An Outline of Philosophy* for *The Nation* (April 11, 1895), Peirce contrasted a new, empiricist way of supporting idealism with the way pursued by "the older generation of idealists," including Watson himself. The empiricist idealism rejects "the notions, the sentiments, and the mode of being which, heretofore accidentally associated with idealism, have their home in the theological seminary" and instead supports itself with "observed fact" (CN 2: 103, 102). But the idealism about which Peirce wrote in this review was not a doctrine about the cognizability of reality. "The strong hold of idealism to-day," said Peirce, "lies in reflections upon the question of how consciousness came into the world" (CN 2: 102). This is true of the form of idealism – *objective idealism* – that Peirce defended in his *Monist* "cosmological series" published from 1891 to 1893.[21] As we will see, his objective idealism is unrelated to his basic idealism, having nothing to do with the question whether reality is cognizable. It is instead a hypothesis about the relationship between mind and matter, and it is consistent with both basic realism and realism about external things.

One of Peirce's earliest statements of objective idealism is as follows: "The one intelligible theory of the universe is that of objective idealism, that matter is effete mind, inveterate habits becoming physical laws" (6.25,

---

[21] Unfortunately, Skagestad uses "objective idealism" to refer to a completely different doctrine that he attributes to Peirce, that "the objects [of knowledge are] external to the individual mind ... As an objective idealist Peirce held that the reality of things depends on their cognizability, while it does not in the least depend on our actual cognition of them" (1981: 63–64). It is true that Peirce held that anything real is capable of being cognized or represented in thought – that is the doctrine that I call "basic idealism." But to say that what can be known is "external to the individual mind" is to imply that we cannot know anything about the internal and therefore (given basic idealism) to imply that there are no real internal facts or states. As we have seen, Peirce was a realist about both the external and the internal.

W 8: 106). This is from "The Architecture of Theories" (AT, 1891), the first article in the cosmological series.[22] In the "The Law of Mind" (LM, 1892), the third article in that series, he stated the view as follows: "matter [is] mere specialized and partially deadened mind" (6.102, W 8: 135). So objective idealism is the claim that any instance of matter is identical with an instance of *a specific kind or form of* mind, viz. mind that is "effete" or "partially deadened." Objective idealism is a form of *monism* (or as Peirce preferred, *hylopathy* – the term is probably derived from the Greek *hule*, meaning matter, and *pathos*, meaning suffering) according to which mind and matter are not "two radically different kinds of substance" (AT, 6.24, W 8: 105).

We must not read into Peirce's uses of "mind" more than he intended. In the cosmological series, that term does not connote intelligence, cognition, thinking, or any other higher-level mental activity. Nor does it necessarily signal a mind that is *the mind of* some person or other conscious entity. A sign of what Peirce meant by "mind" in these papers occurs toward the end of AT, where he summarized his cosmogony:

> [I]n the beginning, – infinitely remote, – there was a chaos of unpersonalized feeling, which being without connection or regularity would properly be without existence. This feeling, sporting here and there in pure arbitrariness, would have started the germ of a generalizing tendency. Its other sportings would be evanescent, but this would have a growing virtue. Thus, the tendency to habit would be started; and from this with the other principles of evolution all the regularities of the universe would be evolved. (AT, 6.33, W 8: 110)

On this account, the universe has evolved, and continues to evolve, from a state of less order to one of greater order. Before this evolution began, there was nothing but "unpersonalized feeling," feeling that was not experienced by any individual person or other conscious being, but that somehow existed on its own – except that, "being without connection or regularity," it was "properly . . . without existence."[23] One way to attempt to explain the fact that there are real things is to hypothesize a point in time before there was anything real and then to give an account of how reality began, despite there having been nothing real at that earlier time. But this is

---

[22] The other articles in the series are: "The Doctrine of Necessity Examined" (6.35–65, W 8: 111–125, 1892), "The Law of Mind" (6.102–163, W 8: 135–157, 1892), "Man's Glassy Essence" (6.238–271, W 8: 165–183, 1892), and "Evolutionary Love" (6.287–317, W 8: 184–205, 1893). Short argues that the ideas that Peirce put forward in this series and related works constituted "a scientific program that he never got very far with and eventually dropped" (2010: 521).

[23] In 1891, Peirce was still using "existence" casually; see Note 16.

doomed to failure, since if at one time there is literally nothing, there cannot *be* anything to cause there to be something at a later time. Peirce tried to have it both ways, with feelings "sporting" despite their not being "properly" real. Short notes the obvious problem with this view: "Peirce's idea of a primordial chaos is not easily freed, if it can be freed at all, from self-contradiction. On the one hand, nothing happens; on the other hand, something happens – feelings sport" (2010: 533).[24]

At any rate, part of Peirce's cosmogony has to do with the emergence of matter from impersonal mind or feeling over the course of the universe's development. But this story about matter and mind/feeling cannot be separated from another thread of that cosmogony: the increasing lawfulness of the universe. At the earliest stage of the world's history, there was maximum disorder. As the universe aged, two sorts of law emerged: *psychical* or *mental* laws, which govern mind, and *physical* laws, which govern matter. But the difference between them is not merely a matter of what they govern; it also has to do with how strictly they govern it. Physical laws are "absolute"; they require "exact relation[s]"; events "must actually take place exactly as required by" a physical law (AT, 6.23, W 8: 105). On the other hand, mental laws require "no exact conformity"; a given mental law "makes a given feeling *more likely* to arise," but does not necessitate its arising (ibid.). That a law can make something more likely to occur without necessitating its occurrence reflects Peirce's *tychism*, the view there is real chance in the universe. Here, "real chance" does not mean "ordinary" chance, which is merely chance "relative to the causes that are taken into account" (W 4: 549, 1883–1884). A roll of a pair of dice involves chance, but only in the sense that the factors that determine how the dice will land are too complicated for us to take all of them into consideration. How they will land is not completely determined by the limited set of influences we *do* take into account, but it is nonetheless determined by the influences acting upon them. The view that ordinary chance is real is consistent with determinism, or, as Peirce called it, "the doctrine of necessity" or "necessitarianism." But tychism asserts the reality of "indeterminacy, spontaneity, or *absolute chance* in nature" (AT, 6.13, W 8: 101).[25]

---

[24] Later, in "Man's Glassy Essence," the fourth article in the cosmological series, Peirce amended this point: "[T]hat primeval chaos in which there was no regularity was mere nothing, from a physical aspect. Yet it was not a blank zero; for there was an intensity of consciousness there in comparison with which all that we ever feel is but as the struggling of a molecule or two to throw off a little of the force of law to an endless and innumerable diversity of chance utterly unlimited" (6.265, W 8: 181).

[25] In "The Doctrine of Necessity Examined," Peirce noted that his belief in absolute chance echoed that of Aristotle, who held that "events come to pass in three ways, namely, (1) by external compulsion, or the action of efficient causes, (2) by virtue of an inward nature, or the influence of

Absolute chance is due "to the imperfect cogency of the law itself, to a certain swerving of the facts from any definite formula" (ibid.). Hence, tychism implies that determinism is false – not that physical laws are to be formulated statistically, but rather that, although they are formulated deterministically, physical laws never apply exactly.[26] Some events occur without being determined to happen in exactly the way that they do in fact happen. Now, there are exactly three ways in which physical and psychical laws can be related to one another:

> [T]he question arises whether physical laws on the one hand, and the psychical law on the other are to be taken –
>
> (A)   as independent, a doctrine often called *monism*, but which I would name *neutralism*; or
> (B)   the psychical law as derived and special, the physical law alone as primordial, which is *materialism*; or
> (C)   the physical law as derived and special, the psychical law alone as primordial, which is *idealism*. (AT, 6.24, W 8: 105)

Peirce rejected neutralism and materialism and accepted idealism, or, as he called it, *objective* idealism (AT, 6.25, W 8: 106).[27]

The two distinctions – between matter and mind/feeling, and between physical laws and mental laws – interlock as follows. At the earliest stages of the universe, there was nothing but unpersonalized mind/feeling, "sporting" in a chaotic fashion. But the world gradually took on "a tendency to habit," so that those sportings became less random and more regular, although they "require[d] no exact conformity" – mental laws do not determine exactly what mind/feeling will do. Eventually, as the universe became even more orderly and habit became even more habitual, stricter laws took hold, and there came to be instances of mind/feeling that behaved in less spontaneous, more deterministic ways. Those feelings, "effete" and "partially deadened," were matter, subject to "absolute," physical laws. Mental law is primordial, and physical law emerged from it as the universe evolved; ergo, what the mental law governs – mind/

---

final causes, and (3) irregularly without definite cause, but just by absolute chance; and this doctrine is of the inmost essence of Aristotelianism" (6.36, W 8: 111).

[26] Short notes that "Peirce did not ... anticipate the idea of quantum mechanics, that laws may themselves be statistical in formulation" (2010: 540).

[27] Peirce rejected neutralism because it violates Ockham's razor by implying that there are "more independent elements ... than necessary. By placing the inward and outward aspects of substance on a par, it seems to render both primordial" (AT, 6.24, W 8: 106). And he rejected materialism, saying that it is "as repugnant to scientific logic as to common sense; since it requires us to suppose that a certain kind of mechanism will feel, which would be a hypothesis absolutely irreducible to reason" (AT, 6.24, W 8: 105).

feeling – is primordial, and matter emerged from it. But matter is not totally free of the spontaneity that is the hallmark of feeling: "matter never does obey its ideal laws with absolute precision, but . . . there are almost insensible fortuitous departures from regularity" (6.264, W 8: 180, 1892). "At any time . . . an element of pure chance survives and will remain until the world becomes an absolutely perfect, rational, and symmetrical system in which mind is at last crystallized in the infinitely distant future" (AT, 6.33, W 8: 110). Since the time at which there is no longer any spontaneity or deviation from physical law – and thus nothing but matter? – is "in the infinitely distant future," it will never actually occur. As Peirce said of external things that cannot be represented by any mind, it is a "limit which the possible cannot attain" (5.311, n. 1, W 2: 238, n. 7). He eventually adopted "the Absolute" as a name, not for an absolute mind of the sort posited by Hegel or Royce, but for the limits at each end of the universe's evolution. For example, in his 1893 "Reply to the Necessitarians," he wrote that in AT he had "carefully recorded [his] opposition to all philosophies which deny the reality of the Absolute" (6.605; the reference is to 6.27–28, W 8: 107–108) and that in "The Doctrine of Necessity Examined" he had

> only propose[d] to explain the regularities of nature as consequences of the only uniformity, or general fact, there was in the chaos, namely, the general absence of any determinate law . . . Somebody may notice that I here admit a proposition as absolutely true. Undoubtedly; because it relates to the Absolute. (6.606 and 606 n)[28]

It is tempting to think that in his cosmogony, Peirce intended to strip "matter" and "mind" of more traditional meanings like, respectively, *that which is extended in space* and *that which thinks or feels*, and to pair each of those terms with new meanings, perhaps something like *that to which deterministic laws apply* and *that to which nondeterministic laws apply.*[29] But that seems not to have been his intention. He understood objective idealism to imply that every instance of feeling/mind has the traditional hallmarks of both mind and matter: "[t]his hypothesis . . . attributes to mind one of the recognized properties of matter, extension, and attributes to all matter a certain excessively low degree of feeling" (6.277, ca. 1893). He made the same point in "Man's Glassy Essence" (MGE, the fourth paper in the cosmological series), albeit less explicitly:

---

[28] See also 6.603, 1893; 7.566, EP 2:1, 1893; 8.277, 1902.

[29] Short's view is that Peirce's use of mentalistic language in these passages was "a rhetorical strategy that served to startle his audience, challenging their Cartesian preconception of matter and mind as utterly different. However, as well as being beneficially leading, it was disastrously misleading" (2007b: 668).

[I]f matter has no existence except as a specialization of mind, it follows that whatever affects matter according to regular laws is itself matter. But all mind is directly or indirectly connected with all matter, and acts in a more or less regular way; so that all mind more or less partakes of the nature of matter. Hence, it would be a mistake to conceive of the psychical and the physical aspects of matter as two aspects absolutely distinct. Viewing a thing from the outside, considering its relations of action and reaction with other things, it appears as matter. Viewing it from the inside, looking at its immediate character as feeling, it appears as consciousness. These two views are combined when we remember that mechanical laws are nothing but acquired habits, like all the regularities of mind. (6.268, W 8: 181–182, 1892)

He eventually qualified this view, requiring as a necessary condition of an "ascertainable degree" of feeling – sentience? – some degree of material organization: "there may be, and probably is, something of the general nature of feeling almost everywhere, yet feeling in any ascertainable degree is a mere property of protoplasm, perhaps only of nerve matter" (7.364, 1902). But remember that in 1891's AT, he described the "feelings" that are the universe's earliest components as "unpersonalized" – not belonging to any person or mind. So even before the 1902 qualification, Peirce did not mean by "feelings" the mental states of a sentient individual.

Peirce restated objective idealism elsewhere in the cosmological series. In LM, he wrote that "what we call matter is not completely dead, but is merely mind hide-bound with habits" (6.158, W 8: 155), and that

> the mind is not subject to "law," in the same rigid sense that matter is. It only experiences gentle forces which merely render it more likely to act in a given way than it otherwise would be. There always remains a certain amount of arbitrary spontaneity in its action, without which it would be dead. (6.148, W 8: 153)

In a draft of MGE, he wrote that "the law of mind ... antedates the very existence of matter. In fact, matter has no existence except as a specialization of mind" (R 961A, W 8: 408, 1892); in the published version of that article, he stated that "physical events are but degraded or undeveloped forms of psychical events ... [T]he phenomena of matter are but the result of the sensibly complete sway of habits upon mind" (6.264, W 8: 180). Elsewhere he put the point in similar ways:

> [I]dealism regards the psychical mode of activity as the fundamental and universal one, of which the physical mode is a specialization; while materialism regards the laws of physics as at the bottom of everything, and feeling as limited to special organizations. (W 8: 43, 1890)

... I suppose matter is merely mind deadened by the development of habit. (8.318, 1891)

Wherein do materialistic monism and idealistic monism differ? Only in this, that the former makes the laws of mind a special result of the laws of matter, while the latter makes the laws of matter a special result of the laws of mind. (CN 1: 200, 1893)

[W]e must ... regard matter as mind whose habits have become fixed so as to lose the powers of forming them and losing them, while mind is to be regarded as a chemical genus of extreme complexity and instability. It has acquired in a remarkable degree a habit of taking and laying aside habits. (6.101, 1902)

Carl Hausman cites a passage we saw earlier – "The one intelligible theory of the universe is that of objective idealism, that matter is effete mind, inveterate habits becoming physical laws" (AT, 6.25, W 8: 106) – as providing "probably the most obvious support for the view that Peirce was committed to metaphysical idealism" (1993: 147). But he then goes on to say that Peirce "did not necessarily claim that his own view is identical with objective idealism" (1993: 149) and to provide reasons for thinking that Peirce did not accept objective idealism. But Hausman's treatment of this issue is flawed. First, he incorrectly runs together objective idealism with what Peirce called conditional idealism (1993: 149), which, as we saw previously, is his pragmatic clarification of the idea of reality. Second, he mistakenly takes Peirce's scholastic realism, i.e., his realism about generals, to be in conflict with objective idealism (1993: 154). Third, he does not clearly distinguish Peirce's concepts of the real and the external: "As early as his 1878 papers on belief and the maxim of meaning, he uses what he says is the commonly adopted meaning [of 'real'], namely that the real is what has characters that are independent of how you or I think (5.405)" (1993: 150). In the paragraph cited by Hausman, which is from HTM (and is also at W 3: 271), Peirce actually distinguished between the real and the external and gave his usual definitions of each. A symptom of this failure clearly to distinguish reality and externality is that Hausman frequently uses the sort of ambiguous language I criticized in the Introduction ("mind-independent," "independent of thought"). Finally, he seems to assume that there is a tension between any theory that Peirce called realism and any that he called idealism. He suggests that "Peirce wanted to move beyond the options, including idealism and realism, as they were available at the time" (1993: 154). But getting clear on exactly what sorts of realism and what sorts of idealism Peirce embraced shows that this is not the case. And given the many assertions quoted earlier of the view that Peirce, in AT, called "objective idealism," it is clear that he *did* accept objective idealism.

As his evolutionism about law suggests, Peirce did not think that the distinction between physical and mental law is absolute. Physical laws are those the violations of which are relatively rare, while mental laws are those that allow for relatively more exceptions. Thus, the difference between the two sorts of law is one of degree, and the same is true of the difference between matter and mind/feeling themselves. Matter is only "*partially* deadened mind"; "what we call matter is not *completely* dead." This is a manifestation of Peirce's *synechism*, a view he sometimes stated as a methodological principle, e.g., "[t]he tendency to regard continuity . . . as an idea of prime importance in philosophy" (6.103, W 8: 136, 1892; see also 6.169, 1902) and sometimes as a metaphysical doctrine, e.g., as the view that "all that exists is continuous" (1.172, R 955, 1893).[30] On the relationship between matter and mind/feeling, synechism

> will say: [the] disparateness [of mind and matter] is a mere matter of degree. Either *mind* is a peculiar kind of *matter*, or else *matter* is a peculiar sort of *mind*. Which is it? If mind is nothing but a highly complicated arrangement of matter, – for which theory there is much to be said, – we are landed in *materialism* . . . But if, on the other hand, matter is nothing but effete mind, – mind so completely under the domination of habit as to act with almost perfect regularity & to have lost its powers of forgetting & of learning, then we are brought to the more elevating theory of *idealism* (R 936: 3, no date; see also NEM 4: 355, 1893; 6.277, ca. 1893; 7.569–570, EP 2: 2, 1893).[31]

We have seen enough of Peirce's objective idealism to recognize that it is logically independent of basic idealism. It does not imply basic idealism: it is possible for matter to be "effete" mind/feeling, and yet for some real things to be incognizable, beyond the ability of humans or other scientific

---

[30] The *Collected Papers* gives "c.1897" as the date of R 955, but the Peirce Edition Project (2001) dates it from the summer of 1893. R 955, part of which is published as 1.141–175, is the second part of a lecture titled "Scientific Fallibilism" by the Peirce Edition Project. The first part of the lecture is in R 860, a portion of which is at 6.492–493.

[31] As I describe in Chapter 4, Peirce maintained in the cognition series of 1868–1869 that a given mind is continuous with the external world that it cognizes. But in that early work he sought to explain how an individual mind can represent objects that are external to it, while his objective idealism was concerned with how, generally speaking, matter can originate from mind/feeling. That matter and mind are continuous was, Peirce believed, a necessary assumption for the solution of each problem. But for each problem he posited a different mind-matter continuity: in the cognition series he maintained that an individual mind is continuous with the world external to it, some of which is physical; and in the cosmological series he held that the difference between matter and mind/feeling is the degree to which each is governed by law. I now think that my earlier treatment of these matters (Lane 2011a and 2011b) overstated the similarities between the cognition series' and the cosmological papers' respective treatments of the continuity of mind and matter.

intelligences to understand. That "matter is effete mind" does not imply that everything real is cognizable by individual minds. And basic idealism does not imply objective idealism. It is possible for any real thing to be a possible object of thought without matter being mind/feeling that is law-governed to a relatively high degree. So objective idealism is not a form of idealism as Peirce understood that term in the 1870s (again, "[t]he main position of idealism ... is that being an object of thought – actual or possible – is an essential part of existence"; R 935: 3, 1872). Why, then, did he call it objective *idealism*? Because it was inspired by the objective idealism of Schelling. As the editors of W 8 note, Peirce's slogan "matter is effete mind" "echoes Schelling, who in his *System des transzendentalen Idealismus* (Tübingen: Cotta, 1800, p.191) called matter 'extinct mind' (*erloschene Geist*)" (W 8: 364), hence Peirce's description of his own objective idealism as "a Schelling-fashioned idealism" (LM, 6.102, W 8: 135). What Peirce called objective idealism was one – but only one – of a cluster of doctrines he attributed to Schelling in his *Century Dictionary* definition of "idealism, objective":

> The doctrine of F. W. J. von Schelling (1775–1854), that the relation between the subject and the object of thought is one of absolute identity. It supposes that all things exist in the absolute reason, that matter is extinct mind, and that the laws of physics are the same as those of mental representations. (CD 2974)

Objective idealism is compatible with basic realism. The former theory *does* imply that every instance of matter is also an instance of mind/feeling and therefore conscious, at least to some minimal degree. And it implies that every instance of mind/feeling is also an instance of matter and therefore extended in space. But these claims are consistent with the view that there are things – including instances of mind and instances of matter – that have the properties that they have whether or not anyone believes that they have them or otherwise represents them as having them. Even if every instance of matter *feels* to some degree, this does not imply that every instance of matter *thinks*, or *cognizes*, or otherwise *represents* the world as being a certain way; nor does it imply that things are a certain way because some instance of matter thinks that they are that way. And even if every instance of mind/feeling is extended in space, this does not imply that matter or mind/feeling is the way it is only because it is thought to be that way, nor does it imply that *everything* is the way it is because it is thought to be that way. It is consistent to maintain that in a world of real things, everything that feels is also extended in space and that everything that is extended in space also feels.

It is more difficult to see whether objective idealism is compatible with realism about the external world. This is because it is not obvious how the distinction between more-deterministic matter and less-deterministic mind/feeling intersects with the distinction between the external and the internal. Again, Peirce defined the external as that which is the way it is regardless of what anyone thinks or feels about anything at all; the fact that the earth orbits the sun is real, since it does not depend on whether anyone thinks that the earth orbits the sun, and it is also external, since it does not depend on what anyone thinks, about the earth or anything else. And he defined the internal as that which *does* depend on what someone or other thinks or feels; emotions and dreams are internal, since my having either is a matter of my thoughts or feelings being in a certain state. Intuitively, everything physical is external, since nothing physical depends on what anyone in particular thinks or feels.[32] Whether objective idealism is consistent with the view that everything physical is external depends on whether the feelings mentioned in Peirce's definitions of "external" and "internal" must belong to a person or other sentient being, or whether dependence on a feeling that is not the feeling of a sentient being is sufficient for internality. If the latter, then objective idealism implies that every physical object is internal. This is akin to Berkeley's ontological idealism, according to which everything real – even those things that we (mistakenly, on Berkeley's view) think of as material objects – are real only if they are ideas or minds. If objective idealism implies that (a) physical objects are internal, and if (b) physical objects are the only candidates for things that are external, then the theory implies that everything real is internal and is therefore inconsistent with realism about external things.

But the textual evidence indicates that Peirce believed neither (a) nor (b).[33]

With regard to (a): so far as I have been able to discover, Peirce never defined "external" or "internal" in terms of feelings or thoughts that are not

---

[32] At least, nothing physical depends *directly* on what anyone thinks or feels. My thinking about having a beer might indirectly result in my getting up and walking to the refrigerator.

[33] The position that I defend here – that Peirce's objective idealism is consistent with his realism about external things – is at odds with Almeder's (1980: 183) conclusion that Peirce was inconsistent when he defended both objective idealism and "epistemological realism," by which Almeder seems to mean the view that there is an external world of which we are capable of having knowledge. This is different than the basic realism that I attribute to Peirce, which (i) allows for there to be both external and internal reals and (ii) does not mention our capacity for knowledge of the real. (On my account, the latter issue is covered by Peirce's basic idealism.) That Almeder formulates epistemological realism in this way is, I think, a symptom of the fact that he pays insufficient attention to Peirce's distinction between the real and the external. Another symptom is his tendency to use phrases like "independent world" and "world existing independently of mind" (1980: 57) – phrases that are ambiguous between what Peirce would characterize as "external," on the one hand, and "real," on the other.

the feelings or thoughts *of someone or other*. In each case, he defined the external or the internal by reference to a being or beings to whose minds the external is external and the internal is internal. For example:

> "[T]he external" means simply that which is independent of what phenomenon is immediately present, that is of how we may think or feel. (8.13, W 2: 470, 1871; quoted approvingly by Peirce at R 641: 13, 1909)

> The internal is that whose real existence depends on what I (or you or somebody) think of something. The external is that which so far as it is real is independent not only of what I think about it but also of what I think about anything. (W 3: 49, 1872)

> An external object is anything that is not affected by any cognitions, whether about it or not, of the man to whom it is external. (5.525, 1905)

> The external is that which is as it is whatever one may think about *anything*. (R 498: 32, no date, but probably 1906 based on its similarity to R 499)

> Externality . . . [is] irrelativity of all direct action of personal Cognition . . . [T]hat which constitutes the Externality of a Fact is that it would remain the very same Fact no matter what or how any given Mind or Group of Minds may Actually Feel, or Think, or Imagine, or within itself might do or suffer. (R 642: 15–16, 1909)[34]

Peirce did not state either his definition of "external" or his definition of "internal" in the cosmological series; all of the passages just quoted are from outside the period of his objective idealism. But neither did he state or imply alternative definitions of those terms in that series.[35] And his uses of "external," "internal," and their cognates in that series are consistent with his usual definitions. In LM, he wrote that "[s]ince space is continuous, it follows that there must be an immediate community of feeling between parts of mind infinitesimally near together. Without this, I believe it would have been impossible for minds external to one another ever to become

---

[34] See also, e.g., 7.339, W 3: 29–30, 1872; W 3: 78, 1873; 5.405, W 3: 271, 1878.

[35] N.b., Peirce's *Century Dictionary* entries for "external" and "internal," written in the years leading up to the cosmological series (he began work on his contributions to the *Dictionary* in 1883 and continued that work until the first edition was published in 1889–1891; see W 5: xliii–xliv), do not include the definitions that he gave so often in his philosophical writing. But they do imply the gloss that I have sometimes employed, that the internal is mental and the external is nonmental. His entry for "external" reads in part: "in *metaph.*, forming part of or pertaining to the world of things or phenomena in space, considered as outside of the perceiving mind" (CD 2094). His entry for "internal" reads in part: "Inner; pertaining to the mind, or to the relations of the mind to itself. [In this sense the word *interior* is preferable]" (CD 3149; the bracketed insertion is Peirce's); and his entry for "interior" contains the following: "Pertaining to the immediate contents of consciousness; relating to that which one can perceive within one's self; inward; inner; inmost; mental" (CD 3144).

coördinated" (6.134, W 8: 148). This indicates that Peirce distinguished between mind/feeling, which is the basic "stuff" of the universe, and the individual minds of persons (a distinction to which I will return); but for present purposes, the point to recognize is that individuals' minds are external to each other. My mind is external to yours and everyone else's, in that it does not depend on what you or anyone else is thinking. Elsewhere in LM, he asserted that his account of mind/feeling overcomes traditional difficulties about "reference to the external" (6.151, W 8: 154), and in describing how one person can come to know the personality of another, he wrote that "the opposition between the two persons is perceived" by the first person, "so that the externality of the second is recognized" (6.160, W 8: 156). In "Evolutionary Love," the final paper in the series, he described a way in which (not mind/feeling, but) thought, i.e., the thought of an individual or group of individuals, can develop:

> The anancastic development of thought will consist of new ideas adopted without foreseeing whither they tend, but having a character determined by causes either external to the mind, such as changed circumstances of life, or internal to the mind as logical developments of ideas already accepted, such as generalizations. (6.307, W 8: 196, 1893)[36]

"External anancasm" is "[d]evelopment under the pressure of external circumstances," while "internal anancasm" amounts to "logical groping" (6.312–313, W 8: 199–200).

But what should we make of the claims, quoted previously, that "[v]iewing a thing from the outside, considering its relations of action and reaction with other things, it appears as matter," and that "[v]iewing it from the inside, looking at its immediate character as feeling, it appears as consciousness" (MGE, 6.268, W 8: 181)? The key is to distinguish between, on the one hand, the claim that there is mind/feeling, and on the other, the claim that there are one or more *minds*, the minds of individual people or other sentient beings. According to Peirce's cosmogony, what there was at the earliest stages of the universe was mind in the sense of "unpersonalized feeling" – feeling not felt by any person. But there were not yet any individual *minds*. In order for there to be an individual mind, there must be a physical being with a significant degree of structural complexity. Now objective idealism implies that all physical objects, even stones, are characterized by at least some minimal level of sensitivity or experience. When we "view" a stone "from the outside,"

---

[36] Peirce distinguished among three kinds of evolution: tychasm, or "evolution by fortuitous variation"; anancasm, or "evolution by mechanical necessity"; and agapasm, or "evolution by creative love" (6.302, W 8: 194, 1893).

i.e., when we consider it as something that can be acted upon by and react to other things, we are attending to its material aspect. But when, having accepted objective idealism and its implications about mind and matter, we "view" a stone "from the inside," "it appears as consciousness" – we think of it as being constituted by feeling, albeit not by feelings that are felt by someone. A stone, while made of effete mind/feeling, does not have a mind. In order for *x* to be internal to a mind, *there must be a mind* in relation to which *x* is internal. Stones are not minds or possessors of minds. So a stone and the effete mind/feeling of which it is constituted are external, i.e., external to my mind, to yours, and to anyone else's. The same holds for every other physical object. And so everything physical is external, in the sense of being external to any*one*'s mind. Objective idealism does not imply that physical objects are internal.

Not all of the cosmological series' references to externality are easy to square with Peirce's usual definition of that term. In LM, he wrote that a

> feeling has a subjective, or substantial, spatial extension ... This is, no doubt, a difficult idea to seize, for the reason that it is a subjective, not an objective, extension. It is not that we have a feeling of bigness ... It is that the feeling, as a subject of inhesion, is big. Moreover, our own feelings are focused in attention to such a degree that we are not aware that ideas are not brought to an absolute unity; just as nobody not instructed by special experiment has any idea how very, very little of the field of vision is distinct. Still, we all know how the attention wanders about among our feelings; and this fact shows that those feelings that are not coördinated in attention have a reciprocal externality, although they are present at the same time. But we must not tax introspection to make a phenomenon manifest which essentially involves externality. (6.133, W 8: 148)

Although much about this passage is obscure, at least this much is clear: Peirce held that the feelings of individual people can have spatial extension (albeit "subjective" extension) and that they can be external in some respect. That a person's feelings can be external does not imply that physical objects are internal, nor does it necessarily undermine realism about the external world in general. But this passage does raise questions about how Peirce was thinking about the distinction between the external and the internal during the early 1890s. On the usual way of thinking about an individual person's feelings, they depend – trivially – on what that person is feeling and are thus internal on Peirce's usual definition of that word. But it is not obvious how that definition and his usual definition of "external" are to be reconciled with the claim that an individual's feelings can be external. So while the textual evidence supports the interpretation on which objective idealism is consistent with physical objects being external to any individual mind, it is not clear what he meant by the claim that an individual's feelings can be external.[37]

Peirce also denied (b), according to which only physical objects are external. Beginning no later than in the cognition series and lasting until the end of his life, Peirce was a realist, not just about individual minds and physical objects, but also about what he called *generals*: universals, including kinds and laws. And he held that generals, although they are not physical objects capable of reacting against other things, are nonetheless external:

> [T]he external world, (that is, the world that is comparatively external) does not consist of existent objects merely, nor merely of these and their reactions; but on the contrary, its most important reals have the mode of being of what the nominalist calls "mere" words, that is, general types and would-bes. The nominalist is right in saying that they are substantially of the nature of words; but his "mere" reveals a complete misunderstanding of what our everyday world consists of. (8.191, ca. 1904)

I will examine Peirce's realism about "general types and would-bes" in Chapters 5 and 6. But first, in the following chapter, I will consider some seemingly anti-realist claims that Peirce made beginning in the 1860s, claims that could be seen as undermining my interpretation of his views of reality and truth. Those apparently anti-realistic claims are included in what he called his idealistic theory of reality.

---

[37] It is also worth noting that in R 942, which I believe to be from the mid- to late 1890s, Peirce used "inner world" and "outer world" to mean something other than what he typically meant by "internal" and "external." In this manuscript, he stated objective idealism, not in terms of stricter law emerging from less strict law, or in terms of matter emerging from mind, but in terms of the outer world emerging from the inner world (NEM 4: 141).

CHAPTER 4

The Idealistic Theory of Reality: Idealism in the Cognition Series

4.1

In Chapter 3, I drew on texts from the 1860s through the 1910s to show that what Peirce took to be the "main position of idealism" – what I have called his basic idealism – is consistent with basic realism and with realism about the external world. But not all of the relevant textual evidence clearly supports this interpretation. Some statements in the cognition series – a series that comprises three papers: "Questions Concerning Certain Faculties Claimed for Man," hereafter QCCF (1868); "Some Consequences of Four Incapacities," hereafter SCFI (1868); and "Grounds of Validity of the Laws of Logic: Further Consequences of Four Incapacities," hereafter GVLL (1869) – are difficult to square with basic realism. These statements have to do with what he called his "idealistic theory of reality" (GVLL, 5.353, W 2: 270). For example: "The real . . . is that which, sooner or later, information and reasoning would finally result in" (SCFI, 5.311, W 2: 239). This could be read as implying that reality is or will eventually be brought about by information and reasoning, that it will be, not discovered, but *created* by investigation. If this is the case, then, for any x and any property F, whether x is F will depend on what is thought about x at the end of investigation, and so basic realism is not true.

Peirce also wrote that "reality consists in the agreement that the whole community would eventually come to . . . [T]his theory of reality . . . makes all reality something which is constituted by an event indefinitely future" (GVLL, 5.331, W 2: 252). This could be read as implying that reality is not simply the *result* of investigation that would lead to a consensus, but that reality *is that consensus itself.* Peirce made similar statements in the years following the cognition series, e.g., "[t]he Real thing is the ultimate opinion about it" (W 2: 440, 1870); "it is a consensus or common confession which constitutes reality" (8.16, W 2: 471, 1871). To identify reality with a consensus does not necessarily mean abandoning basic realism, since whether there is an agreement, and what the content of that agreement is, may well be independent of what anyone thinks about that agreement and its content. But if that agreement is the only thing that is real, then, on the assumption that an agreement comprises various beliefs or opinions that share the same content, a form of ontological idealism is true.

From these statements, one might conclude that the idealistic theory of reality defended in the cognition series is not idealistic because it includes basic idealism, but because it includes some other variety of idealism that is inconsistent with basic realism; and one might conclude that Peirce changed his mind about these matters by the time he wrote *Illustrations of the Logic of Science* (1877–1878), in which his commitment to basic realism and to realism about the external are explicit. But at least once in the years following *Illustrations*, Peirce seemed to reaffirm the view that reality is identical to the final opinion: "the real is the idea in which the community ultimately settles down" (6.610, 1893).

Despite appearances, Peirce's idealistic theory of reality was not antirealist. In writing the cognition series, he was committed to the view that there is a real world and that parts of that world are external to any particular mind. Properly understood, the seemingly anti-realistic claims of the cognition series and later works are compatible with basic realism and with realism about the external. This chapter defends those claims. First I show that the cognition series assumes that there is a real world containing not only minds and mental states, but also things and events that are external to particular minds.[1] Then, after a closer consideration of the seemingly anti-realistic passages in the cognition series, I argue that Peirce intended his idealistic theory of reality to be compatible with basic realism. As a whole, this chapter shores up the arguments of Chapter 3 by showing that the doctrines Peirce defended and labeled "idealism" or "idealistic" are consistent with his basic realism.[2]

---

[1] Murphey has argued that in some works of the 1860s, Peirce was "committed to an extreme semiotic idealism" according to which "[w]hat there are . . . are signs" (1961: 90). I am not sure that this is true even of works dating from earlier than 1868. But my concern here will be only works dating from 1868 and thereafter, and on the reading that I defend Peirce was not committed to that sort of ontological idealism. In an in-progress book, T. L. Short argues that, whether or not Peirce was fully committed, in the cognition series of 1868–1869, to a semiotic or conceptual idealism according to which the only real things there are are thought-signs, the positions that he explicitly defended in that series drove him toward just that sort of idealism. I disagree with Short on this point, but here my task will be to explain the positions Peirce actually took rather than to consider what he might have inadvertently committed himself to by taking those positions.

[2] Almeder argues that "a good case can be made for the claim that Peirce was never an epistemological idealist," by which he means someone who holds that "the existence and properties of physical objects are causally, and therefore logically, dependent upon the noetic act of the sum of finite minds identified as the community of scientific inquirers" (1980: 153, 148). My view is consistent with Almeder's, but my treatment of Peirce's idealism has at least two advantages over his. First, I provide

4.2

By the time Peirce wrote the cognition series, he had already accepted the definition of "reality" as that which is independent of what anyone thinks about it. Perhaps the earliest occurrence of that definition is in a manuscript from 1867: "the essential difference between a reality and a nonreality, is that the former has an existence entirely independent of what you or I or any number of men may think about it" (W 2: 104). In the same manuscript, he illustrated the distinction between reals and figments with the example of dreaming, the same example he provided later in "How to Make Our Ideas Clear" (HTM); and, as he was also to do in HTM, he quoted Thomas Gray's "Elegy Written in a Country Churchyard":

> What I dream, for example, only exists so far as my dreaming imagination creates it. But the fact that I have had such a dream, remains true whether I ever reflect upon that fact or not. The dream, therefore, as a mental phenomenon, is a reality; but the thing dreamed is a figment. If there ever really was such a man as Romulus, he would have existed just the same if history had never mentioned him; but if he is not a reality he exists only in the fables which have been told of the foundation of Rome. When Gray says,
>
> > Full many a gem of purest ray serene
> > The dark unfathomed caves of ocean bear;
> > Full many a flower is born to blush unseen
> > And waste its sweetness on the desert air;
>
> he expresses with precision the essential character of reality. (W 2: 104, 1867)

Peirce did not state his verbal definition of "reality" in the cognition series. However, he did describe the real as "that which . . . is . . . independent of the vagaries of me and you" (SCFI, 5.311, W 2: 239), and that he had his verbal definition in mind when writing that passage is confirmed by the following:

> [I]n a system of signs in which no sign is taken in two different senses, two signs which differ only in their manner of representing their object, but which are equivalent in meaning, can always be substituted for one another. Any case of the falsification of this principle would be a case of the dependence of the mode of existence of the thing represented upon the mode of this or that representation of it, which, as has been shown in the article in the last number [i.e., in SCFI], is contrary to the nature of reality. (GVLL, 5.323, W 2: 245–246)[3]

a much closer analysis of the apparently anti-realistic texts of the 1860s and 1870s. Second, I explain the connection between Peirce's seemingly anti-realistic claims and his pragmatic clarification of the idea of reality.

[3] In a footnote appended to this passage, the editors of the *Collected Papers* direct us back to 5.311, in which occurs the "vagaries" passage.

The verbal definition is also at work later in GVLL:

> If men were not to be able to learn from induction, it must be because as a general rule, when they had made an induction, the order of things (as they appear in experience), would then undergo a revolution. Just herein would the unreality of such a universe consist; namely, that the order of the universe should depend on how much men should know of it. (5.352, W 2: 269)

If how x is depends on what people know about x, then x is unreal. Conversely, if x is real, then how x is does not depend on what anyone knows about x. So Peirce accepted his verbal definition of "real" by no later than 1867, and he assumed that definition in the cognition series.[4]

It is possible, of course, to define a term but then to say that there is nothing to which that term applies. But that is not what Peirce was up to in the cognition series. Throughout that series he asserted that various mental faculties and the "conditions" in which they operate "exist," i.e., are real, e.g., he asserted that the existence of cognitions is "indubitable" (SCFI, 5.267, W 2: 214). Again, that a cognition is a mental state or event does not rule out its being real; mental states and events, and minds themselves, meet the verbal definition of "real" so long as they have the properties they have regardless of whether they are believed to have them. So at the very least, Peirce was a realist about mental items and events during this period. Furthermore, one of his arguments in the cognition series in support of basic idealism assumes that there is a real world:

> [T]he highest concept which can be reached by abstractions from judgments of experience – and therefore, the highest concept which can be reached at all – is the concept of something of the nature of a cognition. *Not*, then, or *what is other than*, if a concept, is a concept of the cognizable. Hence, not-cognizable, if a concept, is a concept of the form "*A*, not-*A*," and is, at least, self-contradictory. Thus, ignorance and error can only be conceived as correlative to a real knowledge and truth, which latter are of the nature of cognitions. Over against any cognition, there is an unknown but knowable reality; but over against all possible cognition, there is only the self-contradictory. In short, *cognizability*

---

[4] Another piece of evidence is found in a late manuscript: "If I have ever done any work of any value in Noölogy, it was in the years 1862–1868; and its results, including the view of Reality and the outlines of most of the opinions in the present paper, are given in three articles in Vol.II of Dr. William T. Harris's *Journal of Speculative Philosophy*," i.e., in the cognition series (R 641: 14, 1909). In this manuscript, Peirce once again affirmed his usual verbal definition of "reality"; see R 641: 12–13, wherein he quoted the definition as he had stated it in his 1871 review of Fraser's edition of Berkeley, and R 641: 17, wherein he quoted the definition – as well as his description of three signs that a given percept is real – as he had stated them in his 1901 review of the second edition of Karl Pearson's *The Grammar of Science* (8.144).

(in its widest sense) and *being* are not merely metaphysically the same, but are synonymous terms. (QCCF, 5.257, W 2: 208)

When S errs in believing that x is F, what is "over against" this cognition – what is apart from the cognition and enables us to understand the cognition as being mistaken – is something *real*. That reality is unknown to S at the time that S is mistaken. But according to Peirce, this point cannot sensibly be generalized to cover all possible beliefs. We cannot understand what it would be for a mistaken belief to be insusceptible to correction – the very concept of a reality that is "over against all possible cognition" is incoherent. Hence, he concluded that the concepts of *cognizability* and *being* are one and the same, and thus that anything that *is*, i.e., anything real, is cognizable. If there is still any doubt that in the cognition series Peirce assumed basic realism, the following should put that doubt to rest:

> [W]e may ... say, in general, that if nothing real exists, then, since every question supposes that something exists – for it maintains its own urgency – it supposes only illusions to exist. But the existence even of an illusion is a reality; for an illusion affects all men, or it does not. In the former case, it is a reality according to our theory of reality; in the latter case, it is independent of the state of mind of any individuals except those whom it happens to affect. So that the answer to the question, Why is anything real? is this: That question means, "supposing anything to exist, why is something real?" The answer is, that that very existence is reality by definition. (GVLL, 5.352, W 2: 269–270)

So when he wrote the cognition series, Peirce accepted basic realism and held that, at the very least, cognitions and other mental events and "states of mind" are real.

On his own later account of the internal/external distinction, all mental events and states are *internal*, i.e., they depend on what someone or other thinks.[5] Given only the textual evidence I have mustered so far, one might conclude that the cognition series' idealistic theory of reality is accompanied by the view that all real things are mental and therefore internal to some mind or other. But there is evidence that in the cognition series Peirce maintained that there are real extra-mental things and thus a real world outside of any particular mind. For example, in QCCF he argued that humans lack the power of introspection, i.e., "a direct perception of the internal world" (5.244, W 2: 206), and that our only way of "investigating a psychological question is by inference from external facts" (5.249, W 2: 207), facts involving "outward things" (5.245,

---

[5] So far as I have been able to discover, he first gave his usual definition of "external" in his 1871 Berkeley review (8.13, W 2: 470) and first gave his usual definition of "internal" the following year (W 3: 49, 1872).

W 2: 206). He also asserted that "[w]e can admit no statement concerning what passes within us except as a hypothesis necessary to explain what takes place in what we commonly call the external world" (SCFI, 5.266, W 2: 213), and he inferred from this that "the only cases of thought which we can find are of thought in signs," since "[p]lainly, no other thought can be evidenced by external facts" (QCCF, 5.251, W 2: 207). And he asserted that of all the different "modifications of consciousness," cognitions are the ones that "most closely follow[] external facts" (SCFI, 5.267, W 2: 214).[6]

So Peirce's view in the cognition series was that there are real, internal, mental states and events and also real things external to all minds. But complicating matters is his view that the distinction between the internal and the external is continuous, not absolute. His position here is difficult to grasp; I will provide only a sketch, just enough to demonstrate that he was committed to the reality of an external world.

Peirce argued that every human cognition is a sign, and he held that each "thought-sign" is a mental event, one that takes place over some period of time rather than instantaneously. A given thought-sign can represent an object x that is outside the mind, but it can do so only mediately, by virtue of representing an earlier thought-sign of x, which itself represents x only in virtue of referring to a still-earlier thought-sign.

> For what does the thought-sign stand – what does it name – what is its *suppositum*?[7] The outward thing, undoubtedly, when a real outward thing is thought of. But still, as the thought is determined by a previous thought of the same object, it only refers to the thing through denoting this previous thought. (SCFI, 5.285, W 2: 224)

This is a consequence of Peirce's view that humans lack the faculty of intuition, i.e., of having "a cognition not determined by a previous cognition of the same object, and therefore so determined by something out of the consciousness" (QCCF, 5.213, W 2: 193).

A subject S can think about an external thing x, but any such cognition represents x indirectly, in virtue of representing an earlier cognition of x by S. This implies that there is an infinite regress leading back from any cognition toward its external object. But Peirce denied that this regress

---

[6] In the opening paragraphs of QCCF, Peirce used Kant's phrase "transcendental object" (5.213–214, W 2: 194). But he did so only for dialectical purposes, in order to sketch the view, which he then argued against, that humans have intuitive cognitions, i.e., cognitions determined immediately by their objects rather than by earlier cognitions. So I do not include this among the evidence that in writing the cognition series he assumed that there is an external world.

[7] Peirce defined "suppositum" as "[t]hat which is supposed; the thing denoted by a name in a given proposition" (CD 6076).

prohibits thought-signs from representing external objects. Let t_1 be the latest time before S begins thinking of some external object x and t_2 a time at which S is thinking of x. There is "an infinite series of finite times" (W 2: 163, 1868) between t_1 and t_2, but this does not mean that the time between t_1 and t_2 is infinitely long. Since cognition is continuous, it does not consist of ultimate, fundamental cognitive events. In the same way that a physical object can occupy an infinite number of positions as it moves along a path in space that is finite in length, an infinite number of cognitive events can occur within a finite time. There is no such thing as S's very first cognition of x, since any of S's cognitions of x is preceded by some earlier cognition by S of x. But on Peirce's view, this does not imply that S's cognition of x has no beginning in time. He was still committed to this view several years later: "the object of the sign, that to which it virtually at least professes to be applicable, can itself be only a sign ... The immediate object which any sign seeks to represent is itself a sign" (R 599: 36–37, ca. 1902). There is no "ultimate reality" that can be accessed via human cognition without being represented and therefore without being represented *mediately*; for any representation r of a real object x, there is always some previous representation that intercedes between r and x. This does not imply that there are no reals, nor does it imply that no reals are external. But it does imply that all reals can be represented and therefore can be the objects of ideas; i.e., it implies basic idealism.

At the time of the cognition series, Peirce understood a continuum to be "precisely that, every part of which has parts, in the same sense" (GVLL, 5.335, W 2: 256). Consider "a piece of glass to be laid on a sheet of paper so as to cover half of it" (GVLL, 5.336, W 2: 256). Is the line lying directly under the edge of the glass covered or not? The answer is that it is partly covered and partly not. Because the sheet is continuous, each part of it has parts "in the same sense," so there is no part of the sheet so small that it cannot be partly covered and partly uncovered. Peirce applied this kind of analysis to the "boundary" between a cognition of an external object x and x itself:

> [T]here is nothing absolutely out of the mind, but the first impression of sense is the most external thing in existence. Here we touch material idealism. But we have adopted, also, another idealistic //conclusion/doctrine//, that there is no intuitive cognition. It follows that the first impression of sense is not cognition but only the limit of cognition. It may therefore be said to be so far out of the mind, that it is as much external as internal (W 2: 191, 1868).[8]

---

[8] The editors of W placed the slashes in this passage to indicate that Peirce had two words in mind – "conclusion" and "doctrine" – but did not indicate in his manuscript which he preferred.

"Material idealism" was Kant's term for the view (which he rejected) that "the existence of objects in space outside us [is] either merely doubtful and indemonstrable, or else false and impossible" (*Critique of Pure Reason* B 274; in Kant [1787] 1998: 326).[9] Peirce saw that his own doctrine that "there is nothing absolutely out of the mind" pulled him toward material idealism, but that he was pulled back by his view that there is no sharp boundary between a cognized external object and someone's cognition of it. "The first impression of sense" – the very beginning of a given process of cognition – is partially external, partially internal. The boundary between the extra-mental and the mental is itself partly extra-mental and partly mental, just as the line under the edge of the piece of glass is partly covered and partly uncovered.[10] There is no absolute boundary between the external and the internal; the difference between them turns out to be a matter of degree. This explains Peirce's statement, early in QCCF, that "[i]t is not intended here to assume the reality of the external world. Only, there is a certain set of facts which are ordinarily regarded as external, while others are regarded as internal" (5.244, W 2: 205). What he wanted to deny was that there are such things as the external and internal *as ordinarily conceived*, viz. as being discontinuous with one another; but this does not mean that nothing external is real. His denial of an absolute boundary between the internal and the external carried forward into later decades, well after he had adopted his usual definitions of "external" and "internal":

[9] Kant attributed the former kind of material idealism to Descartes; in the *Prolegomena to any Future Metaphysics*, he called it "empirical idealism" and described it as "only a problem, the insolubility of which gave everyone the liberty, in Descartes' opinion, to deny the existence of the corporeal world, because it could never be satisfactorily answered" (4: 293; in Kant [1783] 2004: 98); in the B edition of the *Critique of Pure Reason* he called it "problematic idealism" and described it as "profess[ing] only our incapacity for proving an existence outside us from our own by means of immediate experience" (B 275; in Kant [1787] 1998: 326). Kant attributed the latter kind of material idealism to Berkeley; in the *Prolegomena* he called it "mystical and visionary idealism" (4: 293; in Kant [1783] 2004: 99); in the B edition of the *Critique* he called it "dogmatic idealism," asserting that it is "unavoidable if one regards space as a property that is to pertain to the things in themselves; for then it, along with everything for which it serves as a condition, is a non-entity" (B 274; in Kant [1787] 1998: 326). For Peirce's comments on this part of the *Critique*, see W 8: 80 (ca. 1890), a portion of which is at 1.36. Kant insisted that the fact that he had called his own position *transcendental idealism* in the A edition of the *Critique* "cannot justify anybody in confusing it with" either form of material idealism. His transcendental idealism does "not concern the existence of the things [i.e., 'the things that we represent to ourselves through the senses'] (which to doubt properly constitutes idealism in its accepted meaning), for," said Kant, "it has never entered my mind to doubt the latter, but only the sensible representations of the things" (from *Prolegomena* 4: 293; in Kant [1783] 2004: 98–99).

[10] Peirce also used the image of a triangle being dipped apex first into water to illustrate the regress from a given cognition back to the external object that it represents; see W 2: 178, 1868; QCCF, 5.263, W 2: 210–211. For a similar illustration, see W 1: 488–490, 1866.

> We naturally make all our distinctions too absolute. We are accustomed to speak of an external universe and an inner world of thought. But they are merely vicinities with no real boundary line between them ... There is an intermediate world, our own neighborhood, household, and persons, which belongs to us, which we sometimes feel inclined to class with the outer world and sometimes with the inner world. (7.438, ca. 1893)

> [T]he *real* [is] that which is such as it is regardless of what you or I or any of our folks may think it to be. The *external* [is] that element which is such as it is regardless of what somebody thinks, feels, or does, whether about that external object or about anything else. Accordingly, the external is necessarily real, while the real may or may not be external; nor is anything absolutely external nor absolutely devoid of externality. (8.191, ca. 1904)

Given that the dependence mentioned in his definitions of "external" and "internal" can be a matter of degree, so that it makes sense to say that x being F depends to a greater or lesser degree on what someone thinks or feels, his view that there is no absolute distinction between the external and the internal is consistent with those definitions.

Another passage in SCFI might be taken as evidence that Peirce was a phenomenalist of the sort that denies that there is a real external world:

> [W]henever we think, we have present to the consciousness some feeling, image, conception, or other representation, which serves as a sign. But it follows from our own existence (which is proved by the occurrence of ignorance and error) that everything which is present to us is a phenomenal manifestation of ourselves. (SCFI, 5.283, W 2: 223)

But that everything "present to the consciousness" is a phenomenon does not mean that it is internal to someone's mind. Peirce continued: "This does not prevent its being a phenomenon of something without us, just as a rainbow is at once a manifestation both of the sun and of the rain" (5.283, W 2: 223). Without both sun and rain, there is no rainbow. Without both perceiving mind and perceived object, there is no thought-sign. And that every thought-sign is a "phenomenal manifestation" of the mind in which it occurs does not imply that its object is internal to that mind. The view Peirce expressed here was an anticipation of his distinction between two aspects of the *percept*, which is at once the phenomenal presentation of the world to the perceiver and a direct causal interaction between perceiver and environment.[11]

---

[11] Percepts are thoroughly nonrepresentational; the representational aspect of perception is the *perceptual judgment*, the spontaneous belief that occurs along with the percept and which together with the percept forms the *percipuum* (7.619ff., 1903). For more on Peirce's theory of perception, see Haack 1994 and Lane 2007a.

So the theory of cognition that Peirce defended in 1868–1869 assumes both that there are real things and that some of those things are external to any individual mind. The cognition series is no less realist and no less committed to the reality of the external world than 1877–1878's *Illustrations of the Logic of Science*.

4.3

The idealistic theory of reality defended in the cognition series is not a single doctrine. It is a tangle of connected claims only some of which are obviously consistent with basic realism and with realism about externals. One of the claims foreshadows Peirce's pragmatic clarification of the idea of reality:

> [A] proposition whose falsity can never be discovered, and the error of which therefore is absolutely incognizable, contains, upon our principle, absolutely no error. Consequently, that which is thought in these cognitions is the real, as it really is. (SCFI, 5.311, W 2: 239; see also W 2: 163 and 175, 1868)

This is consistent with basic realism. But as we saw at the beginning of this chapter, in explaining his idealistic theory Peirce also asserted two subtly different claims, one of which seems to abandon basic realism, the other of which seems to abandon realism about external things. His statement that "[t]he real ... is that which, sooner or later, information and reasoning would finally result in" (SCFI, 5.311, W 2: 239) might be read as implying that reality is, not discovered, but *created*, by investigation. This is inconsistent with basic realism: if x being F is the "result" of inquirers believing that x is F at the end of investigation, then x does not meet the standard of reality set by Peirce's definition of that term, and so there are no real things in that sense of "real." And his claim that "reality consists in the agreement that the whole community would eventually come to" (GVLL, 5.331, W 2: 252) might be taken to mean that reality is not simply the *result* of investigation ending in consensus, but that reality *is that consensus itself*. A consensus comprises a group of beliefs sharing the same content; it thus comprises a set of mental states and is thus internal. So this view is inconsistent with realism about the external.

The problems with these views are obvious. The view that makes reality dependent on the future outcome of investigation implies that there is nothing real at the present time, and it is not clear what sense can be made of "at the present time" once that view is assumed – if nothing is real, then time is not real. If nothing is real at present, then presently there is no one engaged in the process of experiencing the world and reflecting on those experiences. If "information and reasoning" are eventually to "result in" some set of beliefs, then there must be beings who gather information and reason about it. But those beings could not be real, since, *ex hypothesi*, there is no reality until the investigation is complete. On the other hand, if reality is not simply the result of future inquiry, but the consensus on which that inquiry will settle, the same problem arises: at any time before that consensus is reached, there is no one real to work toward it. These views are bizarre, if not incoherent.

However, Peirce did not have any of this in mind. Properly interpreted, the seemingly anti-realistic statements are consistent with basic realism and with realism about the external. My argument will begin with an analysis of 5.311 (W 2: 238–239, from SCFI), some of which I have already quoted. I focus on this passage because it is the cognition series' lengthiest statement about reality and the mind's ability to cognize external objects. I will have to bypass much in the passage that is of interest, considering only the parts that are relevant to the question of realism and incorporating relevant material from elsewhere in the cognition series and other works from the same period.

Peirce began this statement of his idealistic theory as follows:

> At any moment we are in possession of certain information, that is, of cognitions which have been logically derived by induction and hypothesis from previous cognitions which are less general, less distinct, and of which we have a less lively consciousness. These in their turn have been derived from others still less general, less distinct, and less vivid; and so on back to the ideal first. (SCFI, 5.311, W 2: 238)

Once again, consider a subject S thinking about some external object x at time t. As we have already seen, Peirce maintained that there is an infinite regress of thought-signs leading back in time from S's thinking of x at t toward x itself. S's thinking about x does have a beginning in time – there are earlier times at which S is not thinking about x – but there is no earliest cognition that S has of x. Any cognition in the series was preceded by a prior cognition of the same object:

> [A]lthough the act of perception cannot be represented as whole, by a series of cognitions determining one another, since it involves the necessity of an infinite series, yet there is no perception so near to the object that it is not determined by another which precedes it – for when we reach the point which no determining cognition precedes we find the degree of consciousness there to be just *zero*, and in short we have reached the external object itself, and not a representation of it. (W 2: 179, 1868)

But the external object

> is quite singular, and quite out of consciousness. This ideal first is the
> particular thing-in-itself. It does not exist *as such*. That is, there is no
> thing which is in-itself in the sense of not being relative to the mind, though
> things which are relative to the mind doubtless are, apart from that relation.
> (5.311, W 2: 238–239)

The external thing x that S cognizes *is*, "apart from that relation" – in other
words, x is *real*: that it has some properties and not others does not depend
on whether it is represented as having or not having those properties. And
it is *external*: that it has some properties and not others does not depend on
whether it is represented at all. But this does not imply that it is an
incognizable *Ding an sich*. An external thing-in-itself, something that
cannot be represented by any mind, is a "limit which the possible cannot
attain" – Peirce wrote in a footnote that this is what he meant by describing
the external object of cognition as "ideal" (5.311, n. 1, W 2: 238, n. 7). No x
stands outside of all possible relation to any mind.

The word "possible" here is crucial. As we saw in Chapter 3, Peirce took
"[t]he main position of idealism" to be "that being an object of thought –
actual or possible – is an essential part of existence" (R 935: 3, 1872). His view
in the cognition series was not that all external things must be cognized by
some mind or other, but that all external things are cogniz*able*, capable of
being represented in the thoughts of intelligent beings. It would be absurd to
maintain that everything real will eventually be an object of actual thought:

> [T]he sum of all that will be known up to any time, however advanced, into
> the future, has a ratio less than any assignable ratio to all that may be known
> at a time still more advanced. This does not contradict the fact that every-
> thing is cognizable; it only contradicts a proposition, which no one can
> maintain, that everything will be known at some time some number of years
> into the future. (GVLL, 5.330, W 2: 250–251)[12]

The next portion of this statement of the idealistic theory demonstrates
that the representationalist aspect of Peirce's account of truth was present
in the cognition series:

---

[12] It is surprising to find that in 1869, Peirce saw very clearly the need to explain reality in a way that did
not assume that all real things will at some point actually be represented in the beliefs of inquirers –
surprising given his seeming vacillation on this point in 1878's HTM (as described in Chapter 2).
Still, he was inconsistent in his use of the subjunctive mood in discussing reality in the cognition
series, and even as late as 1893 he wrote, using the indicative mood, that his "theory of reality [is] that
the real is the idea in which the community ultimately settles down" (6.610, 1893). It was only in the
1900s, after he had adopted a strong form of modal realism, that he began consistently to explain
reality in terms of what *would* be believed; see Chapters 6 and 7.

> The cognitions which thus reach us by this infinite series of inductions and hypotheses (which though infinite *a parte ante logice* [i.e., from a logical point of view], is yet as one continuous process not without a beginning *in time*) are of two kinds, the true and the untrue, or cognitions whose objects are *real* and those whose objects are *unreal*. (5.311, W 2: 239)

Here as in the *Illustrations*, Peirce connected the ideas of truth and reality: a true cognition is one that represents something real.

> And what do we mean by the real? It is a conception which we must first have had when we discovered that there was an unreal, an illusion; that is, when we first corrected ourselves. Now the distinction for which alone this fact logically called, was between an *ens* relative to private inward determinations, to the negations belonging to idiosyncrasy, and an *ens* such as would stand in the long run. (5.311, W 2: 239)

In 1867, Peirce noted that in its medieval sense, "*ens*" meant, not something real, but something that can be named, whether or not it is real, and he proposed that that original meaning be adopted once again (W 2: 103). In SCFI, he employed the term to distinguish, not between two kinds of real thing, but between unreal things, i.e., figments or fictions, which are "relative to private inward determinations," and real things, which "would stand in the long run." We can understand what it means to be mistaken, and therefore understand self-correction, only once we understand the latter sort of *ens*. The very idea of error depends on the idea of there being something to be gotten right: a real world.

Up to this point 5.311 has been consistent with basic realism. But next comes the apparently anti-realistic claim that we encountered previously:

> The real, then, is that which, sooner or later, information and reasoning would finally result in, and which is therefore independent of the vagaries of me and you. (5.311, W 2: 239)

Set this aside for now – I will return to it momentarily. The passage continues:

> Thus, the very origin of the conception of reality shows that this conception essentially involves the notion of a COMMUNITY, without definite limits, and capable of an indefinite increase of knowledge. (5.311, W 2: 239)[13]

---

[13] In the original version of SCFI published in the *Journal of Speculative Philosophy*, this passage read: "and capable of a definite increase of knowledge." This is repeated in the *Collected Papers* (5.311). But W 2 changes "a definite" to "an indefinite" to correct a mistake shown on an errata list published in the *Journal*. See W 2: 607–608.

This hints at why Peirce later called his pragmatic clarification of the idea of reality a "social theory of reality" (6.610, 1893): not because it implies that how the world is depends on what society thinks about it, but because it holds that the real is what would be represented in the beliefs of a certain kind of community, viz. a community of inquirers who have employed experience and reasoning to dispel doubt and for whom further investigation would cause no further changes in belief.

The next sentence is an essential piece of evidence for my reading of Peirce's idealistic theory:

> And so those two series of cognitions – the real and the unreal – consist of those which, at a time sufficiently future, the community will always continue to re-affirm; and of those which, under the same conditions, will ever after be denied. (5.311, W 2: 239)[14]

By "series" of "unreal" cognitions, he did not mean cognitions *that aren't* – cognitions which themselves are fictional (e.g., thoughts attributed by an author to the characters in a novel she is writing) or illusory (e.g., thoughts attributed to Napoleon in a hallucination that I have of him contemplating the invasion of Russia). Rather, he was referring to cognitions *about* the unreal, i.e., cognitions that are not true. So the series of "real" cognitions to which he referred is the series of cognitions that *represent* the real; he was using "real" synonymously with "true," to mean "that which represents reality." This makes sense of the seemingly anti-realistic sentence from earlier: "The real, then, is that which, sooner or later, information and reasoning would finally result in." Replace "real" with "true" and the sentence becomes consistent, not only with the explicitly realistic pronouncements of the cognition series, but also with everything that Peirce would later say about truth and reality in the *Illustrations*.[15]

---

[14] At the beginning of this passage, the *Collected Papers* (5.311) mistakenly has "two series of cognition" rather than "two series of cognitions," which is how it reads in the original published version.

[15] In 1910, Peirce wrote that his SCFI description of reality – "that which, sooner or later, information and reasoning would finally result in, and which is therefore independent of the vagaries of me and you" – "is as plain 'as the nose on one's face,' once one looks at truth or a [sic] reality from that point of view called 'cognitionism'" (R 655: 32). So far as I have been able to discover, this is the only occurrence of "cognitionism" in Peirce's oeuvre. It does not appear in the *Collected Papers*, nor is it indexed in any of the volumes (1–6, 8) of W that have appeared to date or in any other collections of Peirce's work. Unfortunately, he did not define "cognitionism" in R 655, but I strongly suspect he meant by it his view that everything real is cognizable, i.e., that he meant what I have called "basic idealism." Here I disagree with Max Fisch, according to whom Peirce meant by "cognitionism," not a single doctrine, but a group of related ideas about cognition and reality, one of which is that "what there is is cognitions" (1986: 186). But the passages Fisch quotes in support of this reading do not show that Peirce thought that "what there is is cognitions" – a claim that sounds more like Berkeley's ontological idealism than anything that Peirce ever asserted. What they show is that Peirce believed that everything that there is is cognizable.

This may seem like an interpretative stretch, but two other works indicate that this is in fact what he intended. The first is a set of lecture notes dating from spring 1870 (W 2: 439–440) wherein Peirce, *inter alia*, did the following. (1) He stated the representationalist aspect of his account of truth: "Truth belongs to signs, particularly, and to thoughts as signs. Truth is the agreement of a meaning with a reality" (to the first sentence, Peirce appended a footnote: "True sign is that which means as something really is" [*sic*]). (2) He stated the verbal definition of "real" – "A real thing is something whose characters are independent of how any representation represents it to be" – and asserted that "Idealism does not falsify [that] definition." (3) He stated an anticipation of the investigative aspect of his account of truth – "by the truth concerning a thing we do not mean how any man is affected by a thing. Nor how a majority is affected. But how a man would be affected after sufficient experience, discussion, and reasoning" – calling it an "idealistic doctrine concerning truth." He then went on to say the following:

> That there is a truth about everything implies that sufficient experience, discussion, and reasoning would lead a man to a certain opinion.
>   Then since to say that a thing is so and so is the same as to say that it is true that it is so and so it follows that
>   . . . The Real thing is the ultimate opinion about it.
>   About *it*[,] that is[,] about the ultimate opinion, but not involving the reflection that the opinion is itself that ultimate one and is the real thing. Indeed this opinion is in one sense an ideal inasmuch as *more* experience and reasoning may always be had. (W 2: 440, 1870)

Taken literally, the claim that "[t]he Real thing is the ultimate opinion about it" renders this passage incoherent. But the reason Peirce gave for making this claim – "to say that a thing is so and so is the same as to say that it is true that it is so and so" – indicates that he did not mean to *identify* reality with a possible outcome of inquiry, but rather to emphasize the close conceptual connection between the ideas of truth and reality: any true belief is a representation of reality, and reality is exactly that which is represented in a true belief.

The second work is a manuscript of 1910 in which Peirce approvingly quoted 5.311's seemingly anti-realistic sentence before stating: "The 'then' shows that this definition results from reasonings set forth in the article [viz. SCFI]; and, of course, a definition of the *real* amounts to a definition of *truth*, which is obviously the character of a representation of the real as it really is" (R 655: 30). Here he was explaining his earlier claim that reality is the "result" of "information and reasoning" by positing that "real" and "truth" are, if not quite synonyms, then so closely related that each can be defined in terms of the other: a true belief is one that represents the world as it really is, and reality is what is represented in a true belief. In this late manuscript, Peirce read 5.311's apparently anti-realistic claim as being, not about things that possess their characters whether or not anyone thinks that they do, but about representations of those things, i.e., not about reality, but about the truths that represent it.[16]

Several of Peirce's apparently anti-realistic claims can be accounted for by noting his tendency to use "reality" to mean *that which represents reality*, e.g.:

> [R]eality consists in the agreement that the whole community would eventually come to ... [T]his theory of reality ... makes all reality something which is constituted by an event indefinitely future. (GVLL, 5.331, W 2: 252)

> [R]eality consist[s] in the ultimate agreement of all men. (GVLL, 5.351, W 2: 269)

> [T]hat ideal perfection of knowledge by which ... reality is constituted. (GVLL, 5.356, W 2: 271)

> [I]t is a consensus or common confession which constitutes reality. (8.16, W 2: 471, 1871)

> [T]hat thought to which we struggle to have our thoughts coincide, is the reality. (W 3: 47, 1872)

> [T]he real is the idea in which the community ultimately settles down. (6.610, 1893)[17]

Read as Peirce later read 5.311, each of these passages is consistent with basic realism. And that so much of the cognition series is committed to the existence of a real world, part of which is external to any mind, indicates that Peirce intended these seemingly anti-realistic statements to be read in the same way.

The statement of the idealistic theory of reality in 5.311 concludes as follows:

---

[16] Another example of his use of "truth" and "reality" as near synonyms is in this passage from 1901: "the scientific interest is [not] a mere poetical interest in the ideas as images; but solid truth, or reality, is demanded" (7.186, EP 2: 86).

[17] Note also the following use of "Truth" to mean what he usually refers to as "reality": "For the sole purpose of reasoning is ... to ascertain the Truth, in the sense of that which is SO, no matter what be thought about it ... [T]here is such a thing as Truth which is independent of what you or I or any group or generation of men may opine upon the subject" (2.153, 1902).

> Now, a proposition whose falsity can never be discovered, and the error of which therefore is absolutely incognizable, contains, upon our principle, absolutely no error. Consequently, that which is thought in these cognitions is the real, as it really is. There is nothing, then, to prevent our knowing outward things as they really are, and it is most likely that we do thus know them in numberless cases, although we can never be absolutely certain of doing so in any special case. (W 2: 239)

Human cognitions are capable of representing the "outward" (external) world as it really is. And how that world really is does not depend on any individual human representing it to be that way. While we can never know with certainty that a given cognition accurately represents its objects, very many of our current beliefs do accurately represent the world.

4.4

My argument that the cognition series' idealistic theory of reality is consistent with basic realism is nearly complete. But I still need to consider two claims Peirce made in SCFI, each concerning the dependence of something – either reality itself, or the reality of thought in particular – on something occurring in the future. The claims are italicized in the following quotation:

> [A]s what anything really is, is what it may finally come to be known to be in the ideal state of complete information, so that *reality depends on the ultimate decision of the community*; so thought is what it is, only by virtue of its addressing a future thought which is in its value as thought identical with it, though more developed. In this way, *the existence of thought now, depends on what is to be hereafter*; so that it has only a potential existence, dependent on the future thought of the community. (SCFI, 5.316, W 2: 241, emphases added)

The first claim, that reality itself "depends on" what the community eventually believes, is simply another way of putting a point that he made in 5.311, viz., that there is a series of cognitions "which, at a time sufficiently future, the community will always continue to re-affirm" and that "that which is thought in these cognitions is the real, as it really is." Since *x* is real exactly when it is the object of beliefs that the community would permanently accept as a consequence of investigation, the reality of *x* at a given time depends on the fact that those beliefs would eventually be accepted. But this does not imply, what would be inconsistent with basic realism, that the reality of *x* today is somehow causally dependent on someone's having beliefs about *x* in the future. We have seen that, even before he explicitly formulated the pragmatic maxim, Peirce sometimes interpreted claims about the present state of things as conditional claims about the future. He did this in the cognition series, e.g.:

> [I]f we consider the manner in which ... a proposition [such as "If there is smoke, there has been fire"] became known to us, we shall find that what it really means is that "If we find smoke, we *shall* find evidence on the whole that there has been fire"; and this, if reality consists in the agreement that the whole community would eventually come to, is the very same thing as to say that there really has been fire ... [T]his theory of reality ... makes all reality something which is constituted by an event indefinitely future. (GVLL, 5.331, W 2: 251–252)

And he did the same in slightly later works, e.g., "We must mean by how things are, how we are affected by them," i.e., "how [we] would be affected after sufficient experience, discussion, and reasoning" (W 2: 440, 1870). His SCFI claim that "reality depends on the ultimate decision of the community" means only this: to say that x is real is to say that investigation pushed sufficiently far would result in the community's having beliefs in which x is represented.

One of Peirce's clearest statements of this first claim about dependence on the future, one that demonstrates how it is related to his pragmatism, occurs in a manuscript dating from fall 1872. After reiterating the cognition series' view that "the conception of an object which ... [is] beyond all possible thought is an absurdity," noting that this does "not annul the distinction between a reality and a fiction," giving his usual definitions of those two terms, providing an account of reality that anticipates his eventual pragmatic clarification ("[t]he object of that final settled opinion to which it is supposed that an investigation will lead, if carried far enough"), and asserting that that account "satisfies [his] definition of reality," he went on to say that the following two statements express the same "strange fact," although (ii) does so "in a more familiar way" than (i):

(i)   "the new elements of belief that spring up in the mind, no matter how we vary them by changing the circumstances of their emergence, will inevitably be such as shall lead us at last to a destined conclusion";

(ii) "[the] origins of belief are produced in us by the action of realities upon sense and must therefore be relative to these fixed realities" (W 3: 58).

These claims state the same fact because the objects of "the destined conclusion" mentioned in (i) just *are* the realities mentioned in (ii):

> [I]n the one case we have said that the observations are determined by what is to be finally believed in, and in the other case we have said that they are determined by the realities. But ... the object finally believed in (if investigation is pushed so far) is absolutely identical with the realities. (W 3: 58–59)

Thus, "the existence of a present reality is in one sense made by a contingent event" (W 3: 59). But the "making" of present realities by future beliefs cannot be a matter of causal dependence, since "the belief is future and may even not ever be attained, while the reality actually exists ... [T]he act of believing is one thing, the object of belief another" (W 3: 59). The general point that Peirce was making here, about the relation between present realities and future (actual or merely possible) beliefs, results from applying his pragmatic approach (but again, before he had explicitly formulated the pragmatic maxim) in order better to understand a claim about some *specific* sort of present reality. For example,

> a leaden weight resting upon a table is really heavy. Yet to say that it is heavy only means that if it be so placed that it is free to move it will approach the earth ... We have only to extend this conception to all real existence and to hold these two facts to be identical, namely that they exist and that sufficient investigation would lead to a settled belief in them, to have our Idealistic theory of metaphysics. This doctrine is that observation and reasoning are perpetually leading us towards certain opinions and that the fact of such a perpetual tendency is otherwise expressed by saying that the objects of those final opinions have a real existence. (W 3: 59)

As I suggested in Chapter 2, the dependence that Peirce had in mind here was not causal, but logical. Pragmatically understood, the idea that x is real depends on the idea of future investigation permanently settling beliefs about x. Thus, as Peirce said in a later statement about pragmatism, "whatever means anything means that something will happen (provided certain conditions are fulfilled) ... the future alone has primary reality" (8.194, 1904). Peirce's statement in SCFI that "reality depends on the ultimate decision of the community" is better put as follows: the idea of reality, pragmatically clarified, depends on the idea of the community's ultimate opinion.[18]

To understand the second dependence claim, that "the existence of thought now, depends on what is to be hereafter," we will need to delve a bit more deeply into Peirce's semiotic, beginning with his view that the

---

[18] R 370 (7.340–344, W 3: 30–31, fall 1872) and R 379 (W 3: 80–81, March 1873) also contain explanations of this dependence claim in the context of pragmatic clarifications of more specific ideas, including those of weight, force, matter, and mental abilities.

sign relation is triadic: "a sign has, as such, three references: 1st, it is a sign *to* some thought which interprets it; 2d, it is a sign *for* some object to which in that thought it is equivalent; 3d, it is a sign, *in* some respect or quality, which brings it into connection with its object" (SCFI, 5.283, W 2: 223). Any instance of the sign relation relates three things: the sign itself, the object that it represents, and the sign's *interpretant*, the thing to which the sign represents its object, e.g., a thought in the mind of the sign's interpreter. As we have seen, Peirce held that no cognition represents an external object directly and that there is an infinite regress of thought-signs back from a given cognition to its external object. Peirce also held that any thought-sign is, not just preceded by, but also followed by, an infinite sequence of thought-signs. He held this because of his belief that any interpretant must itself be a sign that is interpreted in later thought:

> [I]f a train of thought ceases by gradually dying out, it freely follows its own law of association as long as it lasts, and there is no moment at which there is a thought belonging to this series, subsequently to which there is not a thought which interprets or repeats it. There is no exception, therefore, to the law that every thought-sign is translated or interpreted in a subsequent one, unless it be that all thought comes to an abrupt and final end in death. (SCFI, 5.284, W 2: 224)[19]

Peirce also believed that a given sign has no meaning apart from the triadic relationship in which it stands with its object and its interpretant. My thought that this kumquat is sweet lacks meaning at the time that it occurs and comes to have meaning only at a later time, when it is interpreted by my later thought(s) to be a sign of the kumquat:

> [N]o present actual thought (which is a mere feeling) has any meaning, any intellectual value; for this lies not in what is actually thought, but in what this thought may be connected with in representation by subsequent thoughts; so that the meaning of a thought is altogether something virtual. (SCFI, 5.289, W 2: 227)

The meaning that a thought-sign possesses at the time that it occurs is virtual, i.e., potential.[20] At that time, the thought-sign has not yet been

---

[19] For many years Peirce continued to believe that the interpretant of a sign is always a subsequent sign and thus that there is an infinite *progressus* following any thought-sign (e.g., see 1.339, NEM 4: 309–310, ca. 1893). But he eventually abandoned this view and came to hold that some signs have interpretants that are not necessarily signs, e.g., the command "Ground arms!" might have as an interpretant the action that soldiers perform upon hearing it (5.473–475, 1907).

[20] See Peirce's *Century Dictionary* definition of "virtual": "1. Existing in effect, power or virtue, but not actually; opposed to *real, actual, formal, immediate, literal* . . . 2. Pertaining to a real force or virtue; potential" (CD 6766).

interpreted by a later thought-sign in that person's mind or by any other sort of interpretant. Things can be "fit to be signs" of specific objects even at times when they have not yet been interpreted as representing those objects. But "they are [signs] in the same sense, for example, in which an unseen flower can be said to be *red*, this being also a term relative to a mental affection" (SCFI, 5.287, W 2: 225). Both "red" and "sign" are "relative to . . . mental affection[s]" – each refers in part to the effect that a given item can bring about in an individual mind. "Red" means, in part, a quality that one may experience in visual sensation, but it nonetheless makes sense to say that a flower is red at *t*, even if no one is viewing the flower and therefore not experiencing that sensation at *t*. At *t* the redness of the flower is merely potential. Likewise, a thought-sign, at the time that it is occurring, has a virtual or potential meaning; it is fit to be interpreted in a specific way by a subsequent thought-sign, but has not yet been interpreted. In defending the counterintuitive idea that the thoughts that I am having now are not yet meaningful, Peirce drew an analogy between cognition and motion:

> It may be objected, that if no thought has any meaning, all thought is without meaning. But this is a fallacy similar to saying, that, if in no one of the successive spaces which a body fills there is room for motion, there is no room for motion throughout the whole. At no one instant in my state of mind is there cognition or representation, but in the relation of my states of mind at different instants there is. (SCFI, 5.289, W 2: 227)[21]

The virtual meaning of a thought I am having now thus gets actualized by being interpreted by future thoughts. But those future thoughts need not be limited to my own. My thought that this fossilized jawbone is from the Jurassic period can have as an interpretant a later thought-sign occurring in my own mind, and it can also have as interpretants the thoughts of others. I can express the thought by communicating it orally or in writing, and in this way it can "address itself to thought of another person" (SCFI, 5.284, W 2: 223), including to the thoughts of people not currently living. This means that the virtual meaning of my initial thought can be actualized in the subsequent thoughts of people belonging to later generations, including others who also investigate the fossil record and add to the community's collective knowledge of it.

---

[21] To this passage Peirce appended the frequently misunderstood footnote: "Accordingly, just as we say that a body is in motion, and not that motion is in a body[,] we ought to say that we are in thought, and not that thoughts are in us" (5.289, n. 1, W 2: 227, n. 4). He did not mean that we are surrounded by thought, but that thinking is something that we do and thus no instance of it is complete at any one moment.

Now we are in a position to understand what Peirce meant when he wrote that "the existence of thought now, depends on what is to be hereafter; so that it has only a potential existence, dependent on the future thought of the community" (SCFI, 5.316, W 2: 241). He did not mean that no one in the present has thoughts or cognitions. He meant that the *meaning* of thoughts in the present depends on the interpretants to which those thoughts eventually give rise. The potential meaning of a present thought is not completely actualized until it has been maximally developed in an interpretation by the community of inquirers – something that may never actually happen with regard to any given thought. This is consistent with there now being a real world that includes real individual thinking subjects. In sum, the idealistic theory of reality that Peirce defended in the cognition series and thereafter is consistent with both his basic realism and his realism about the external world.[22]

---

[22] I would be remiss to omit from my reading of Peirce's idealistic theory of the late 1860s and early 1870s a jarring claim that occurs in the three pages of R 393, a manuscript dated summer–fall 1872 and consisting of notes for a lecture. Therein Peirce wrote that "the real is something ideal and never actually exists ... We ought ... to discard the conception of the real as something actual and to say simply that only thought actually exists" (W 3: 9). Peirce had defined "real" in his usual way in 1867 (W 2: 104), and he had made the real/external distinction explicitly in 1871 (8.13, W 2: 470), so by the time he wrote R 393, he recognized the importance of keeping the concepts of the real and the external distinct. What's more, he defined "real" in that way no fewer than seven different times in his 1872–1873 notes toward a logic book (W 3: 29, 46, 49, 54, 58, 60, 78), and in that same material he defined "external" in his usual way at least three times (W 3: 29, 49, 78). Given these facts, and given the extensive textual evidence that Peirce accepted basic realism and realism about the external world during this period, I believe that the extant portion of R 393 contains a *reductio* of the definition of "reality" as that which is independent of all possible thought, one that ends in the absurdity that "the real is something ideal and never actually exists." In these lecture notes, Peirce was not asserting that "the real ... never actually exists," but tracing the consequences of a concept of reality that he believed to be defective.

CHAPTER 5

Generals: Early Scholastic Realism

5.1

Peirce believed that "there are real generals" (5.503, 1905). By "generals," he meant what have more frequently been called *universals*: types of which particular things are instances, as, for example, a single pear is an instance of the general *pear*.[1] He also understood natural laws to be generals; they are, in fact, "the kind of universals to which modern science pays most attention" (4.1, 1898). He called the view that there are real generals *scholastic realism* – scholastic because of its roots in the philosophy of the medieval period. Peirce was committed to this kind of realism from early on: "never, during the thirty years in which I have been writing on philosophical questions, have I failed in my allegiance to realistic opinions and to certain Scotistic ideas" (6.605, 1893)[2] – Scotistic because his realism about generals was influenced by that of Duns Scotus.[3] In the editorial notes accompanying Peirce's 1871 review of Fraser's edition of the works of Berkeley (W 2: 552), the editors of the *Writings* misquote Peirce as having

---

[1] In his Baldwin's *Dictionary* entry for "universal," Peirce wrote that it is the "word . . . used in the middle ages where we should now use the word General" (2.367, 1902).

[2] The context of Peirce's claim that he had "never . . . failed in [his] allegiance to realistic opinions" makes clear that he had in mind scholastic realism rather than basic realism. In his rejoinder to Paul Carus's critical response to "The Architecture of Theories" and "The Doctrine of Necessity Examined," Peirce wrote that Carus "pronounces me to be an imitator of David Hume, or, at least, classes my opinions as closely allied to his. Yet be it known that never, during the thirty years in which I have been writing on philosophical questions, have I failed in my allegiance to realistic opinions and to certain Scotistic ideas; while all that Hume has to say is said at the instance and in the interest of the extremest nominalism" (6.605, 1893). As we will see, nominalism, the traditional opponent of scholastic realism, implies that there are no real generals.

[3] "Duns Scotus . . . first stated the realistic position consistently, and developed it with great fulness and applied it to all the different questions which depend upon it"; however, Scotus's realism was "separated from nominalism only by the division of a hair" (8.11, W 2: 466–467, 1871). Peirce eventually came to believe that Scotus "incline[d] too much toward nominalism" (1.560, EP 2: 424, 1907; see also 8.208, ca. 1905; R 641: 13, 1909). For more on the medieval roots of Peirce's scholastic realism, see Boler 1963 and 2004. For competing accounts of the differences between Peirce's and Scotus's respective forms of scholastic realism, see Boler 1963, Almeder 1980, and Mayorga 2007.

written that that review was where he "first declared" for scholastic realism; what he actually wrote was that "[i]n a long notice of Frazer's [*sic*] *Berkeley* . . . I declared for realism" (1.20, 1903). He explicitly argued for scholastic realism three years before that review, in 1868's "Some Consequences of Four Incapacities" (SCFI). Max Fisch held that it was in SCFI that Peirce took his "first step toward [scholastic] realism" (1986: 187). But there is evidence that Peirce was committed to scholastic realism before he penned the published version of SCFI. In R 920, a late attempt to revise *Illustrations of the Logic of Science*, he wrote that by 1865, he was "more or less a scholastic realist though not yet the more than scholastic realist which riper studies have converted me [*sic*]. I did not then go further than the stand-point of Scotus, – a half-baked, apologetic, diffident realism that I have long since outgrown" (ILS 188).[4]

Peirce's realism about generals is a familiar topic to students of his work, but new insights can be had by seeing how it is related to some of the results of previous chapters. To begin with a basic question: on Peirce's view, are generals external or internal? We have seen that Peirce defined the internal as that which is dependent on what someone thinks, so something internal is internal to the mind of *someone or other*. The fact that I am now thinking about eating lunch is a fact about how things are in *my* mind. And we have seen that a thing's being internal is consistent with its being real. So were generals internal, they would not necessarily be figments. But if a given real general were internal, it would depend on how someone thinks; it would be like the occurrence of a thought in someone's mind. Were the general *pear* internal, it would not be a single thing exemplified by particular pears. Instead, there would be multiple *pear* generals – mine, yours, and those of others. But on Peirce's view, real generals are external (8.191, ca. 1904); they are outside the mind of any individual person and therefore outside the minds of all individual people. So not only are they independent of what anyone thinks *about them*, they are also independent of what anyone thinks *about anything at all*.

Nominalism is a very different view about generality. Nominalists acknowledge that there are general words, but they believe that the generality of those words is only a matter of their being used to signify multiple distinct things. Peirce defined nominalism as

> [t]he doctrine that nothing is general but names; more specifically, the doctrine that common nouns, as *man, horse*, represent in their generality

---

[4] In Lane 2004, I argue that claims that Peirce made prior to 1868 that appear to suggest anti-realism about generals are in fact consistent with his scholastic realism.

nothing in the real things, but are mere conveniences for speaking of many things at once, or at most necessities of human thought; individualism. (CD 4009)

"Pear" is a general word, in that we use it to refer indiscriminately to many particular pears. But according to nominalism, there is nothing general over and above such words. Hence, *nomin*alism: the only things truly general are general *names*. So the disagreement between scholastic realism and nominalism is, in part, over whether generals are real, and "the question between [them] is, in its nature, susceptible of but two answers: yes and no" (1.27, ILS 219, 1909).

In the definition quoted earlier, Peirce identified nominalism with *individualism* – the view that all real things are individuals – and this is because the general is antithetical to the individual.[5] This is not to say that individual pears are not in some sense characterized by generality. It is to say that, despite the fact that they are external to the mind, generals themselves are not individual things. But caution is needed here, since on Peirce's view, "individual," as well as "singular," have multiples senses:

> "Singular" and "individual" are equivocal terms. A singular may mean that which can be but in one place at one time. In this sense it is not opposed to general. *The sun* is a singular in this sense, but, as is explained in every good treatise on logic, it is a general term.[6] I may have a very general conception of Hermolaus Barbarus, but still I conceive him only as able to be in one place at one time. When an image is said to be singular, it is meant that it is absolutely determinate in all respects. Every possible character, or the negative thereof, must be true of such an image. (5.299, W 2: 233, 1868)

Following what Peirce said elsewhere, I will call a thing that can be in only one place at one time a *concrete* individual, and I will call a thing that is completely determinate with respect to every property, such that it either does or does not have that property, a *strict* individual.[7] A concrete individual

---

[5] Peirce defined the relevant sense of "individualism" as: "The tendency to the doctrine that nothing is real but individual things. The doctrine is, for example, that the laws of nature are not real, but only the things whose mode of behavior is formulated in these laws" (CD 3065). He held that nominalism, in implying that only individuals are real, has unpalatable moral implications (8.38, W 2: 486–487, 1871). On the connection between Peirce's views on ethics and his scholastic realism, see Mayorga (2012).

[6] For example, in Whately's *Easy Lessons on Reasoning* (1848: 45).

[7] I take "concrete" from Peirce's use at W 3: 235, 1877. I take "strict individual" from R 300, 4.561, n. 1, ca. 1907–1908; see also W 1: 461, 1866; W 3: 93, 1873. Peirce noted in his *Century Dictionary* entry for "singular" that "Scotus and others define the singular as that which is here and now – that is, only in one place at one time. The Leibnitzian school define the singular as that which is determinate in every respect" (CD 5648). In other words, Scotus et al. understood the singular in terms of concrete individuality while the Leibnizians understood it in terms of strict individuality.

exemplifies real generals: a particular pear exemplifies, *inter alia*, the general *pear*; a particular event of a pear being eaten exemplifies, *inter alia*, the general *eat*; etc. It is in this sense that individuality "is not opposed to [the] general." But generals themselves are not concrete individuals; they do not occupy only one place at one time because they do not occupy places at all; they are not spatially extended. For a particular pear to be real, it must occupy time and space, and the event of its being eaten occurs over a specific duration and only in a specific place at any one time. The relationship between generality and strict individuality is more difficult to explain. For now, it will suffice to say that Peirce believed that there is no such thing as an individual in the strict sense of the term.[8] I return to this topic later.

Peirce noted that some partisans in the debate over whether generals are real take a position called *conceptualism*, according to which "universals are real, indeed; but they are only real thoughts" (1.27, ILS 220, 1909). So conceptualists believe that there is something general over and above general words, viz. general thoughts. But given that every thought is internal to some individual mind or other, conceptualism does not imply that there is anything outside of individual minds that is general, and so it is consistent with the view that anything that is real and that is external to all minds is a particular thing. At first blush, it seems that Peirce should have counted conceptualism as a form of realism about generals, since he was a realist about mental states and events. But instead he viewed it as "essentially the same thing" as nominalism. To see why, recall his distinction between *thinking*, which is a mental process in which each person engages on her own, and *thought*, which is, at least in part, a content that can be shared by multiple thinkers and the character of which does not depend on anyone actually thinking it.

> [T]hinking always proceeds in the form of a dialogue, – a dialogue between different phases of the *ego*, – so that, being dialogical, it is essentially composed of signs . . . Not that the particular signs employed *are* themselves the thought! . . . One selfsame thought may be carried upon the vehicle of English, German, Greek, or Gaelic; in diagrams, or in equations, or in graphs: all these are but so many skins of the onion, its inessential accidents. (4.6, LI 353–354, 1906)[9]

Thoughts, unlike thinking, are external. If you and I are each thinking that the skin of a Bartlett pear turns yellow as it ripens, each of our respective

---

[8] For example, see 3.93, n. 1, W 2: 390–391, n. 8, 1870; 8.208, ca. 1905.
[9] See also W 3: 46–47, 1872; W 3: 58, 1873; 2.53, 1902; 8.256, 1902; R 683: 26–27 alternative run of pages, ca. 1913; R 735: 3–4, no date.

instances of thinking is a distinct event, mine occurring in my mind and yours in your mind. But the thought we are thinking is the same – each instance of thinking instantiates the same thought. In this way,

> the general ... is of the nature of what is thought, but ... our thinking only apprehends and does not create thought, and ... that thought may and does as much govern outward things as it does our thinking ... The conceptualist doctrine is an undisputed truism about *thinking*, while the question between nominalists and realists relates to *thoughts*, that is, to the objects which thinking enables us to know. (1.27, ILS 220, 1909)

If conceptualism were a claim only about thinking, it would be correct. But conceptualists have taken themselves to be contributing to the debate over generals, and on Peirce's view, that debate is not about internal processes of thinking, but about some of the external realities that we can come to know by way of thinking. Conceptualism "seek[s] to wedge in a third position conflicting with the principle of excluded middle" (1.27, ILS 219–220, 1909): generals are not fictions (since conceptualism is not nominalism), but they are also not (fully, genuinely) real (since conceptualism is not scholastic realism). But for Peirce, the real and the fictional are exhaustive categories – there is no *tertium quid* between them.

Although he believed that there are real generals, Peirce denied that generals *exist*. In his early writings he used "existence" in a casual sense (e.g., when he wrote that "generals must have a real existence"; 5.312, W 2: 239, 1868), but he eventually assigned it a specific meaning distinct from that of "reality," reserving "existence" to mean "reaction with the environment" (5.503, 1905); "existence ... is the mode of being of that which reacts with other things" (8.330, SS 26, 1904).[10] An existing thing is something that can respond to or resist the action or power of something else.[11] Generals, therefore, do not exist: "The realist ... does not say that *any* generals *exist*. Existence is a *dynamic* condition, that of reacting with the rest of the universe. What he says is, that some generals, such as the law of gravitation, are *real*" (R 290: 15–16, 1905). It makes sense, then, that Peirce would say that "individuals alone exist" (5.429, EP 2: 342, 1905; see also R 329:17, ca. 1904): concrete individuals, which can be in only one place at a given time, are the only reals capable of reacting or

---

[10] Peirce seems to have adopted this use of "existence" by ca. 1896 (1.457). See also, e.g., 6.349, 1902–1903; 6.495, ca. 1906; 6.328, 336, ca. 1909. He associated existence with his universal category of Secondness, which in its phenomenological aspect encompasses reaction and resistance; see, e.g., 1.527, 532, 1903. But on at least a few occasions after 1896, he used "existence" in a looser, nontechnical sense; see, e.g., 3.460, 1897.

[11] Here I am taking advantage of Peirce's definition of "reaction," which reads in part: "Any action in resistance or response to the influence of another action or power" (CD 4981).

responding to things in their environment. "[A]n individual is something which reacts. That is to say, it does react against some things, and is of such a nature that it might react, or have reacted, against my will" (3.613, 1901).[12] In a manuscript of ca. 1899 (R 1292), Peirce wrote that

> the existence of a thing consists in its reacting against the other things in the universe; and action and reaction is something which takes place at a given place in a given time and has no generality in it . . . but is mere brute force. But existence is the smallest element of the reality even of those things that exist. (HP 1124)

The existence of a concrete individual "has no generality in it," but this is not to say that concrete individuals do not instantiate generals. It is to say that the existence of a concrete individual, its being in *this* place at *this* time, does not depend on which generals it exemplifies. Exactly which generals an individual instantiates is irrelevant to the fact of its existence and to the fact that it continues to exist through time:

> [T]he qualities of the individual thing, however permanent they may be, neither help nor hinder its identical existence. However permanent and peculiar those qualities may be, they are but *accidents*; that is to say, they are not involved in the mode of being of the thing; for the mode of being of the individual thing is existence; and existence lies in opposition merely. (1.458, ca. 1896)

But Peirce also wrote that since "action and reaction is something which takes place at a given place in a given time and has no generality in it, [it] consequently [has] no intelligibility" (R 1292, HP 1124, ca. 1899). This might seem to contradict his basic idealism, according to which everything real is capable of being represented in thought. But the contradiction is merely apparent. Any existing thing can be represented in thought. I can now think about the ripening pear that is in my kitchen, and I can know any number of things about it. But there is something about such an individual that remains unintelligible, i.e., something about it of which no one can have a concept: its own specific existence, that which makes it numerically distinct from other existents and makes possible its reactions

[12] This is the second of two definitions of "individual" Peirce stated in his Baldwin's *Dictionary* article for that term. He wrote that it was preferable to the first, which states: "an object (or term) not only actually determinate in respect to having or wanting each general character and not both having and wanting any, but is necessitated by its mode of being to be so determinate" (3.611, 1901). This corresponds to what I called a "strict individual" previously. That of the two definitions he offered in 1901, one was of strict individuality as he had defined it in 1868, and the other was not of concrete individuality as he had defined it early on, suggests that the definition in terms of reaction may have replaced that in terms of time and space in Peirce's thinking.

against and responses to them. In the mid-1880s, Peirce adopted Scotus's term *haecceity* to refer to this aspect of a concrete individual, and thereafter he frequently spoke of such an individual's *here-and-nowness*, of its being *hic et nunc*.[13] A thing's *haecceity* is something that we can experience, as when we touch or bite into a pear. But it is not something that we can *understand*, since the relevant general concepts – the concepts of touching and biting, the concept of pear, and even of the concept of existence – do not convey a given individual pear's specific reactions, which are unique to it.[14] As Peirce wrote, "a reaction may be experienced, but it cannot be conceived in its character of a reaction; for that element evaporates from every general idea" (3.613, 1901). Peirce's recognition of *haecceity* is consistent with his denial that there are strict individuals, since even though a given concrete individual has its own unique *haecceity*, there is still no limit to the specificity with which it can be represented and so no maximally specific representations of it.

Peirce dubbed the view that "generals *exist*" *nominalistic Platonism* (5.503, 1905) – nominalistic, since to characterize generals as existents is to imply that they are individuals and thus to deny that they are really generals at all, and Platonism, since this would make generals akin to Platonic forms, abstract entities to which the particulars that exemplify them are somehow related.[15] Some contemporary philosophers characterize universals as entities,[16] and some Peirce scholars have used the word to

---

[13] The earliest of Peirce's uses of the term *haecceity* that I have been able to locate is in his 1869 review of Noah Porter's *Human Intellect* (W 2: 277), but there he used it only in passing as he was criticizing Porter's misunderstanding of Scotus. Its next occurrence in his corpus seems to be among definitions written in 1886 for the *Century Dictionary* (W 5: 389). But the first time he employed the word to expressly state one of his own philosophical views was in 1887–1888's "A Guess at the Riddle" (1.383, W 6: 187; 1.405, W 6: 205). Short argues that Peirce's recognition of *haecceity* in the mid-1880s was required by his new conception of indexical signs, which, according to Short, may have been motivated by his introduction of quantifiers into formal logic (2007a: 48–51). For uses of the phrase *hic et nunc* to describe the individual, existent, or anti-general, see, e.g., R 787, 1.566, 1896; 6.82, RLT 212, 1898; R 141, 7.532, 1899; 1.212, 1902; 2.146, 1902. Peirce wrote that the phrase was "perpetually in the mouth of Duns Scotus, who first elucidated individual existence" (1.458, ca. 1896).

[14] On this point I agree with Mayorga (2007: 131). The view that we cannot articulate what it is for a particular to be the particular thing that it is has found some purchase in contemporary metaphysics, e.g., David DeGrazia, citing both Saul Kripke and Duns Scotus, writes that "the criteria determining what counts as some particular human organism may be impossible to articulate fully, beyond ostension – literally, pointing – or rigid designation with a name" (2005: 256, n. 20).

[15] As an illustration of nominalistic Platonism, Peirce cited the views of Bernard of Chartres (Bernardus Carnotensis), a twelfth-century French neo-Platonist who "combined scholastic realism with individualism" (5.502, 1905). Note his characterization of Berkeley as illustrating "that strange union of nominalism with Platonism, which has repeatedly appeared in history, and has been such a stumbling-block to the historians of philosophy" (8.10, W 2: 464, 1871).

[16] For examples, see Armstrong (2004), Ney (2014), and the introduction to Galluzzo and Loux (2015). Haack (1992: 36) notes Armstrong's earlier uses of the word to refer to universals.

describe his view.[17] But so far as I have been able to discover, Peirce never described generals as entities. He emphasized the fact that the Scotists had never done so (6.361, 1902), and he complained about the vagueness of the term in his *Century Dictionary* entry for it:

> An independent ens; a thing; a substance; an ontological chimera. As a concrete noun, it is chiefly used to express the current notion of the mode of being attributed by scholastic metaphysicians to general natures and to formalities. Modern writers have generally said the schoolmen made *entities* of words, a judgment which seems to espouse the nominalistic side of the great dispute, although the writers who use this phrase are not decided nominalists. Such being the connection which by its associations give the word *entity* its meaning, the latter is necessarily vague. (CD 1951)[18]

On Peirce's view, generals are neither abstract entities nor material entities, and so they are not entities at all.[19] His use of the plural noun "generals" obscures this; it would have been less misleading had he said that there is real *generality* in the world and that this is illustrated in different ways by different particular things.

But if generals are not individual entities, not even *abstract* individual entities, then what *are* they? How can they be real, i.e., "[i]n what way can a general be unaffected by any thought about it?" (5.503, 1905). The answer is to be found by examining an argument for scholastic realism that Peirce employed in both 1868's "Some Consequences of Four Incapacities" and the 1871 Berkeley review. Before considering that argument, though, we must carefully examine a distinction that he introduced in the Berkeley review, between what he called the realist and the nominalistic conceptions of reality.

---

[17] For example: "[Peirce's] position is as extreme a realism as Plato's, since for both the referent of the universal is a real general entity" (Murphey 1961: 401); "[O]nce [Peirce] has shown to his satisfaction that there are real generals, he will go on to discuss the nature of these entities" (Boler 1963: 72); "Scholastic realism holds that certain abstract entities are real ... and that it is to such entities that abstract terms refer" (Skagestad 1981: 59). On the other hand, Misak correctly notes that "when Peirce says that ... generals ... are real, he does not mean that they actually exist as objects or entities" (1991/2004: 135).

[18] For Peirce's account of the use and misuse of "entity" in debates between Scotists and natural scientists, see 6.361, 1902.

[19] Michael Dummett's view that realism should be understood as a semantic theory is motivated by his assumption that, if realism is understood as a metaphysical theory, then it can apply only to entities: "[I]t seems preferable to say that realism is a view about a certain class of *statements* – for instance, statements in the future tense, or ethical statements – since certain kinds of realism, for instance realism about the future or about ethics, do not seem readily classifiable as doctrines about a realm of entities" (1982: 55). Dummett does not say exactly what he means by "entity." Still, the position he takes precludes without argument a view like Peirce's realism about generals.

5.2

In the Berkeley review, Peirce complained that "current explanations of the realist-nominalist controversy are equally false and unintelligible" and then attempted to "state the matter [so] that no one shall fail to comprehend what the question [is], and how there might be two opinions about it. Are universals real?" (8.12, W 2: 467). This led him to state some definitions that are by now familiar:

> Objects are divided into figments, dreams, etc., on the one hand, and realities on the other. The former are those which exist only inasmuch as you or I or some man imagines them; the latter are those which have an existence independent of your mind or mine or that of any number of persons.[20] The real is that which is not whatever we happen to think it, but is unaffected by what we may think of it. The question, therefore, is whether *man, horse*, and other names of natural classes, correspond with anything which all men, or all horses, really have in common, independent of our thought,[21] or whether these classes are constituted simply by a likeness in the way in which our minds are affected by individual objects which have in themselves no resemblance or relationship whatsoever. (8.12, W 2: 467)

He then distinguished "two widely separated points of view, from which *reality*, as just defined, may be regarded" (8.12, W 2: 467). These points of view, which he also called "conceptions" of reality, are not competitors or revisions of his usual definition.[22] Instead, they are answers we might give, once we have accepted that definition, to the question: in the most general terms, what is it to which that definition applies? In other words, exactly what is it that is independent of what anyone thinks about it?

---

[20] Here Peirce should have written: "have an existence independent of *what is thought about them in your mind or mine or that of any number of persons*." As this passage stands, it refers not to the real, which includes both external and internal things, but only to the external. That he intended this phrase to be about all of the real rather than only the external is shown by the fact that he employed his usual definition of the real in this same paragraph – "unaffected by what we may think *of it*" (emphasis added) – and that he explicitly distinguished the real from the external in the next paragraph – "'the external' means simply that which is independent of what phenomenon is immediately present, that is of how we may think or feel; just as 'the real' means that which is independent of how we may think or feel *about it*" (8.13, W 2: 470, emphasis in the original).

[21] At this point, we might expect Peirce to have written "independent of our thought *about them*" (i.e., real) and take his omission of "about it" to have been another error (see Note 20). While that might be the case, it is also plausible to think that he did in fact mean "independent of our thought," i.e., independent of our thought *about anything* and thus external. If there is something that all horses have in common independently of what we think *about horses*, then, since horses are external things, that which they really have in common would be independent of what we think, full stop; i.e., it would be external.

[22] Here I disagree with Hookway, who writes that "[t]he relations between the two conceptions of reality are not very clear. They 'define' reality according to different characteristics" (2000: 91).

According to the first conception,

> there is something . . . which influences our thoughts, and is not created by them . . . [Our] thoughts . . . have been caused by sensations, and those sensations are constrained by something out of the mind. This thing out of the mind, which directly influences sensation, and through sensation thought, because it *is* out of the mind, is independent of how we think it, and is, in short, the real. (8.12, W 2: 468)

On this conception, something is real, i.e., independent of what anyone thinks about it, only if it is an external cause of sensation and perception; "the absolutely external causes of perception are the only realities" (W 2: 490, 1871). Peirce held that "from this point of view . . . the nominalistic answer must be given to the question concerning universals" (8.12, W 2: 468). Once this conception has been accepted, "it may be admitted to be true as a rough statement that one man is like another," but all that that statement can mean is "that the realities external to the mind produce sensations which may be embraced under one conception," i.e., "that the one mental term or thought-sign 'man' stands indifferently for either of the sensible objects [i.e., for either of the sensations] caused by the two external realities" (8.12, W 2: 468). On this view, generality is a characteristic only of internal thinking, i.e., thinking that occurs within the mind of some individual or other. I am caused by external realities to have different sensations, and I *think* of each of those sensations as being sensations of *men*. But "it can by no means be admitted that the two real men have really anything in common," and "not even the two sensations have in themselves anything in common" (8.12, W 2: 468). Generality being a characteristic only of internal thinking, and reality being limited to the external causes of sensations, generality is not real.[23] I will call the view that reality consists exclusively of external causes of sensation the *nominalistic conception of reality.*

Given that Peirce held generals to be external, why, on his view, must a theory that begins with the nominalistic conception imply that generals are not real? Because the nominalistic conception limits the real, not just to the external, but to external *causes* of sensation. And although on Peirce's view generals are external to any individual mind and therefore to all individual

---

[23] Berkeley held a subtly different view of generality than that implied by the nominalistic conception of reality. On his view, "an idea which, considered in itself, is particular, becomes general by being made to represent or stand for all other particular ideas of the same sort" (*Principles of Human Knowledge*, introduction, §12; Berkeley [1710] 1998: 94). For example, the mental image of a particular man, while itself a particular thing, can be used in a general way, as a sign that stands indifferently for all other particular mental images of men. On this view, the generality of an image is a matter of how it is employed rather than a matter of its content.

minds, they do not cause sensation. That is, they are not *efficient* causes of sensation. A single pear, which is a concrete individual, is an efficient cause of my visual sensation of a pear, but the general *pear* is not. To cause sensation, a general would have to be a concrete individual thing; it would have to *exist*.[24] So the fact that a given object exemplifies the general *pear* is causally relevant to my having a visual sensation of the object. After all, any particular must instantiate *some* generals, since it is impossible for a thing to exist that is characterized only by its own *haecceity*. But it is not the general itself with which I am causally interacting when I see the pear.[25]

Because it implies scholastic realism, Peirce called the second conception of reality the *realist conception* (8.12, W 2: 468). He stated it as follows:

> All human thought and opinion contains an arbitrary, accidental element, dependent on the limitations in circumstances, power, and bent of the individual; an element of error, in short. But human opinion universally tends in the long run to a definite form, which is the truth. Let any human being have enough information and exert enough thought upon any question, and the result will be that he will arrive at a certain definite conclusion, which is the same that any other mind will reach under sufficiently favorable circumstances . . . On many questions the final agreement is already reached, on all it will be reached if time enough is given. The arbitrary will or other individual peculiarities of a sufficiently large number of minds may postpone the general agreement in that opinion indefinitely; but it cannot affect what the character of that opinion shall be when it is reached. This final opinion, then, is independent, not indeed of thought in general, but of all that is arbitrary and individual in thought; is quite independent of how you, or I, or any number of men think. Everything, therefore, which will be thought to exist in the final opinion is real, and nothing else. (8.12, W 2: 468–469)

This conception echoes one aspect of the idealistic theory of reality that he had defended in the cognition series of 1868–1869, and it anticipates the pragmatic clarification of the idea of reality that he stated in 1878's "How to Make Our Ideas Clear."[26] As we saw in Chapter 2, this clarification

---

[24] Peirce seems to have walked back from this view decades later when he wrote that "generals . . . may . . . be *physically efficient*"; but he then immediately hedged this claim: "*physically efficient*, not in every metaphysical sense, but in the commonsense acception in which human purposes are physically efficient" (5.431, EP 2: 343, 1905; see also 1.213, EP 2: 120–121, 1902).

[25] A full accounting of this matter would attend to Peirce's theory of perception, on which see Haack (1994) and Lane (2007a). On the perception of generals, see Wilson (2012) and Short (2015).

[26] I do not identify this earlier, realist conception of reality with his eventual pragmatic clarification, for reasons explained in Chapter 2. However, Peirce evidently came to think of the realist conception as stated in the Berkeley review as having, at the very least, anticipated his pragmatic clarification of the idea of reality. In a 1904 letter to James in which he referenced the Berkeley

depends on the investigative aspect of his account of truth: the real is exactly what will – or, on his considered view, would – be represented in a belief permanently fixed by investigation, i.e., by the method of science.[27] According to the realist conception, "reality belongs to what is present to us in true knowledge of any sort" (W 2: 490).

Peirce pointed out that Berkeley had characterized real experience, as opposed to imagination, as constituted by, first, its greater vividness, and second, and more important, "its connected character. Its parts hang together in the most intimate and intricate conjunction, in consequence of which we can infer the future from the past" (8.30, W 2: 479).[28] Peirce initially wrote that this was either "a third new conception of reality," distinct from both the nominalistic and realist conceptions, "or if [it] is to be identified with either of those, it is with the realist view" (8.30, W 2: 479), presumably because of its emphasis on the future. But ultimately he judged that in characterizing reality in this way, Berkeley was using "reality" to mean something other than "*an object's independence of our thought about it*" (8.30, W 2: 480), and this implies that what Berkeley said about the connected character of experience does not count as a conception of reality *at all*. But, wrote Peirce, Berkeley *did* assume a conception of reality, i.e., of what counts as real once the usual definition of that term has been accepted: "being in the mind of God," "who has created our spirits [and] has the power immediately to raise ideas in them" (8.30, W 2: 480).[29] Berkeley therefore assumed that the real (in the usual sense) is that which is outside of human minds and that causes sensations in them, i.e., he assumed the nominalistic conception of reality after all. But Berkeley's nominalism was a nominalistic Platonism, since it assumed that "the reality of sensible things resides only in their archetypes in the divine mind" (8.30, W 2: 480).

The nominalistic and the realist conceptions are not necessarily at odds on the issue of what *specific* things are real. If the only things that are represented in the final opinion are external causes of sensation, then the two conceptions will yield an identical ontology. But this is an unlikely result. A belief that belongs to the final opinion could represent an external cause of sensation – the sun, say – without there being a difference in the

---

review, Peirce wrote that "[t]he most important consequence of [pragmatism], by far, . . . is that under [the realist] conception of reality we must abandon nominalism" (8.258).

[27] The choice between "will" or "would" represents Peirce's early vacillation between understanding pragmatic clarifications as better expressed by indicative or by subjunctive conditionals, as described in Chapter 2. That vacillation ceased in the 1900s, as I explain in Chapter 6. For the remainder of this chapter, I will describe Peirce's pragmatic clarification of reality in terms of the beliefs that *would* be fixed by investigation, but n.b. that he himself was unclear on this point during the 1860s and 1870s.

[28] See Berkeley, *Principles of Human Knowledge*, especially §§33, 36, and 59.

[29] See *Principles* §33.

respective ontologies associated with the nominalistic and realist conceptions. But it could not represent the sun as an external cause *of sensation*
without thereby yielding such a difference. The belief that the sun's light is
a contributing cause of the visual sensations in many organisms is, in part,
about sensations, which are *internal* events. On the realist conception, that
that belief is part of the final opinion would imply that sensations are real,
even though they are internal. And this *would* be a deviation from the
nominalistic conception's ontology, which consists exclusively of external
causes of sensation. So the two conceptions do not necessarily commit their
partisans to different ontologies, but if they are to yield the same ontologies, the course of investigation would eventually have to eliminate beliefs
about mental states (as well as beliefs that represent external things that are
not causes of sensation – I return to this point in what follows).

As the example of the sun shows, even if the two conceptions yield
different ontologies, those ontologies might overlap, i.e., it is possible that
a given thing meet both the nominalistic criterion and the realist criterion
for being real.[30] If the final opinion includes any beliefs about the sun,
conceived as an external cause of sensation, then the realist conception
will, like the nominalistic conception, imply that the sun is real. And this
point – that, even on the realist conception, there *are* external causes of
sensation – is, I believe, the crux of the following passage:

> What is the POWER of external things, to affect the senses? To say that
> people sleep after taking opium because it has a soporific *power*, is that to say
> anything in the world but that people sleep after taking opium because they
> sleep after taking opium? To assert the existence of a power or potency, is it
> to assert the existence of anything actual? Or to say that a thing has a
> potential existence, is it to say that it has an actual existence? In other
> words, is the present existence of a power anything in the world but a
> regularity in future events relating to a certain thing regarded as an element
> which is to be taken account of beforehand, in the conception of that thing?
> If not, to assert that there are external things which can be known only as
> exerting a power on our sense, is nothing different from asserting that there
> is a general *drift* in the history of human thought which will lead it to one
> general agreement, one catholic consent. And any truth more perfect than
> this destined conclusion, any reality more absolute than what is thought in
> it, is a fiction of metaphysics. (8.12, W 2: 469)

There *are* external things that have the power to cause sensation. But what
are we saying when we attribute such a power to an external thing? Once

---

[30] In this sense, I agree with Misak (1991/2004: 133) that the realist (or as she says, the pragmatic) and
nominalist conceptions of reality are compatible.

again anticipating his pragmatic approach to answering such questions, Peirce maintained that the attribution of such a power amounts to a claim about future events. The claim that opium has the power to put people to sleep means that *if* anyone ingests opium, they will fall asleep; and to think of opium as *now* having that power is simply to take account of those contingent future events in our present idea of opium. As he would later say, it is to have a pragmatically clarified idea of opium. The claim that an external thing has the power to affect people's senses, and (as he emphasized in his initial description of the nominalistic conception) thereby to cause them to have thoughts, means that *if* we use experience and reasoning in an attempt to dispel doubt and fix belief, we will end up with beliefs in which that external thing is represented. And to think of an external thing as *now* having that power is to take account of that contingent future event in our present concept of the thing. So the realist conception is consistent with, and as Peirce insisted, also "highly favorable to[,] a belief in external realities" (8.13, W 2: 470). He did not hesitate to affirm that belief:

> [O]bserving that "the external" means simply that which is independent . . . of how we may think or feel; just as "the real" means that which is independent of how we may think or feel *about it*; it must be granted that there are many objects of true science which are external, because there are many objects of thought which, if they are independent of that thinking whereby they are thought (that is, if they are real), are indisputably independent of all *other* thoughts and feelings. (Ibid.)

Peirce insisted that the realist conception

> is instantly fatal to the idea of a thing in itself, – a thing existing independent of all relation to the mind's conception of it. Yet it would by no means forbid, but rather encourage us, to regard the appearances of sense as only signs of the realities. Only, the realities which they represent would not be the unknowable cause of sensation, but *noumena*, or intelligible conceptions which are the last products of the mental action which is set in motion by sensation. (8.13, W 2: 469–470)

That last statement is a dependence claim of the sort described in Chapter 4, and it raises the same sorts of question we encountered previously: If "the realities" are "products of mental action," how can any of them be external? And if they are "*the last* products of mental action," how can there ever *be* anything – i.e., be anything *real* – that can engage in that mental action to begin with? But this passage is consistent with his basic realism and realism about the external. The "appearances of sense" *are* signs of realities. But whereas the nominalistic conception implies that they are signs of external realities solely in virtue of having been caused by those realities, the realist conception brings with it a more complicated story. Sensations "set in motion" our processes of thinking, and the "last products of [that] mental action" – the *very* last products of it – are true beliefs, which Peirce here described as "intelligible conceptions" and "*noumena*" (8.13, W 2: 470). But those true beliefs represent, *inter alia*, external realities which are the causes of sensation. "[R]eality [i.e., true beliefs, those that represent reality, is] the normal product of mental action," and while some reals are external causes of sensation and mental action, none are "*incognizable* cause[s] of it" (8.15, W 2: 471, emphasis added). This interpretation is supported by a manuscript from 1872 in which Peirce once again considered the nominalistic and realist conceptions of reality:

> We have particularly drawn attention to the point to which thought flows, and that it finally reaches; a certain level, as it were – a certain basin, where reality becomes unchanging. It has reached its destination, and that permanency, that fixed reality, which every thought strives to represent and image, we have placed in this objective point, towards which the current of thought flows. But the matter has often been regarded from an opposite point of view; attention being particularly drawn to the spring, and origin of thought. It is said that all other thoughts are ultimately derived from sensations; that all conclusions of reasoning are valid only so far as they are true to the sensations; that the real cause of sensation therefore, is the reality which thought presents. Now such a reality, which causes all thought, would seem to be wholly external to the mind – at least to the thinking part of the mind, as distinguished from the feeling part; for it [i.e., the feeling part] might be conceived to be, in some way, dependent upon sensation. (7.337–338, W 3: 29)

On the nominalistic conception, the real is the external cause of our beliefs, and on the realist conception, the real is that toward which thought is flowing, i.e., that about which investigation is leading us to have beliefs. Peirce denied that "the two views are absolutely irreconcilable" and asserted that "the realists need not, and should not, deny that the reality exists externally to the mind" and that "there is no objection to saying that this external reality causes the sensation, and through the sensation has caused all that line of thought which has finally led to the belief" (7.339, W 3: 29–30, 1872).

The foregoing interpretation of the 1871 Berkeley review helps make sense of what Peirce wrote in two manuscripts dating from the next year. In one, he wrote that the following statements "assert[] the very same fact": (i) "there are external things, and ... observations are only the appearances which these things produce upon sense by their relations to us," and (ii) "observations inevitably carry us to a predetermined conclusion" (W 3: 47). And in the other, discussed in Chapter 4, he wrote that the following state the same fact: (i) "the new elements of belief that spring up in the mind . . . are produced in us by the action of realities upon sense and must therefore be relative to these fixed realities" – "they are determined by the realities"; and (ii) "the new elements of belief that spring up in the mind . . . will inevitably be such as shall lead us at last to a destined conclusion" – "the observations are determined by what is to be finally believed in" (W 3: 58). Each statement (ii) is somewhat like a pragmatic clarification of the corresponding statement (i). But as we saw in Chapter 2, a pragmatic clarification does not invalidate or undermine the item that is being clarified. Each pair of statements is consistent, since "the object finally believed in (if investigation is pushed so far) is absolutely identical with the realities" (W 3: 58–59).

5.3

Again, the nominalistic conception implies that no general is real: on that conception, only external causes of sensation are real, and while generals are external, they do not cause sensation. On the other hand, the realist conception implies realism about generals. The first publication in which Peirce argued from the realist conception to scholastic realism was 1868's "Some Consequences of Four Incapacities" (SCFI), the second article in his so-called cognition series. As we saw in Chapter 4, in that series Peirce defended an "idealistic theory of reality" consisting of a group of connected claims; one of those claims was the realist conception. In SCFI, he stated that conception as follows: "a proposition whose falsity can never be discovered, and the error of which therefore is absolutely incognizable, contains . . . absolutely no error. Consequently, that which is thought in these cognitions" – that is, in true cognitions – "is the real, as it really is" (5.311, W 2: 239). From this he concluded that "[t]here is nothing . . . to prevent our knowing outward things as they really are, and it is most likely that we do thus know them in numberless cases" (5.311, W 2: 239); it is possible for our thinking to represent the external world accurately, and it is likely that much of our thinking about the external does just that. However, "no cognition of ours is absolutely determinate," and so he concluded that "generals must have a real existence" (5.312, W 2: 239), that is, they must be real.[31] He went on to note that

> scholastic realism is usually set down as a belief in metaphysical fictions. But, in fact, a realist is simply one who knows no more recondite reality than that

---

[31] As noted previously, Peirce did not begin reserving "existence" to refer to a special mode of reality until ca. 1896.

which is represented in a true representation. Since, therefore, the word "man"
is true of something, that which "man" means is real. (5.312, W 2: 239)[32]

Peirce had anticipated this argument in draft material for the cognition
series: "there is nothing to prevent universal propositions from being absolutely true, and therefore universals may be as real as singulars" (W 2: 175,
1868), i.e., as real as concrete individuals. And he went on to use the same
reasoning in the Berkeley review:

> It is plain that [the realist conception] of reality is inevitably realistic;
> because general conceptions enter into all judgments, and therefore into
> true opinions. Consequently a thing in the general is as real as in the
> concrete. [For example, the general *man* is just as real as a particular
> human being, who is a concrete individual.] It is perfectly true that all
> white things have whiteness in them, for that is only saying, in another form
> of words, that all white things are white; but since it is true that real things
> possess whiteness, whiteness is real. It is a real which only exists by virtue of
> an act of thought knowing it, but that thought is not an arbitrary or
> accidental one dependent on any idiosyncrasies, but one which will hold
> in the final opinion. (8.14, W 2: 470, 1871)

That is, the general *white* does not depend on any *actual* act of thinking that
occurs in someone's mind; rather, it depends on the fact that a *thought*,
which can be had by any number of individuals, would be had by any who
investigate sufficiently. Like the statement of the argument in SCFI, this one
relies on the realist conception of reality: "the realist defends his position
only by assuming that the immediate object of thought in a true judgment is
real" (8.17, W 2: 471). Peirce's reasoning can be reconstructed as follows:

1. Anything that is represented by a true belief, i.e., by the proposition
    that is the content of a true belief, is real.
2. The content of any belief, *a fortiori* of any true belief, is expressible as a
    proposition some of the constituent signs of which are general.
3. General signs represent generals.
4. Therefore, there are real generals.

I will call this *the Early Argument* for scholastic realism.[33] Formulated in
this way, it contains an important ambiguity. As applied to signs, "general"

---

[32] For a very different interpretation of this argument, see Skagestad (1981: 65–66). Skagestad also
attributes to Peirce a very different pragmatic argument for scholastic realism, one on which it
follows directly from the pragmatic maxim itself (1981: 60).

[33] My concern in this chapter and the next will be narrow, focusing on only one early argument and
one later argument for scholastic realism. But as Haack (1992: 20) points out, Peirce's defense of the
theory "marshall[ed] together arguments both logical and phenomenological from his theory of

has a wider and a narrower sense. From the 1860s into at least the 1880s, Peirce held that *all* signs, even proper names, are general in the wider sense. But the Early Argument concerns only signs that are general in the narrower sense. In order to understand the distinction, we need to look more closely at Peirce's early theory of signs.

Peirce used "general" and "indeterminate" as synonyms during this early period; i.e., early on he recognized no difference between the generality and the indeterminacy of a sign.[34] But in what sense of "indeterminacy"? In 1868, Peirce defined "determined" as "fixed to be *this* (or *thus*), in contradistinction to being this, that, or the other (or in some way or other)" (6.625, W 2: 155–156). This is consistent with one of his *Century Dictionary* definitions of "determinate": "Having defined limits; fixed; definite; clearly defined or definable; particular: as, a *determinate* quantity of matter" (CD 1572). I agree with Short that we should understand "determine" to mean "to limit, as in, 'The water's edge determines where your property ends'" (2007a: 167).[35] For a sign to be determinate is for its meaning to be limited, narrowed, more specific than it otherwise might be. Hence, "all determination is by negation" and so "whatever is absolutely universal" – i.e., absolutely general, absolutely indeterminate – "is devoid of all content or determination" (5.223, n. 2, W 2: 200, n. 4, 1868).

What's more, Peirce held that no sign is completely determinate. His view was that any sign is general/indeterminate to some degree, in that it is always possible for its meaning to be more determinate than it actually is.

> We can . . . say, in a general way, that a term, however determinate, may be made more determinate still, but not that it can be made absolutely determinate. Such a term as "the second Philip of Macedon" is still capable of logical division, – into Philip drunk and Philip sober, for example. (3.93, W 2: 390, 1870)[36]

As this example suggests, semiotic indeterminacy amounts to *underspecificity*; an indeterminate or general sign is one that is not maximally specific. The sign "the second Philip of Macedon" is less specific (more general)

---

categories, arguments from the history of philosophy, arguments from the philosophy of language, [and] arguments from the philosophy of science."

[34] See 5.306, 1868; 3.124, 1870; W 3: 84, 1873; W 3: 105, 1873; 2.696, W 4: 411, 1883.

[35] Short (2007a: 168, n. 9) provides references to other works that consider what Peirce meant by "determine." Riley (1974: 161ff.) traces the idea that determination requires limitation and negation back to Hegel, who, according to Riley, was influenced in this regard by Spinoza.

[36] By the 1900s, Peirce had begun to distinguish two species of semiotic indeterminacy, which he called *generality* and *vagueness*. But he continued to hold that every sign is indeterminate – either general or vague (e.g., 5.506, 1905). I will consider these later views in Chapter 6.

than "the second Philip of Macedon drunk," which is less specific than "the second Philip of Macedon drunk on wine," which is less specific than "the second Philip of Macedon drunk on wine and lying flat on his back next to the Skopje Aqueduct at 4 a.m." Thus, Philip "is logically divisible into Phillip drunk and Phillip sober; and so on; and you do not get down to anything completely determinate till you specify an indivisible instant of time" (W 3: 235, 1877).[37] But given Peirce's view of continuity during this period, specifying an indivisible instant of time is impossible.[38]

So a proper name, or any other sign that can serve as the subject term of a proposition, will be general: "every cognition we are in possession of is a judgment both whose subject and predicate are general terms" (W 2: 180, 1868). But the reason "the second Philip of Macedon" is general is not that it is opposed to *concrete* individuality; that name represents a concrete individual, something that can be in only one place at a time. It is general because it is opposed to *strict* individuality. A strict individual would be "absolutely determinate in all respects" (5.299, W 2: 233, 1868); it would be maximally specific and therefore not general to any degree. Peirce's basic idealism implies that if x were a strict individual, it would be possible for every aspect of x to be accurately represented in thought. But accurate representation of a strict individual would require thought-signs that are completely determinate, for, if a thought-sign representing x were less than completely determinate, then there would be some aspect of x not represented by that thought-sign. Anything that exists for any time whatsoever "will undergo some change in its relations" during that time (3.93, n. 1, W 2: 391, n. 8, 1870). For any x and any duration d through which x endures, there is a property, F, that x will have during only part of d. So x will be "logically divisible" into x that is F and x that is not F. It follows that "the second Philip of Macedon" is not a strictly individual sign, that Philip is not a strict individual, and, more broadly, that strict individuals are not real. Since "[t]here actually are no individual [i.e., strictly individual, or absolutely determinate] terms," "[t]he

[37] Peirce took this example from a story told by Plutarch. "When a wife petitioned Philip of Macedon on behalf of her husband, he happened to be in his cups and dismissed her. 'I shall appeal' she told him. 'To whom?' he asked, confident that there was no higher authority than himself. 'From Philip drunk to Philip sober' she replied, and in due course her appeal succeeded" (Wilkinson 2013: 116). Peirce frequently used the Philip example to illustrate semiotic indeterminacy; see W 3: 84–85, 1873; W 3: 235, 1877; 1.494, ca. 1896; 5.506, 1905; R 515: 25, no date.

[38] "A *continuum* (such as time and space actually are) is defined as something any part of which however small itself has parts of the same kind" (W 3: 106, 1873; see also 5.335, W 2: 256, 1868). This implies that a continuum, such as space or time, is infinitely divisible. According to his own later testimony, at this time he held that infinite divisibility was one and the same property as the property of having parts all of which have parts of the same kind; he later came to think that they are not the same property and that only the former amounts to continuity (6.168, PM 138, 1903).

object denoted by any sign whatever is more or less indeterminate" (W 3: 84, 1873). Thus, everything that can be represented by any sort of sign has some degree of indeterminacy/generality. And since everything real is capable of being represented, every aspect of reality is general to some degree. "[N]o object is [strictly] individual but . . . the things the most concrete have still a certain amount of indeterminacy" (W 3: 235, 1877).[39] There are real concrete individuals, including Philip of Macedon, but there are no strict individuals, no absolutely determinate (non-general) entities.

Noting the distinction between strict and concrete individuals helps clarify an 1868 passage that otherwise might seem shocking: "every cognition we are in possession of is a judgment both whose subject and predicate are general terms. And, therefore, it is not merely the case . . . that universals have reality on this theory, but also that there are nothing but universals which have an immediate reality" (W 2: 180). This seems to imply that particular things are not real. But Peirce continued:

> [H]ere it is necessary to distinguish between an individual in the sense of that which has no generality [i.e., a strict individual] and which here appears as a mere ideal boundary of cognition, and an individual in the far wider sense of that which can only be in one place at one time [i.e., a concrete individual] . . . To the former I have denied all immediate reality. (W 2: 180)

Concrete particulars, like Philip, are universal in the sense that they are not strict individuals, and it is in that sense of "universal" that Peirce asserted that only the universal is real and that "being at all is being in general" (5.349, W 2: 268, 1869).[40]

Like "the second Philip of Macedon," the common noun "human" is a general sign, in that it is less than maximally specific. But unlike "the second Philip of Macedon," "human" is true of more than one concrete individual. Given the investigative aspect of Peirce's account of truth, this means that investigation would lead inquirers to believe about more than one concrete

---

[39] Short (2007a: 46–47) characterizes this denial that there is individuality as Peirce's "last restatement of idealism" before a radical change occurs in "The Fixation of Belief" (FOB), in which Peirce committed to a real "external permanency" (5.384, W 3: 253). He takes this as evidence that by FOB, Peirce had abandoned an earlier idealism. As noted in Chapter 4, Note 1, I disagree with Short's view that the positions Peirce defended in the cognition series of 1868–1869 imply a semiotic or conceptual idealism according to which the only real things are thought-signs. And I think that in the broader sense of "idealism" in which Peirce embraced that doctrine during the 1860s and 1870s – that of *basic idealism* – he continued to be an idealist for the rest of his life.

[40] Hookway cites the statement just quoted, as well as 3.93, n. 1 (W 2: 390n, 1870), to support his claim that "before the mid-1880s . . . [Peirce] denied that any true individuals existed" (1985: 167). But in those passages Peirce denied the reality only of strict individuals, not concrete individuals.

individual that it is human; the permanently fixed beliefs resulting from the method of science would be such as to apply the sign "human" to more than one thing. So "human" is general in a narrower sense: not only does it *not* represent a *strict* individual, it *does* represent more than one *concrete* individual.[41] While "Philip of Macedon" is a general sign of one particular thing, "human" is a general sign that represents multiple particular things, and it is the latter type of general sign that is relevant to scholastic realism. The second and third premises of the Early Argument have to do with signs that are general in this narrower sense.

There is one further distinction from Peirce's semiotic that is relevant here, that among *icons, indices*, and *symbols*. Roughly, an icon is a sign that represents its object in virtue of a resemblance between it and its object; an index is a sign that represents its object in virtue of some actual connection between it and its object; and a symbol is a sign that represents its object in virtue of a convention or rule by which it is taken to represent its object.[42] Indices and symbols are especially pertinent to present purposes, for the following reasons. First, in order for a proposition to represent something in the actual world, it must contain an index, a sign that serves to connect the proposition to an object about which something might then be said.

> The index asserts nothing; it only says "There!" It takes hold of our eyes, as it were, and forcibly directs them to a particular object, and there it stops. Demonstrative and relative pronouns are nearly pure indices, because they denote things without describing them; so are the letters on a geometrical diagram, and the subscript numbers which in algebra distinguish one value from another without saying what those values are. (3.361, W 5: 163, 1885)

Proper names, like "the second Philip of Macedon," are indices (8.335, 341, 1904).[43] Second, in order for the proposition to *say something* about the thing that the index represents, it must also contain a symbol.

> Any ordinary word, as "give," "bird," "marriage," is an example of a symbol. It is *applicable to whatever may be found to realize the idea connected with the*

---

[41] This explanation of the narrower sense of "general" is sufficient for my explanation of Peirce's early scholastic realism. But in order to understand the later version of the theory, it is necessary to see that a sign that is general in this sense is applicable, not just to more than one actual concrete particular, but to any number of particulars whatsoever. I return to this point in Chapter 6.

[42] Peirce first made this distinction in 1867's "On a New List of Categories" (1.558, W 2: 56); however, see W 1: 484–485 (1866) for an anticipation of it. The distinction occurs frequently in his writings beginning in 1885.

[43] However, cf. 2.283–284, EP 2: 274, 1903. As Short (2007a: 225, 276ff.) points out, Peirce's understanding of proper names as indexical signs anticipated the work of Kripke.

word; it does not, in itself, identify those things. It does not show us a bird, nor enact before our eyes a giving or a marriage, but supposes that we are able to imagine those things, and have associated the word with them. (2.298, ca. 1895)

The fact that Philip is drunk can be expressed only by a proposition that includes both an index – a term that singles him out, like "the second Philip of Macedon" – and a symbol – a term, like "drunk," by which the proposition represents him as being drunk. Any true belief, i.e., the propositional content of any belief that would eventually be fixed by investigation, will be expressible only by a combination of indexical and symbolic signs. On Peirce's view, this is the case for *any* proposition that represents the actual world. As Short puts it, "there must be an indexical component of knowledge, an immediate connection of the particular thought to its particular object, via which general concepts can be predicated of particulars" (2007a: 49). So not every sign in a true proposition must correspond to a particular.

After stating the Early Argument in SCFI, Peirce went on to say that

> [t]he great argument for nominalism is that there is no man unless there is some particular man. That, however, does not affect the realism of Scotus; for although there is no man of whom all further determination can be denied, yet there is a man, abstraction being made of all further determination. (5.312, W 2: 240)

No human being is a strict individual, i.e., an individual "of whom all further determination can be denied"; indeed, *nothing* is a strict individual. Still, we can think of a particular man (who is a concrete individual) *as a man* without thinking of him as having or lacking any other properties. So it is possible to derive, by way of abstraction, the general concept *human* from our experience of a particular human or humans.[44] Furthermore, "[t]here is a real difference between man irrespective of what the other determinations may be" – i.e., the general *human* – "and man with this or that particular series of determinations" – i.e., some particular human – "although undoubtedly this difference is only relative to the mind and not *in re*" (5.312, W 2: 240). The distinction between the general *human* and any one or more individual humans is one made only by the mind, but not by the mind of some particular person; that would make any such distinction internal. The general itself is external; it is not dependent on what any one or more people think. So the distinction between that general and any particular human must also be external. That the general

---

[44] The sort of abstraction that is relevant here is what Peirce called *prescission*. I say more about this later.

human is "relative to the mind" means that it is relative to how anyone who investigates would eventually come to represent some one or more particulars. Investigation would permanently fix the belief that some things are human, and so the general *human* is real. That it is not *in re* – not in individual humans, apart from how they might be represented in thought – does not imply that it is internal or that it is a fiction.

After pointing out that the view he has just described "is the position of Scotus," Peirce continued: "Occam's great objection is, there can be no real distinction which is not *in re*, in the thing-in-itself; but this begs the question, for it is itself based only on the notion that reality is something independent of representative relation" (5.312, W 2: 240). Occam begged a crucial question by assuming that it is possible for there to be real distinctions that cannot be represented in thought. Peirce's basic idealism implies that this is not the case. The distinction between the general *human* and particular humans is one that can be made by individual minds, but that is no reason for denying that it is real, or even for denying that it is external. An actual instance of abstraction within the mind of an individual person results in a general concept that is part of the actual thinking of that individual. My instance of the concept *human* is the result of a specific instance (or instances) of abstraction, which is one of *my* internal mental processes. Of course, this is no guarantee that that concept represents anything real, since the same is true of my concept of *vampire*. One's general concepts that represent real, external generals are the ones that appear in her *true* beliefs, i.e., beliefs that would survive investigation pushed so far as to permanently dispel doubt. On the assumption that *human* is such a general, it is real even if *my* thinking it has resulted from an internal instance of abstraction. The question is whether the sign "human" will appear in a proposition that is the content of a belief that would survive investigation. If so, then the general *human* is real and particular humans are human whether or not anyone actually believes that they are human. According to nominalism, "human"

> is a *mere* name. Strike out the "mere," and this opinion is approximately true. The realists say it *is* real. Substitute for "is," *may be*, that is, *is* provided experience and reason shall, as their final upshot, uphold the truth of the particular predicate, and the natural existence of the law it expresses, and this is likewise true. It is certainly a great mistake to look upon an idea, merely because it has not the mode of existence of a hecceity, as a lifeless thing. (3.460, 1897)[45]

---

[45] This is an exception to the general point that after about 1896, Peirce reserved "existence" to mean the mode of being of things that can react to other things. Here he was using it synonymously with "reality."

Peirce's comment that a given general *may be* real reflects his complaint that the Scotists "were utterly uncritical in accepting classes as natural, and seemed to think that ordinary language was a sufficient guarantee in the matter" (6.361, 1902). The Early Argument implies that which generals are real is to be discovered through investigation, so, as Haack (1992: 23) notes, "there are real generals" is preferable to "generals are real" as a statement of scholastic realism.

In drafts of the cognition series, Peirce described his scholastic realism as "nominalistic," which seems contradictory. But he continued: "nominalistic, inasmuch as it bases universals upon signs" (W 2: 175, 1868). Genuine nominalism identifies generals with internal signs, maintains that those signs are not real, and implies that only external individual things are real. Peirce inferred the reality of generals from the fact that true propositions contain general signs, and his realism about generals is "quite opposed to that individualism which is often supposed to be coextensive with nominalism" (W 2: 175, 1868). He also described his theory of cognition as having a "nominalistic element." But this was simply the view that "nothing out of cognition and signification generally," i.e., outside of what is cognizable, "has any generality" (W 2: 180).[46] He illustrated the nominalistic element as follows:

> [I]s the blackness of *this*, identical with the blackness of *that*? I cannot see how it can help being; the determinations which accompany it are different but the blackness itself is the same, by supposition. If this seems a monstrous doctrine, remember that my nominalism saves me from all absurdity. This blackness, upon my principles, is purely significative[,] purely cognitive; there is nothing I suppose to prevent signs being applied to different individuals in precisely the same sense ... [B]lackness in general, is shown to be real, by the testimony of the senses, and its cognitive or significative character does not stand in the way of this, at all. (W 2: 181, 1868)

We are now in a position to develop a better understanding of what generals *are*, if they are not abstract entities. The reality of a given general amounts to this: inquirers who attempt permanently to settle their beliefs by way of investigation, i.e., by the method of science, would eventually have beliefs the propositional contents of which contain some general sign – general in the sense that it applies to more than one particular thing. We cannot think of particulars in terms of their respective *haecceities*; we can only think of them by way of signs that are general. That such inquirers

---

[46] For very different understandings of the "nominalistic element" in Peirce's scholastic realism, see Michael (1988) and Short (1996).

would end up with such beliefs follows trivially from Peirce's view that *all* beliefs have such propositional contents. But that investigation would permanently fix some beliefs and not others is not trivial, since the beliefs that it would permanently fix are those that correspond with reality. Since investigators will inevitably have beliefs that *classify* particular things and events into general kinds, those kinds are real: "[a]ny class which, in addition to its defining character, has another that is of permanent interest and is common and peculiar to its members, is destined to be conserved in that ultimate conception of the universe at which we aim, and is accordingly to be called 'real'" (6.384, 1901).[47] The reality of a given general consists, then, in the fact that investigation, if pushed so far as to dispel doubt and settle belief permanently, would eventually lead to a specific belief. Thus does Peirce's scholastic realism follow from the conjunction of his views about truth and reality and his belief that every proposition contains one or more general signs.[48]

5.4

Peirce recognized two different processes of abstraction, each of which can give rise to general concepts and is thus relevant to scholastic realism. In 1867's "On a New List of Categories," he described a sort of "mental separation . . . which arises from *attention to* one element and *neglect of* [another]. Exclusive attention consists in a definite conception or *supposition* of one part of an object, without any supposition of the other" (1.549, W 2: 50). He called this process *prescission* (1.353, W 5: 238, 1885; 2.428, 1893; 2.364, 1902; 4.235, 1902).[49] Prescission is not simply the act of paying attention, but also the formation of a concept of that which is attended to; the quoted passage suggests that the formation of that concept is a necessary condition of the act of exclusive attention. In ca. 1903, Peirce indicated more explicitly that prescission culminates in the formation of a concept that is *general*, in the sense that it is predicable of more than one

[47] This is from Peirce's Baldwin's *Dictionary* definition of "kind." He mentioned "permanent interest" in order to contrast his definition of "kind" with Mill's definition of "character," as a property that is "interesting to us."

[48] I argued in Chapter 2 that the claim that a given inquirer has a given belief is pragmatically respectable – it can be clarified in terms of actions and their experiential results. If that argument succeeds, then there is no tension between Peirce's pragmatic maxim and his scholastic realism. For different views on this question, see Boler (1963), Murphey (1968), and Skagestad (1981).

[49] He also called it *precision* (1.549, W 2: 50, 1867; EP 2: 270n, 1903), *prescisive abstraction* (4.235, 1902), *precission* (EP 2: 270, 1903), and *precisive abstraction* (4.463, ca. 1903). On the etymology of "to prescind," see 5.449, 1905.

particular; he described it as the "psychological act by which, for example, on seeing a theatre, one is led to call up images of other theatres which blend into a sort of composite in which the special features of each are obliterated" (4.463).[50] Since prescission is a mental act or process, it is internal, something that is done by, or that occurs within the mind of, a particular inquirer. A specific instance of prescission will yield a general concept in that inquirer's mind, but it cannot result in a real, external general. What's more, prescission can yield, not just the general concepts *pear* and *human*, but also *vampire*, and so it is not guaranteed to result in a concept that corresponds to a real general.

Beginning in the mid-1880s, Peirce distinguished prescission from *hypostatic abstraction* (4.235, 1902; R 288: 41, 1905; 4.346, 1905; 5.447, n. 1, 449 and 455, EP 2: 351–352 and 356, 1905), which is the "consideration of abstractions as if they were objects" (3.509, 1897).[51] This consideration is the result of an inference from a premise in which a general concept is predicated of a subject to a conclusion in which that general concept has been transformed into a subject in its own right, as in the inference from "honey is sweet" to "honey possesses sweetness" (4.235, 1902). As with prescission, any instance of hypostatic abstraction is internal, something that is done by or occurs within the mind of an individual thinker. In what follows, I will use "hypostatic abstraction" to refer both to the internal mental process and to the concept that an inquirer might come to have as a result of that process; what I mean in a given instance should be clear from the context.

Peirce described hypostatic abstraction as

> a necessary inference whose conclusion refers to a subject not referred to by the premiss . . . But how can it be that a conclusion should necessarily follow from a premiss which does not assert the existence of that whose existence is affirmed by it, the conclusion itself? The reply must be that the new individual spoken of is an *ens rationis*; that is, its being consists in some other fact. (4.463, ca. 1903).[52]

In what other fact? The fact that is represented in a true "ordinary predication" (3.642, 1902).[53] Concepts that result from the process of

[50] Skagestad (1981: 68–69) emphasizes the role that prescision plays in the formation of general concepts.
[51] He also called it *hypostatization* (1.385, W 6: 187, 1887–1888), *hypostatisation* (3.509, 1897), *subjectual abstraction* (NEM 3: 917, 1904), and sometimes simply *abstraction* (1.83, ca. 1896; NEM 4: 49, 1902; EP 2: 270n, 1903; 4.463, ca. 1903).
[52] This is one of the rare passages from the 1900s in which Peirce seems to have used "existence" loosely and other than in the technical sense explained earlier.
[53] See also 6.382, 1902; 4.370, ca. 1903; 5.447, n. 1, EP 2: 350–351n, 1905; R 291, 5.534, 1905.

hypostatic abstraction do not necessarily add anything to our ontology. The general *sweet* is real, since it is true that honey is sweet. Hypostatic abstraction can infer from that belief the further belief that honey possesses sweetness, but this does not necessarily commit us to saying that there is an entity that the concept of *sweetness* represents. "'Sweetness' might be called a fictitious thing, in one sense. But since the mode of being attributed to it consists in no more than the fact that some things are sweet, and it is not pretended, or imagined, that it has any other mode of being, there is, after all, no fiction" (4.235, 1902). So the hypostatically abstract concept of *sweetness* does not correspond to anything real other than what is already represented in the belief that honey is sweet. One may be a realist about the general *sweet*, and one may hypostatically abstract the concept *sweetness*, without committing to the reality of something over and above the general *sweet*, which, again, is not an abstract entity. To infer that there is such an abstract individual would commit one to nominalistic Platonism.

The foregoing helps explain some of Peirce's early claims about concepts that he would eventually think of as resulting from hypostatic abstraction. In passages quoted previously, he claimed that both blackness (W 2: 180, 1868) and whiteness (8.14, W 2: 470, 1871) are real. In the following passage from about the same time, he initially seems to have taken a different position:

> Two things are alike in a certain respect[,] that is to say[,] the same predicate can be applied to either of them. Then the capacity of having that predicate applied to it with truth is called an attribute[,] that is[,] a thing to which it can be applied. The attribute is therefore an abstract term. Terms are divisible into concrete and abstract. The concrete are such as white[,] virtuous &c.[,] the abstract such as whiteness[,] virtue, etc. Abstract terms do not denote any real thing but they denote fictitious things. An object's being white is conceived as being due to its being in some relation with a certain fictitious thing[,] whiteness. (W 3: 99, 1873)

That an abstract term like "whiteness" denotes nothing real seems to signal a change in views. But he continued:

> In point of fact that the object is white may in a certain sense be said to be due to its connection with the sign or predicate white[,] that is to say[,] it must be in such a relation to the name white that this name may be applied to it with truth or else it cannot be white. There is no falsity in this statement[,] although it is more natural to state the matter in the inverse way and to say that its having that connection with that name is due to the fact that it is white. One statement is as true as the other. (W 3: 99, 1873)

This is consistent with everything we have seen so far about Peirce's realism about generals. It is true that some particular things are white, and what is represented in a true belief is real, so the general *white* is real. We can express this point differently by saying that some things possess whiteness, but this does not commit us to the reality of *whiteness* conceived as an abstract individual entity.[54] Hypostatic abstraction does not always lead to an expanded ontology.

On the other hand, sometimes it *does*. One of Peirce's favorite illustrations of hypostatic abstraction was the inference from the premise that opium puts people to sleep to the conclusion that it has *a dormitive power* or *virtue*.

> Abstractions have been a favorite butt of ridicule in modern times. Now it is very easy to laugh at the old physician who is represented as answering the question, why opium puts people to sleep, by saying that it is because it has a dormative [*sic*] virtue. It is an answer that no doubt carries vagueness to its last extreme. Yet, invented as the story was to show how little meaning there might be in an abstraction, nevertheless the physician's answer does contain a truth that modern philosophy has generally denied: it does assert that there really is in opium *something* which explains its always putting people to sleep. This has, I say, been denied by modern philosophers generally. Not, of course, explicitly; but when they say that the different events of people going to sleep after taking opium have really nothing in common, but only that the mind classes them together – and this is what they virtually do say in denying the reality of generals – they do implicitly deny that there is any true explanation of opium's generally putting people to sleep (4.234, 1902).[55]

The power to put people to sleep is a general, since it is something possessed by multiple individual things.[56] Understood pragmatically, the

---

[54] The view I defend here is consistent with what I argued in Lane (2004), that when Peirce wrote in 1865 that terms like "whiteness" denote only "fictions" (W 1: 287), and that "[q]*ualities* are fictions ... redness is nothing, but a fiction framed for the purpose of philosophizing" (W 1: 307), he was not denying that the generals *white* and *red* are real, but only that they are entities, things, or individuals. It is possible that commentators who have mistakenly claimed that Peirce was a nominalist during the 1860s and 1870s, despite his explicit avowals of scholastic realism beginning in 1868, might have been misled due to their failure to distinguish between generals and the abstract individual entities that could (mistakenly, on Peirce's view) be thought to correspond to hypostatically abstract concepts.

[55] For other uses of the opium example, see 8.12, W 2: 469, 1871; 4.463, ca. 1903; R 291, 5.534, 1905. Short suggests that the point of the example was that the abductive conjecture that opium has a power of putting people to sleep "was that such an abstraction is nevertheless the beginning, or could be, of an inquiry aimed at explanation. Without supposing a cause, no search for it can be made. The dormitive virtue is *that which* in opium puts people to sleep. The words 'that which' are a placeholder for further characterization. Empirical inquiry is needed to fill in the blank" (2007a: 268). His account of hypostatic abstraction (2007a: 264ff.) is worth reading in full.

[56] I am grateful to T. L. Short for helping me see this point and for other insights that helped me get clear on the relationship between hypostatic abstraction and scholastic realism.

question whether opium's dormitive virtue is real is the question whether the belief that opium puts people to sleep would be permanently fixed in the minds of investigators. If investigation would permanently fix that belief, then that power is real. But this does not imply that the reality of that power amounts to something over and above the real fact that that general belief is true.

> On pragmatistic principles *reality* can mean nothing except the *truth* of statements in which the real thing is asserted . . . [W]e shall if we incline to believe there is something in pragmatism also incline to believe that an abstraction may be a real substance. At the same time nobody for many centuries, – unless it was some crank, – could possibly believe that an abstraction was an ordinary primary substance. You couldn't load a pistol with dormitive virtue and shoot it into a breakfast roll. Though it is in opium, it is wholly and completely in every piece of opium in Smyrna, as well as in every piece in every joint in the Chinatown of San Francisco. It has not that kind of existence which makes things *hic et nunc*. What kind of being has it? What does its reality consist in? Why it consists in something being true of something else that has a more primary mode of substantiality. Here we have, I believe, the materials for a good definition of an abstraction.
>
> An abstraction is a substance whose being consists in the truth of some proposition concerning a more primary substance. (NEM 4: 162, PM 73, 1903)[57]

So the process of hypostatic abstraction will sometimes result in concepts that correspond to real generals, hence Peirce's description of the view that "realistic hypostatization of relations . . . is something to be avoided" as "very shallow" and "in accord with the spirit of nominalism" (1.383, W 6: 187, 1887–1888). But the real generals that correspond to hypostatically abstracted concepts are not abstract individuals, and so Peirce's realism about such generals does not amount to nominalistic Platonism.[58]

This account of Peirce's scholastic realism implies that concepts corresponding to real generals need not originate in the natural sciences. The

---

[57] This is from R 303, a notebook containing material written for his Harvard pragmatism lectures of 1903 but not delivered. A note Peirce attached to the notebook indicates that he rejected it, but not because he was unhappy with its contents: "No time for this and it would need two if not three lectures."

[58] On Boler's interpretation of Peirce's scholastic realism, "the predominance of continuity tends to eliminate the concept of substance" and a particular human such as Socrates "comes to be treated as a process. What we call 'things' are not strictly individuals but generals" (1963: 141). On my interpretation, Socrates is an individual, but he is a *concrete*, not a *strict*, individual, something that Peirce called a first substance. Boler cites 4.5 (1898) to support the interpretation that "Socrates is not just a member of a collection, partaking in generality through his similarity to other men; he is a fragment of a system" (1963: 141). But neither that claim nor what Peirce says regarding systems at 4.5 is inconsistent with the view that particular things are concrete individuals and first substances.

criterion for the reality of a general is that it be represented in a belief that the method of science would permanently settle. But as we saw in Chapter 1, what Peirce called "the method of science" in his account of truth is simply *investigation* – the attempt to dispel doubt and permanently establish belief through the use of both experience and reason – and investigation is not exclusive to the natural sciences. So any belief that would be permanently fixed by that method represents one or more real generals, whether or not it originated within the natural sciences, the social sciences, history, economics, philosophy (including ethics), or any other area of inquiry. The same is true for permanently fixed beliefs the propositional contents of which contain signs that express general concepts derived from hypostatic abstraction, e.g., *humanity, race, gender, justice, love,* etc. – so long as those terms are not taken to refer to abstract individual entities.

Peirce's Baldwin's *Dictionary* article entitled "Truth and Falsity and Error" indicates that he would have approved of these implications. Therein he was careful to distinguish the concepts of truth and reality, and he first illustrated this distinction with regard to a historical truth:

> The truth of the proposition that Caesar crossed the Rubicon consists in the fact that the further we push our archaeological and other studies, the more strongly will that conclusion force itself on our minds forever – or would do so, if study were to go on forever. An idealist metaphysician may hold that therein also lies the whole *reality* behind the proposition; for though men may for a time persuade themselves that Caesar did *not* cross the Rubicon, and may contrive to render this belief universal for any number of generations, yet ultimately research – if it be persisted in – must bring back the contrary belief. But in holding that doctrine, the idealist necessarily draws the distinction between truth and reality. (5.565, 1902)

As I argued in Chapter 3, Peirce was exactly the sort of idealist metaphysician to whom he alluded here: pragmatically clarified, the claim that Caesar *really* crossed the Rubicon – the claim that he crossed that river whether or not anyone believes that he did – amounts to the claim that the fact that Caesar crossed the Rubicon would be represented in a belief that would be permanently fixed by investigation. Peirce went on to apply these views to both ethics and mathematics:

> [T]he same definitions equally hold in the normative sciences. If a moralist describes an ideal as the *summum bonum* . . . [and if] the future development of man's moral nature will only lead to a firmer satisfaction with the described ideal, the doctrine is true. A metaphysician may hold that the fact that the ideal thus forces itself upon the mind, so that minds in their

development cannot fail to come to accept it, argues that the ideal is *real:* he may even hold that that fact (if it be one) constitutes a *reality* . . .

These characters equally apply to pure mathematics . . . The pure mathematician deals exclusively with hypotheses. Whether or not there is any corresponding real thing, he does not care. His hypotheses are creatures of his own imagination; but he discovers in them relations which surprise him sometimes. A metaphysician may hold that this very forcing upon the mathematician's acceptance of propositions for which he was not prepared, proves, or even constitutes, a mode of being independent of the mathematician's thought, and so a *reality*. (5.566–567, 1902)

So long as investigation is the means by which a belief is permanently established, what is represented in that belief is real, whether it has to do with the physical world, the objects of mathematics, or moral values.

Misak has sketched a Peircean theory of ethics on which "ethics falls under the scope of truth, knowledge, and what [Peirce] calls the scientific method of inquiry" (1991/2004: 185), and this is in line with the interpretation I have presented here. However, she also cites "Truth and Falsity and Error" in support of the view, which she shares with Hookway (2000), that Peirce eventually came to distance his accounts of truth and reality, so that "[t]ruth . . . may be indeterminate and the underlying reality determinate" (1991/2004: 186). But there is no indication in that work that Peirce abandoned the representationalist aspect of his account of truth, according to which a true belief represents the real world, or his pragmatic clarification of the idea of reality, according to which the real is that which is represented in a true belief, i.e., a belief that would be fixed by investigation. Peirce *distinguished the concepts* of truth and reality, but he did not sever the ties between those concepts which he had previously forged. Furthermore, and as we will see in Chapter 7, Peirce maintained not only that a proposition might be of indeterminate truth value, but also that its "underlying reality" might be indeterminate as well. But before considering those views, we need to examine Peirce's later scholastic realism, which encompasses not just generals, but also what he called *vagues*: mere possibilities.

CHAPTER 6

Generals and Vagues: Late Scholastic Realism

6.1

In the early 1900s, Peirce's metaphysics and his semiotic underwent parallel developments.[1] On the one hand, his scholastic realism expanded so as to become realism about both generals and what he called *vagues*. On the other, he came to recognize two kinds of semiotic indeterminacy: generality (which he had first acknowledged in the 1860s) and what he called *vagueness*. One might predict that during these later years he argued for the reality of vagues in the same way that he had argued for the reality of generals early on: since the real is what is represented in a true proposition, and since true propositions (or at least some true propositions) contain vague signs, there must be real vagueness. But this would be inaccurate. Although there is a connection between his realism about vagues and his recognition of semiotic vagueness, it is not so straightforward.

I will begin my explanation of these changes with an argument for the reality of generals that Peirce gave in 1905's "What Pragmatism Is" (WPI), the first of a projected series of articles on pragmatism for the *Monist*.[2] After stating his usual definition of "real" – "[t]hat is *real* which has such and such characters, whether anybody thinks it to have those characters or not" – he argued as follows:

> [T]hought, controlled by a rational experimental logic, tends to the fixation of certain opinions, equally destined, the nature of which will be the same in the end, however the perversity of thought of whole generations may cause the postponement of the ultimate fixation. If this be so, as every man of us virtually assumes that it is, in regard to each matter the truth of which he seriously discusses, then, according to the adopted definition of "real," the state of things which will be believed in that ultimate opinion is real. But, for

---

[1] Portions of this chapter were published in Lane (2007b).

[2] The original plan was that the series consist of three articles: WPI, "The Consequences of Pragmaticism," and "The Evidences for Pragmaticism." This plan changed, though, and although two additional papers – "Issues of Pragmaticism" and "Prolegomena to an Apology for Pragmaticism" – were published, the series was never completed (EP 2: 331).

the most part, such opinions will be general. Consequently, *some* general objects are real. (5.430, EP 2: 342–343)

His reasoning here was as follows:

1. The real is what is represented by a true belief, i.e., by a belief that would be permanently settled were we to attempt to settle our beliefs by way of investigation.
2. Most such beliefs are general.
3. Therefore, there are real generals.[3]

Unlike the Early Argument of the 1860s and 1870s, this *Late Argument* assumes, not that every true proposition contains a sign that is general, but only that "most" true beliefs are general in some sense. But in what sense?

While the first premise states the pragmatic clarification of the idea of reality, the second is supported by his assumption that any true proposition can be clarified by way of the pragmatic maxim and that the conditionals that convey those clarifications are general in the sense that they do not apply only to specific, individual circumstances: "the pragmaticist maxim says nothing of single experiments or of single experimental phenomena (for what is conditionally true *in futuro* can hardly be singular), but only speaks of *general kinds* of experimental phenomena" (WPI, 5.426, EP 2: 340); "the pragmaticistic meaning is undoubtedly general" (WPI, 5.429, EP 2: 341). As we saw in Chapter 5, Peirce held that all signs, even proper names, are general in the sense that none of them represents a strict individual. But some signs are also general in a second, narrower sense: they apply to more than one *concrete* individual. By 1905, Peirce had come to think of the general as applying, not just to multiple individual things, but to *any number* of particular things whatsoever. The reasons behind this change will be made clear in what follows.

This conception of the general can, by way of contrast, help us understand his conception of vagueness. Here we must tread lightly, since his

---

[3] This is not the only argument that Peirce deployed in support of scholastic realism during the 1900s. For example, during his 1903 Harvard lectures on pragmatism he reasoned as follows. I hold a rock in my hand, and I can predict with justification that if I release it, it will fall. According to Peirce, I know that the rock will fall because I know from past experience that *objects of this kind* always do fall in *conditions of this kind*. That is, I know that "all solid bodies fall in the absence of any upward forces or pressure," and "[i]f I *truly know* anything, that which I know must be *real*" (5.94–96, EP 2: 181). So that which is represented by the general proposition "All solid bodies fall in the absence of any upward forces or pressure" is real. This law is an "*active general principle*" that is "really operative in nature" (5.100–101, EP 2: 183).

idea of vagueness is quite different from the contemporary one.[4] In 1905's "Issues of Pragmaticism" (IP), the sequel to WPI, Peirce illustrated generality with the example of the word "man" in the proposition "Man is mortal" (5.447, EP 2: 350–351); broadly speaking, he considered terms that would be symbolized in predicate logic using a universal quantifier to be general. In Peirce's sense, a vague sign is one that picks out some *limited* number of individual things but without specifying exactly *which* things those are. He considered expressions that would be symbolized using existential quantifiers to be vague signs, e.g., "a man" in the proposition "A man whom I could mention seems to be a little conceited" (5.447, EP 2: 351). According to this classification, a sign that is applicable to only one particular thing and that specifies exactly which thing that is, is neither general nor vague, but *singular*. This would include proper names, such as "the second Philip of Macedon," but again, such names are general in a broader sense: they do not refer to a strict individual: "A proper name is set down as singular, although in absolute strictness, of course it is not so" (NEM 3: 812, 1905). Hence, "a sign can only escape from being either vague or general by not being indeterminate. But ... no sign can be absolutely and completely []determinate" (R 291, 5.506, 1905).[5]

During this late period, Peirce sometimes defined a general sign as one to which the principle of excluded middle (PEM) does not apply and a vague sign as one to which the principle of contradiction (PC) does not apply (e.g., IP, 5.448, EP 2: 351). These claims do not mean that general signs give rise to propositions that are neither true nor false or that vague signs give rise to true contradictions.[6] By "principle of excluded middle," he meant "the principle that no pair of mutually contradictory predicates are both false of any individual subject" (R 611: 13, 1908), i.e., of any concrete individual. "The general term, in so far as it is, and in those respects in which it is, general, is not subject to the principle of excluded middle. That 'Men are wise' and that 'men are foolish' ('men' being taken generally) may be alike false"

---

[4] Although he at least once associated vagueness with terms that give rise to sorites paradoxes (R 283: 137–138 alternative run of pages, 1906), the vast majority of his comments on vagueness indicate that he had something different in mind.

[5] Peirce wrote "indeterminate" rather than "determinate," but as the editors of the *Collected Papers* (5.506, n. 1) noted, this was obviously an error on his part.

[6] We will see in Chapter 7 that Peirce did eventually reject the principle of bivalence, according to which each proposition is true or else false, but that this was unrelated to his claim that PEM does not apply to the general.

(NEM 3: 812–813, 1905).[7] If there are substitution instances of "S is P" and "S is not-P" neither of which is true, then "S" is general and PEM does not apply to it. It does not follow from this that there are propositions that are neither true nor false.[8]

Peirce's definition of the vague as that to which PC does not apply is equally innocuous. By "principle of contradiction," Peirce meant "the principle that a pair of contradictory predicates, such as 'is P' and 'is not P' (or other than every P) are both true only of Nothing, and not of any definite [i.e., non-vague[9]] subject" (R 611: 12–13, 1908). If there are substitution instances of "S is P" and "S is not-P" both of which are true, then "S" is vague and PC does not apply to it. Consider one of his examples of a vague – or as Peirce sometimes also said, indefinite – sign: "an animal" in the proposition "An animal is male." He wrote that "[t]he *vague* might be defined as that to which the principle of contradiction does not apply. For it is false neither that an animal (in a vague sense) is male, nor that an animal is female" (R 291, 5.505, 1905). If "An animal is male" and "An animal is female" are interpreted such that both are true, their respective subject terms do not refer to one and the same animal; each refers to only one animal, but neither specifies exactly which animal that is. As it occurs in "A man whom I could mention seems a little conceited," "a man" is vague in the same way; it refers to some particular man without conveying exactly which one. But given that the subject terms of "An animal is male" and "An animal is female" each refer to a different animal, the conjunction of those propositions is not a contradiction. Why, then, did Peirce maintain that PC does not apply to such terms? In fact, it was the irrelevancy of

---

[7] So far as I have been able to discover, Peirce first wrote that PEM does not apply to the general in ca. 1896 (1.434). For other instances of this claim, or of the claim that PEM applies only to the individual, see, e.g., R 530:15, ca. 1903; NEM 2: 514, 1904; NEM 3: 913, 1904; 5.505, 1905; R 200: 79 second sequence of pages, 1908; ILS 257n, 1909; R 516: 39 second pagination, no date; R 145s: 24, no date.

[8] Peirce also explained the difference between general and vague signs in terms of the "rights" of a sign's utterer and its interpreter. A general sign is one that extends to its interpreter the right to further specify its meaning, while a vague sign is one that reserves that right for its utterer (e.g., R 530: 14–15, ca. 1903; 5.447, EP 2: 350–351, 1905). For more on this game-theoretical account of indeterminate signs, as well as on Peirce's explanations of generality and vagueness in terms of PEM and PC, see Lane (1997).

[9] Peirce sometimes used "indefinite" and "vague" synonymously and used "definite" to describe signs that are not vague. For examples, see IP, 5.449, EP 2: 351, 1905; R 291, 5.506, 1905; NEM 3: 812, 1905; 5.448n, EP 2: 393, 1906. In at least one late manuscript, he opted to use "indefinite" as he had previously used "general" – "It will be observed that what is called by other Logicians (and by me previously) a *general* I now call an Indefinite" – and seemingly to use "general" as he had previously used "indeterminate," as a general term of which both *would be's* and *may be's* are species – "how ever far we carry investigation its results will always be more and more *truly* General, that is, *Would-bes* and the *May-bes* will not tend to be eliminated except in certain directions" (R 1601: 5, 7, ca. 1909).

PC to such a conjunction that Peirce meant to underscore. His view was not that what PC implies about "an animal" is *false*, but instead that the principle *does not apply* to such terms.

> I do not say that the Principle of Contradiction is *false* of Indefinites [i.e., of vague signs]. It could not be so without applying to them which is precisely what I deny of it. An argument against what I say, namely, that the Principle of Contradiction does not apply to "A man" because "A man is tall" and "A man is not tall," can only amount to saying that *that* man that is tall is not, while tall, not tall. That is true; and that is what I mean by refusing to say that the Principle of Contradiction is *false* of "A man" but when it is said of that man that is tall, that he is not not-tall, this is said of the existing man, which is not Indefinite, but is, on the contrary, a certain man and no other. (R 641: 24 2/3–24 3/4, 1909)

So Peirce's view that PC does not apply to vague signs does not imply that vague signs give rise to true contradictions.[10]

Peirce also used PEM and PC to explain necessity and possibility, respectively, and the latter explanation is particularly important for a proper understanding of his realism about vagues. "Necessity ... is that mode of being which is not subject to the principle of excluded middle, since it may neither be that A is necessarily B, nor that A is necessarily not B" (NEM 3: 762, no date). PEM does not apply to statements of necessity, including statements of law, since "'S shall be or would be P' and 'S shall be or would be not-P' may both at once be false" (R 642: 21, 1909). Since both "S must/shall/would be P" and "S must/shall/would be not-P" may be false at the same time, PEM does not apply to necessity, which is therefore the general modality. Analogously, "a state of things has the Modality of the possible, – that is, of the merely possible, – only in case the contradictory state of things is likewise possible, which proves possibility to be the vague modality" (IP, 5.454, EP 2: 355). PC does not apply to assertions of possibility, freedom or

---

[10] To my knowledge, the earliest instance of Peirce's claim that PC applies only to the definite and not to the vague or indefinite occurs in R 690, HP 2: 738, 1901. For other examples, including passages where he used "indefinite" synonymously with "vague," see R 530: 14, ca. 1903; NEM 3: 913, 1904; NEM 3: 813, 1905; 5.498, n. 1, ca. 1905–1907; EP 2: 479, SS 80, 1908; R 516: 39 alternative run of pages, no date. The examples I provide in this chapter are all of propositional subject terms, but predicate terms can be vague as well. Consider Peirce's examples of "little" and "much" (R 530: 14, ca. 1903). "S is much" and "S is not much" might both be true, and they might both be false. But this does not mean that "S is much and not much (in the same sense)" is true. Peirce thought of a sentence containing a vague predicate as somewhat like an existential quantification over legitimate interpretations of that predicate. "S is much" means that S is much in *some* legitimate sense, while "S is not much" means that S is not much in some *other* legitimate sense. I believe this interpretation best explains Peirce's connection of his concept of vagueness to sorites paradoxes, mentioned in Note 4. I defend this reading in Lane (1997).

capacity, since "'S can be or may be P' and 'S can be or may be not-P' may both at once be true" (R 642: 21, 1909). "It is possible for me to sin and possible not to sin"; "[p]ossibly I shall vote for Roosevelt; possibly not" (R 137, NEM 2: 528, 531, 1904). Since each member of the pair "S may/can/could be P" and "S may/can/could be not-P" can be true, PC does not apply, and so possibility is the vague modality.[11]

We are now in a position to understand Peirce's later scholastic realism, his realism about both generals and vagues. In IP he wrote that

> the scholastic doctrine of realism . . . is usually defined as the opinion that there are real objects that are general . . . But the belief in this can hardly escape being accompanied by the acknowledgment that there are, besides, real *vagues*, and especially, real *possibilities*. For possibility being the denial of a necessity, which is a kind of generality, is vague like any other contradiction of a general. Indeed, it is the reality of some possibilities that pragmaticism is most concerned to insist upon. (5.453, EP 2: 354)

He illustrated this realism about mere possibility with an example he had used to illustrate the pragmatic maxim in "How to Make Our Ideas Clear" (HTM): a diamond that is destroyed before it is ever exposed to pressure (other than that of the atmosphere and that which was necessary to create it in the first place). During the diamond's existence, was it hard? The answer depends on how we understand the conditionals that pragmatically clarify the idea of hardness. We saw in Chapter 2 that throughout most of HTM, Peirce had understood the clarificatory conditionals generated by the maxim as being in the indicative mood and thus as covering only actual events. Neither "If I try to scratch the diamond with glass, it will be scratched" nor "If I try to scratch the diamond with glass, it will not be scratched" says anything about actual circumstances, since their antecedent was never fulfilled. It follows that the truth value of those conditionals does not depend on how things actually are – hence Peirce's claim that it is merely a matter of language whether we say that the diamond was hard or soft (HTM, 5.403, W 3: 267). But in IP, he took a very different view.

> Nomenclature involves classification; and classification is true or false, and the generals to which it refers are either reals in the one case, or figments in the other . . . [T]he question is, not what *did* happen, but whether it would have been well to engage in any line of conduct whose successful issue depended upon whether that diamond *would* resist an attempt to scratch it, or whether all other logical means of determining how it ought to be classed *would* lead to

---

[11] For other passages in which Peirce claimed that PEM does not apply to necessity and that PC does not apply to possibility, see 4.640, 1907; R 678: 28, 34, 1910; R 686: 2–3, late.

the conclusion which, to quote the very words of that article, would be "the belief which alone could be the result of investigation carried *sufficiently far.*" Pragmaticism makes the ultimate intellectual purport of what you please to consist in conceived conditional resolutions, or their substance; and therefore, the conditional propositions, with their hypothetical antecedents, in which such resolutions consist, being of the ultimate nature of meaning, must be capable of being true, that is, of expressing whatever there be which is such as the proposition expresses, independently of being thought to be so in any judgment, or being represented to be so in any other symbol of any man or men. But that amounts to saying that possibility is sometimes of a real kind. (5.453, EP 2: 354)

His reasoning here extends the Late Argument that he had begun in WPI by using his earlier conclusion that there are real generals as a premise in support of realism about unactualized possibilities:

1. There are real generals.
2. Generals are applicable not only to actual individual things and events, but also to merely possible things and events.
3. Therefore, the conditionals that state the pragmatic clarification of a general concept must be in the subjunctive mood, in order to cover merely possible circumstances.
4. Those conditionals are capable of being true.
5. Therefore, merely possible circumstances are real.

The first inference in this argument illustrates Peirce's view that "pragmaticism could hardly have entered a head that was not already convinced that there are real generals" (R 291, 5.503, 1905), while the second reflects his characterization of scholastic realism, which by this time included realism about mere possibility, as "an essential consequence of" pragmaticism (IP, 5.453, EP 2: 354).[12]

Recall Peirce's dual-aspect account of truth: a true belief is one that represents reality *and* that would be permanently settled in the minds of those who use the method of science, i.e., investigation, in order to dispel doubt. If it is true that the untouched diamond was hard, then (i) the proposition "The diamond was hard" represents something real and (ii) investigation would permanently settle the belief that it was hard. Let's consider each of these points in turn.

According to the representative aspect of his account of truth, if it is true that the diamond was hard, then it is a real fact that the diamond was hard,

---

[12] For very different interpretations of Peirce's view of the relationship between scholastic realism and pragmatism, see Almeder (1980: 179), Skagestad (1981: 60), and Haack (1992: 29).

and so it really would have resisted pressure had it been touched; and if it is true that the diamond was soft, then it is a real fact that it was soft, and so it really would not have resisted that pressure. So the question which general term – "hard" or "soft" – is truly predicable of it cannot be settled by stipulation.

> The question is, Was that diamond *really* hard? It is certain that no discernible *actual* fact determined it to be so. But is its hardness not, nevertheless, a *real* fact? To say, as [HTM] seems to intend, that it is just as an arbitrary "usage of speech" chooses to arrange its thoughts, is as much as to decide against the reality of the property, since the real is that which is such as it is regardless of how it is, at any time, thought to be. (IP, 5.457, EP 2: 356)

Whether the untouched diamond really was hard, and so whether "hard" is truly predicable of it, does not depend on whether anyone now represents it as having been hard; this follows from the definition of "real." What's more, whether it really was hard is also independent of any treatment it actually received when it existed. So the conditional pragmatic clarifications of "The diamond was hard" and those of "The diamond was soft" will have to cover non-actual circumstances. For any of those conditionals to be true, there must be something real in addition to actual circumstances, i.e., it must be the case that reality is not exhausted by actuality. This is why an adequate pragmatic clarification of the idea of hardness must be stated in subjunctive conditionals, which cover, not just actual cases but also merely possible ones.

The example of the untouched diamond yields counterfactuals, conditionals that describe events that could have occurred in the past, but in fact did not. But if any currently existing objects are really hard, then a pragmatic clarification of the idea of hardness will apply to them as well. Part of what it means to say that a currently existing diamond is hard is that, e.g., if I were to try to scratch it with glass, it would not be scratched, so the conditionals that convey that clarification will need to cover future events, some of which may never come to pass. Thus, Peirce's later pragmatism implies that

> the *will be's*, the actually *is's*, and the *have beens* are not the sum of the reals. They only cover actuality. There are besides *would be's* and *can be's* that are real. The distinction is that the *actual* is subject both to the principles of contradiction and of excluded middle; and in *one* way so are the *would be's* and *can be's*. In *that* way a *would be* is but the negation of a *can be* and conversely. But in another way a *would be* is not subject to the principle of excluded middle; both *would be X* and *would be not X* may be false. And in

this latter way a *can be* may be defined as that which is not subject to the principle of contradiction. On the contrary, if of anything it is *only* true that it *can be X* it *can be not X* as well.

It certainly can be proved very clearly that the Universe does contain both *would be's* and *can be's*. (8.216–217, ILS 273, 1910)[13]

Would be's are facts about what would occur were some condition fulfilled, and they are independent of any predictions that anyone might actually make or of any other representations. They are both real and external:

> [T]he external world ... does not consist of existent objects merely, nor merely of these and their reactions; but on the contrary, its most important reals have the mode of being of what the nominalist calls "mere" words, that is, general types and would-bes. The nominalist is right in saying that they are substantially of the nature of words; but his "mere" reveals a complete misunderstanding of what our everyday world consists of. (8.191, ca. 1904)

Notably, Peirce's eventual position about the untouched diamond also committed him to the reality of *would have been's*, facts about what would have happened had some condition been fulfilled in the past.[14]

What does the investigative aspect of Peirce's account of truth imply about the conditionals generated by the pragmatic maxim? If it is true that the untouched diamond was hard, then investigation would permanently settle the belief that it was hard. *Ex hypothesi*, no investigator will ever have had direct experiential evidence of the resistance of the diamond. But this does not stand in the way of a settled belief about its hardness, which, after all,

> is not an isolated fact. There is no such thing; and an isolated fact could hardly be real. It is an unsevered, though presciss, part of the unitary fact of nature. Being a diamond, it was a mass of pure carbon, in the form of a more or less transparent crystal (brittle, and of facile octahedral cleavage, unless it was of an unheard-of variety), which, if not twinned after one of the fashions in which diamonds may be twinned,[15] took the shape of an octahedron, apparently regular (I

---

[13] For other references to *would be's*, see R 633: 9–17, 1910; R 671: 20, ca. 1911; NEM 3: 243, ca. 1912; R 683: 27–28 variant pages, 1913; R 680: 21, 27 alternative run of pages, late; R 390: 22, late.

[14] As noted in Chapter 2, this makes possible one sort of response to the buried secrets objection to his pragmatic clarification of the idea of reality, viz., that the real includes what is represented, not just in beliefs that *would be* fixed by investigation, but also in beliefs that *would have been* fixed had investigation been conducted while there was still relevant evidence. Peirce endorsed this response at least once, in 1911 (EP 2: 457).

[15] Where EP 2 has "twinned," the *Collected Papers* and the original version of IP in the *Monist* have "trimmed." The headnote of IP at EP 2: 346 indicates that the editors followed pp. 481–486 of the *Monist* article, but then followed Peirce's manuscript. The relevant passage occurs on p. 495 of the *Monist* version, so presumably Peirce had written "twinned" rather than "trimmed." Note that one

need not go into minutiae), with grooved edges, and probably with
some curved faces. Without being subjected to any considerable
pressure, it could be found to be insoluble, very highly refractive,
showing under radium rays (and perhaps under "dark light" and
X-rays) a peculiar bluish phosphorescence, having as high a specific
gravity as realgar or orpiment, and giving off during its combustion
less heat than any other form of carbon would have done. From some
of these properties hardness is believed to be inseparable. For like it
they bespeak the high polymerization of the molecule. But however
this may be, how can the hardness of all other diamonds fail to
bespeak *some* real relation among the diamonds without which a
piece of carbon would not be a diamond? (IP, 5.457, EP 2: 356)

Investigators can have excellent reasons for believing that a specific diamond
was hard even if its hardness was never experientially manifested to them.
Given their interactions with other diamonds, and given their belief that some
properties that are truly predicable of the diamonds with which they have
interacted are also truly predicable of the diamonds with which they have not
interacted, it is plausible to think that the belief that the untouched diamond
was hard *would* be permanently fixed. And if that belief would be permanently
fixed among investigators, i.e., among inquirers who use the method of
science, then it is true. What's more, given Peirce's pragmatic clarification of
the idea of reality, what is represented by that belief – the fact that the
untouched diamond was hard – is real. Pragmatically clarified, the claim
that the untouched diamond was hard means that, *inter alia*, if someone
had really attempted to scratch it with glass, it really would not have been
scratched. And so pragmatism is committed to the reality of the vague, the
non-actual, the merely possible.

6.2

In manuscripts written in the same year as IP, Peirce traced his realism about
possibility to two articles published in the previous decade. He wrote that in
1897's "The Logic of Relatives" (LOR) he had "quite assertorically," and in
1892's "The Doctrine of Necessity Examined" he had "more tentatively,"

repudiated the nominalistic view of possibility, and explicitly return[ed] to
the Aristotelian doctrine of a *real possibility*. This was the great step that was
needed to render pragmaticism an intelligible doctrine. The paper of Jan.

of Peirce's *Century Dictionary* definitions of the verb form of "twin" is: "Specifically, in *mineral.*, to
form or unite into a compound or twin crystal by a reversal of the molecular structure according to
some definite law" (CD 6553).

1878 [HTM] wavers palpably at this point, sensible of the advantages of a real possibility, yet wishing to save pragmaticism in case that doctrine should prove untenable. (R 288: 129, 1905)

In another 1905 manuscript, he wrote:

In [LOR] the objectivity of possibility was asserted; and the hypothesis defended in ["The Architecture of Theories" and "The Doctrine of Necessity Examined," viz., tychism] supposes possibility to be real. It was, indeed, *implied* in the scholastic realism maintained in the [1871 Berkeley review]. But [HTM] evidently endeavors to avoid asking the reader to admit a real possibility. The theory of modality is far too great a question to be treated incidentally to any other. But the distinct recognition of real possibility is certainly indispensable to pragmaticism. (R 291: 50, 5.527)[16]

Peirce clearly took LOR to contain a decisive step, one anticipated in the cosmological papers of the 1890s, toward the modal realism that he eventually took to follow from the pragmatic clarification of the idea of reality. LOR, published in the *Monist* in January 1897, was the second in a two-part series of review articles on Ernst Schröder's *Vorlesungen über die Algebra der Logik*. The first article in that series, published in October 1896, was "The Regenerated Logic" (RL).[17] Therein Peirce had asserted that every type of possibility can be defined in terms of states of information: "[P]ossibility may be understood in many senses; but they may all be embraced under the definition that that is possible which, in a certain state of information, is not known to be false" (3.442). But by the time he penned its sequel, he had changed his mind:

I formerly defined the possible as that which in a given state of information (real or feigned) we do not know not to be true. But this definition today seems to me only a twisted phrase which, by means of two negatives, conceals an anacoluthon. We know in advance of experience that certain things are not true, because we see they are impossible. (LOR, 3.527)[18]

---

[16] Unaltered, the first sentence quoted here reads: "In the *Monist* (vol. VII p. 206 *et seq.*) the objectivity of possibility was asserted; and the hypothesis defended in Vols. I and II supposes possibility to be real." "The Architecture of Theories" appeared in *Monist* vol. I, and while both "The Doctrine of Necessity Examined" and "The Law of Mind" appeared in vol. II, the latter's emphasis is on synechism, not tychism.

[17] LOR was published in January 1897. The article that preceded it, RL, was written from May 20–25, 1896 (R 519), and so LOR must have been written at some point later in 1896.

[18] An anacoluthon is a change within a sentence to a second grammatical construction inconsistent with the first. It is not clear to me what anacoluthon Peirce held to be concealed by the two negatives in the quoted statement, which is grammatically correct.

Prima facie, the "great step" that Peirce took in LOR was simply a change from an anti-realistic view, on which possibility amounts to nothing but ignorance in some state of information or other, to realism about possibility. But this interpretation is too simple to be correct. First, Peirce was a realist about modality prior to 1896. As explained in Chapter 3, and as he himself alluded to in the 1905 manuscripts quoted earlier, his tychism, which he adopted no later than 1883–1884's "Design and Chance" (W 4: 544–554), is the view that there is *real chance*, i.e., real contingency and therefore real possibility, in the world. What's more, natural laws are a kind of general, and so scholastic realism, which includes realism about natural laws, implies realism about necessity; he began defending that theory no later than 1868, and his first explicit commitment to realism about natural laws came no later than 1873 (W 3: 81). Furthermore, he continued to rely on the "states of information" account – or as I will call it, the *Information-Relative (IR) account*[19] – after criticizing it in LOR. For example, in 1902 he defined the physically possible as "that which a knowledge of the laws of nature would not enable a person to be sure was not true" (6.371), and he used it in his interpretation of the modal part of his system of existential graphs (4.573, 1906). So the interpretation of his "great step" as a simple move from anti-realism to realism about modality will not do.

In this section and the next, I argue that the great step was in fact a move from a weak to a strong form of modal realism and that the medium through which that move eventually affected Peirce's pragmatism was his conception of continuity. In short, his move from weak to strong realism about possibility enabled him to reconceive continuity, and therefore generality, as requiring unactualized possibilities. It was only after he began thinking of real generality as requiring real unactualized possibility that he revised his pragmatism and fully committed to the view that pragmatic clarifications must be stated in the subjunctive mood. In better understanding the motivation behind that revision, we will better understand the role that real vagues play in his later pragmatism.[20]

Again, prior to 1896 Peirce held that all senses of the modal terms could be analyzed in terms of states of information.[21] On this IR account, the claim that

---

[19] I take this name from Morgan (1979, 1981).

[20] What follows is far from an exhaustive account of Peirce's views on modality. There are several other issues on which a complete account would have to touch and about which I say little or nothing. These include his association of the concepts of *possibility* and *quality*, and his integration of each into his system of universal categories; improvements in his theory of signs that followed on the heels of his rejection of the IR account; his changing views about the nature of probability; and the gamma portion of his existential graphs.

[21] For representative passages, see 3.374, W 5: 169–170, 1885; W 5: 330, 372, 1886; 4.65, 1893; 3.442, 1896.

it is possible that *p* means that *it is not known to be false that p*, the claim that it is necessary that *p* means that it is known to be true that *p*, and the different senses of the modal terms are defined by reference to different states of information. I will call the state of information that defines a given type of modality its *designated state of information (DSI)*. *Subjective* modality is defined by reference to a DSI in which an actual person might find herself:

> One who knows that Harvard University has an office in State Street, Boston, and has [the] impression that it is at No. 30, but yet suspects that 50 is the number, would say "I think it is at No. 30, but it *may be* at No. 50," or "it *is possibly* at No. 50." Thereupon, another, who does not doubt his recollection, might chime in, "It *actually is* at No. 50," or simply "it *is* at No. 50." . . . Thereupon, the person who had first asked what the number was might say, "Since you are so positive, it *must be* at No. 50," or "I know the first figure is 5. So, since we are both certain the second is a 0, why 50 it *necessarily is.*" . . . [W]hen knowledge is indeterminate among alternatives, either there is one state of things which alone accords with them all, when this is in the Mode of *Necessity*, or there is more than one state of things that no knowledge excludes, when each of these is in the Mode of *Possibility*. (IP, 5.454, EP 2: 355)

There are also types of modality that go beyond what an actual subject knows or fails to know. For example, the DSI for *physical* possibility and necessity is that of a hypothetical person who is "thoroughly acquainted with all the laws of nature and their consequences, but . . . ignorant of all particular facts" (4.66, 1893). The physically possible is that which someone in that DSI would not know to be false, the physically necessary that which someone in that DSI would know to be true. Similarly, the *practical* modalities are to be defined by "imagin[ing] ourselves to know what the resources of men are, but not what their dispositions and desires are," and the DSI of the *mathematical* and *metaphysical* modalities are, respectively, the states of information of "the most perfect mathematician or metaphysician" (4.66, 1893).

Peirce described two types of modality that are "of special interest to the logician more than to other men" (4.67, 1893). The DSI of *essential* or *logical* modality is that of someone who knows "*nothing*, except the meanings of words, and their consequences" (4.67, 1893). On the other hand, the DSI of *substantial* modality is that of someone who knows "everything now existing, whether particular fact or law, together with all their consequences"; this is not the omniscience of a trans-temporal God, but rather the state of information of a hypothetical subject who knows all natural laws and all *present* facts; it is "supposed information of the present in the present" (4.67, 1893). A subject in this DSI would know all there is to know about the world as it actually is at present, including all present facts and laws. The only present state of things that a subject of this DSI would not know not to obtain would be the one state of things that he knows *does* obtain: the *actual* present state of things. So in the substantial sense, there are no present *contingent* states of things. That is, there are no states of things that are substantially possible (states that the subject does not know *not to* obtain), but not substantially necessary (states that the subject *does* know to obtain).

Peirce's IR account of substantial modality implies that if determinism is true, then there are no future substantial contingents. Again, a subject in the DSI of substantial modality would know all present facts and laws and their consequences. If determinism is true, those present facts and laws together determine *all* future facts. So, assuming determinism, there would be no present *or future* truths that the subject of the DSI of substantial modality would not know. Every proposition about the future that such a subject would not know to be false would be a proposition that that subject would know to be true, and so all substantially possible truths about the future would be substantially necessary.

But Peirce did not have to accept this consequence of the IR account of substantial modality. This is because he rejected determinism and accepted tychism, which asserts the reality of "indeterminacy, spontaneity, or absolute chance in nature" (6.13, W 8: 101, 1891). With regard to some future events, it is possible both that those events happen and that they not happen, even given previous conditions and governing laws. Tychism is thus the view that, in addition to real necessity, there is real contingency in the world. But the contingency the reality of which tychism asserts is not, or not only, physical contingency. In the substantial sense of the modal terms,

> everything in the present which is possible is also necessary, and there is no present contingent. But we may suppose there are "future contingents." Many men are so cocksure that necessity governs everything that they deny that there is anything substantially contingent. But . . . they are unwarrantably confident, . . . wanting omniscience we ought to presume there may be things substantially contingent, and further that there is overwhelming evidence that such things are. (4.67, 1893)

If the foregoing is correct, the tychistic contingency of a future event is not a matter of anyone's *actual* ignorance. Actual ignorance, the ignorance of someone in the DSI of subjective modality, reflects mere ordinary chance. When I roll a pair of dice, it is subjectively possible (for me) both that they land double-sixes and that they land otherwise. In contrast, the absolute chance of tychism transcends anyone's actual ignorance. The DSI in terms of which absolute chance should be defined is a hypothetical one: the state of information of a hypothetical being who knows all present facts and laws, plus all of their consequences. In this state of information, anything about the present not known to be false is known to be true, so there is no present substantial contingency. But there is *future* substantial contingency, i.e., possible but not necessary truths about the future. According to tychism, even a quasi-omniscient subject with complete knowledge of all present laws and facts and their consequences would not know everything about the future.

So at least through the time he wrote RL, Peirce defined all senses of the modal terms in terms of the knowledge of some subject, either actual or hypothetical. During this same period, he held that there is both real necessity and real contingency in the world. But as we have seen, from at least 1867 Peirce defined the real as that which is independent of what anyone thinks about it. How, then, could he consistently maintain that some events are really necessary or really contingent while at the same time defining "necessary" and "contingent" in terms of states of information? He anticipated this objection:

> To conclude from [the IR account] that there is nothing analogous to possibility and necessity in the real world, but that these modes appertain only to the particular limited information which we possess, would be even less defensible than to draw precisely the opposite conclusion from the same premises. It is a style of reasoning most absurd. (4.68, 1893)

Clearly, he saw no conflict between the IR account and modal realism, nor should he have. After all, the IR account does not say, e.g., that it is contingent that *p* exactly when a hypothetical subject *thinks* that it is contingent that *p*. That would imply that contingency is a figment, for it amounts to the claim that contingency depends on what someone thinks *about contingency*. On the other hand, the IR account does imply that one sort of modality – subjective modality – is internal to the minds of actual people. If it is subjectively possible that it will rain, it is subjectively possible *for someone* that it will rain, in that that possibility consists of that person's not knowing that it will not rain. And since that person's ignorance is a matter of how he thinks, the subjective possibility of rain is internal to his mind. But the DSIs for other types of modality are given in terms of the states of information of hypothetical, not actual, subjects. Whether it is physically possible that p depends on what a hypothetical person, one with full knowledge of the laws of physics, would be ignorant of. But this does not mean that the physical modalities are internal. As we saw in Chapter 3, in Peirce's technical sense of "internal," it refers to that which is internal to some particular person and therefore to some *actual* person. So the IR account is consistent with the view that some kinds of modality are both real and external.

Nevertheless, Peirce eventually became dissatisfied with the IR account as applied to one form of modality in particular – substantial modality – and his rejection of the IR account for that sort of modality enabled important revisions in his accounts of continuity, generality, and pragmatism. To understand why he came to question the IR account, we need to distinguish two kinds of question:

(1) *Questions about which modalities are exemplified.* Assuming that every actual event is possible, are there actual events that are contingent? Or are all actual events necessary?

(2) *Questions about the nature of modality.* Is modality real (i.e., independent of what anyone thinks about it)? Can all modal terms be adequately defined in terms of states of information?[22]

The first sort of question concerns whether there are events that fall under concepts such as *necessary* and *contingent*, while the second asks about the nature of necessity, contingency, and possibility themselves. Peirce's tychism addresses a type-1 question and asserts that some future events are substantially contingent. On the other hand, the IR account addresses a type-2 question about the nature of modality itself. Prior to writing LOR in 1896, Peirce held that all types of possibility, necessity, and contingency ought to be understood in terms of (actual or hypothetical) states of information and that this was compatible with there being something "analogous" to modality "in the real world." This suggests a range of responses to type-2 questions, with Peirce's 1893 view occupying a relatively weak realist position between two extremes:

---

[22] This distinction is analogous to that between normative ethical questions regarding certain types of action (e.g., are there any supererogatory actions, or are all morally permissible actions either obligatory or morally neutral?) and meta-ethical questions regarding the nature of morality (e.g., is morality objective or subjective? do moral judgments convey truths, or do they merely express emotion?).

(a) *strong realism*: modality is real, and at least some types of modality cannot be defined in terms of states of information, even those of a hypothetical subject.

(b) *weak realism*: modality is real, and all types of modality can be defined in terms of states of information.

(c) *anti-realism*: modality is not real.

His rejection of the IR account of substantial possibility was a move from weak to strong realism. Prior to that rejection, Peirce took modality, including future substantial contingency, to be real, yet he took the IR account to be sufficient to define all types of modality. What he changed his mind about was not whether certain modal concepts are exemplified, but whether substantial possibility can be defined in terms of states of information.[23]

As mentioned earlier, Peirce's view in RL was that the IR account was sufficient to define all senses of the modal terms. But his view changed shortly thereafter. In a manuscript dating from around May 1896 (R 787), he characterized the IR account as providing an analysis of only "negative" possibility and asserted that there was, in addition, "positive" possibility:

> In its primitive sense, that which is *possible* is a hypothesis which in a given state of information is not known, and cannot certainly be inferred, to be false. The assumed state of information may be the actual state of the speaker, or it may be a state of greater or less information. Thus arise various kinds of possibility. All these varieties of possibility are *ignorantial*, or *negative*. *Positive* possibility arises when our knowledge is such as is represented by a disjunctive proposition, that either A, or B, or C, or D, etc., is true. A, B, C, D, etc., are then the positively possible cases. Thus, in playing

---

[23] It is widely acknowledged that Peirce eventually adopted a more realist view of modality, but only a few commentators have taken note of his criticism of the IR account in LOR and his later comments about it. Fisch (1986: 194) mentions that criticism, noting that Peirce took it to be a significant step toward realism, but he does not mention Peirce's later reliance on that account. Hookway (1985: 178–179, 243) refers to Peirce's first criticism of the IR account, mentions "the development in Peirce's views of modality during the 1890s," and connects that development with Peirce's thoughts on continuity, scholastic realism, and pragmatism, but he does not mention Peirce's continued use of the IR account after the 1890s. Morgan (1981) acknowledges Peirce's criticism and subsequent use of the IR account without attempting to explain the apparent inconsistency. Noble (1989) correctly identifies one consequence of Peirce's rejection of the IR account for substantial modality, viz. a revision in Peirce's thinking about continuity, but he does not mention Peirce's continued reliance on the IR account. Thompson (1953: 289, n. 22) quotes Peirce's statement that he "formerly defined the possible" in terms of states of information and mentions his 1905 distinction between "subjective" and "objective" modality, but he does not note Peirce's continued use of the IR account. None of these commentators notes the tension between Peirce's shift toward an apparently new realism about modality and his earlier realism about necessity and contingency.

backgammon, there are twenty-one possible throws of the dice, at each play. The aggregate of the positively possible cases is the *range* or *universe* of possibility. (2.347)

The positive possibility described in this passage is still a matter of what someone knows. Peirce wanted to go beyond the IR account, but nevertheless continued to assume that all senses of "possible" could be defined in terms of knowledge.[24]

It was in LOR that Peirce first articulated a concept of possibility that could not be defined in that way. Therein he asked: "Is it, or is it not, logically possible for two collections to be so multitudinous that neither can be put into a one-to-one correspondence with a part or the whole of the other?" (3.526). In effect, he was asking whether the *cardinal comparability theorem* is true. According to that theorem, "for any two sets A and B, either A can be put into a one-to-one correspondence with a subset of B, or *vice versa*" (Myrvold 1995: 530). Peirce's answer was that the theorem *is* true and that it is *not* logically possible for there to be two sets so large that neither can be mapped one-to-one onto even a part of the other.[25] He thought that in order to support this conclusion he needed to revise his views about possibility; on his view, the IR account did not capture the sense of "logically possible" relevant to questions of set theory,[26] and answering the question about the theorem required "not a mere *application* of logic, but a further *development* of the conception of logical possibility" (LOR, 3.526, 1897; see also R 14, NEM 3: 50, 1896).

His attempt to further develop that conception began with the denial that the IR account is adequate to explain substantial possibility, one of the two types of possibility that he had earlier characterized as being of special interest to logicians (4.67, 1893). Peirce had understood the IR account of substantial possibility to imply that it is substantially possible that p because a subject in the relevant DSI would not know that it is false that p and that it is substantially impossible that p because such a subject would know that it is false that p. But in LOR he objected that this explanation gets things backward: "We know in advance of experience that certain

---

[24] It is from Cornelis de Waal (personal correspondence) that I learned that Peirce probably wrote R 787 in May 1896. If he wrote R 787 between writing RL and LOR, then the passage just quoted is Peirce's first step away from the IR account. Still, it would make sense that he viewed LOR as containing "the great step" toward a new position on modality, since it was therein that he first insisted on a sort of modality that cannot be defined in epistemic terms.

[25] Peirce argued in support of the cardinal comparability theorem at R 14, NEM 3: 49–50, 1896; 3.548–550, 1897; 4.179, 1897; NEM 3: 958–962, 1903.

[26] He expressed this same concern a few years later in his Baldwin's *Dictionary* entries for "Modality" (2.383, 1902) and "Possibility, Impossibility and Possible" (6.367, 1902).

things are not true, because we see they are impossible" (3.527). That is, pointing out that someone knows, prior to experience, that p is not true does not help to explain why it is impossible that p. But pointing out that it is impossible that p can help to explain how it is that someone knows, prior to experience, that p is not true. "It is not that certain things are possible because they are not known not to be true, but that they are not known not to be true because they are, more or less clearly, seen to be possible" (6.367, 1902).

So Peirce's move from weak to strong realism was motivated by the belief that substantial possibility cannot be adequately explained in terms of states of information. But he never articulated an alternative account of substantial possibility with which he was satisfied.[27] Had he written nothing else about possibility, we might conclude that his rejection of the IR account of substantial possibility was merely an attempt to articulate a conception of logical possibility not based on the IR account, an attempt which he ultimately found wanting, which he never significantly improved upon, and which had no impact on the rest of his thinking. But as we saw previously, he eventually came to view that rejection as "the great step that was needed to render pragmaticism an intelligible doctrine" (R 288: 129, 1905). To understand its eventual effects on his pragmatism, we next need to consider its connection with his thinking about continuity and generality. As we will see, it was in the year following his move from weak to strong modal realism that he first articulated a conception of continuity and generality on which they have as a necessary condition real unactualized possibility.

6.3

Early on, Peirce defined continuity as the property a thing has when all of its parts have parts "in the same sense," i.e., when it has no "ultimate parts" (5.335, W 2: 256, 1869).[28] He later commented that he had taken this

---

[27] Peirce did proceed to give a new account of substantial modality in LOR, in terms of an "ideal world of which the real world is but a fragment" (3.527). On this account, something is substantially possible exactly when it occurs in the ideal world and substantially impossible exactly when it does not. Peirce mentioned substantial modality and "the ideal world" separately in a handful of other works over the next few years, but so far as I have been able to discover, LOR was the only work in which he defined substantial possibility in terms of the ideal world. In around 1905 he wrote of LOR's discussion of the ideal world analysis of substantial possibility that "it by no means affords a completely satisfactory account" of that sort of possibility (R 288: 128). For more on these concepts, see Lane (2007b).

[28] The following account of the evolution of Peirce's thinking about continuity supersedes those given in Lane (1999, 2007b). For alternative accounts of the evolution of Peirce's view of continuity, see

property to be the same as infinite divisibility (6.168, PM 138, 1903), which he called *Kanticity*.[29] In his *Century Dictionary* entry for "continuity," he rejected this definition along with two others: "The old definitions – the fact that adjacent parts have their limits in common (Aristotle), infinite divisibility (Kant), the fact that between any two points there is a third (which is true of the system of rational numbers) – are inadequate" (6.164, CD 1229). He then went on to state that

> [t]he less unsatisfactory definition is that of G. Cantor, that continuity is the *perfect concatenation* of a system of points . . . Cantor calls a system of points *concatenated* when any two of them being given, and also any finite distance, however small, it is always possible to find a finite number of other points of the system through which by successive steps, each less than the given distance, it would be possible to proceed from one of the given points to the other. He terms a system of points *perfect* when, whatever point not belonging to the system be given, it is possible to find a finite distance so small that there are not an infinite number of points of the system within that distance of the given point. (6.164, CD 1229)[30]

Although this statement of Cantor's definition refers to possibility, it does not characterize any part of a continuum as being merely possible. What is possible is, with regard to concatenation, the identification of a finite number of points, and, with regard to perfection, the identification of a finite distance, and so this definition is consistent with the view that, e.g., a continuous line consists of actual points separated by actual distances.

By 1892, Peirce had changed his mind yet again, defining a continuum as that which has *both* Kanticity and Aristotelicity, the latter being the property of any series that "contains the end point belonging

---

Potter and Shields (1977), Potter (1996), and Havenel (2008); the latter is the most detailed account of that evolution to date. There is also valuable commentary in Moore's introductions to some of the chapters of PM. My account of the emergence of Peirce's modal conception of continuity and its connection to his rejection of the IR account can be read as a supplement to the very detailed account given in Myrvold (1995). Potter, Shields, and Myrvold do not emphasize the modal nature of the conception of continuity Peirce adopted in the 1890s or connect that conception to his rejection of the IR account. Havenel does emphasize the modal nature of that conception, but, like the others, he fails to connect it to Peirce's rejection of the IR account. In tracing Peirce's revision of his definition of continuity to his rejection of the IR account, I agree with Noble (1989).

29   It is clear from his own later criticisms that Peirce believed this definition to be the same as Kant's (NEM 3: 780, 1899; 3.569, 1900; 6.168, 1903). He used the term "Kanticity" to describe this property at 6.166, ca. late 1891 to 1892; 6.122, 1892; 4.121, 1893. On the dating of 6.166 and 168, see Lane (1999: 306–307, n. 21).

30   Here I have corrected a mistake introduced in the *Collected Papers*, in which Peirce's statement of Cantor's definition of "perfect" reads in part: "whatever point belonging to the system be given, it is not possible to find a finite distance so small"; see Fisch (1986: 199, n. 22); Havenel (2008: 95); and Moore (2010: 329).

to every endless series of points which it contains" (6.123). But he eventually described this view as "blundering" (R 300, 6.174, 1908).[31] He had abandoned it by 1893, when he described continuity as "unbrokenness"[32] and "fluidity[,] the merging of part into part," and wrote that "a continuum is merely a discontinuous series with additional possibilities" (1.164 and 170, PM 155 and 157).[33] So far as I have been able to discover, this was his first characterization of a continuum as containing or being composed of possibilities. However, it implies that no purported continuum is genuinely continuous! If a line is a "discontinuous series" of points, it lacks true continuity, even if there are merely possible points between each actual point on the line.

In that same year, Peirce drafted an advertisement (R 397) for a projected book – *How to Reason*[34] – in which he indicated that in that volume he would adopt "Cantor's analysis," albeit "with some correction" (NEM 4: 355), but he did not indicate what that correction would be. In this same draft advertisement, he for the first time identified continuity with generality: "every general concept is, in reference to its individuals, strictly a continuum ... [T]he general is ... precisely the continuous. Thus, the doctrine of the reality of continuity coincides with that opinion the schoolmen called realism" (NEM 4: 358, 1893).[35] He did not say enough here to make clear exactly why he had begun to identify generality and continuity. But he returned to the subject in early 1896, in a manuscript (R 14) entitled "On Quantity" (OQ):

> In the English logic of this century, generals appear as "class-names"; and a class is a multitude, or collection, of individual things, each having its distinct, independent, and prior existence. Such a class cannot have as many individuals as there could be; because "as many as there could be" is not a possible grade of multitude; and the result of insisting upon that would inevitably be that the individuals would be sunk to a potential being, and would no longer be unconditionally and *per se* there. (NEM 3: 58, PM 160–161)[36]

Peirce was struggling to understand the nature of the particulars to which a given general predicate applies. Any general predicate can apply to more

---

[31] I take the date of R 300 from LI 375, n. 1.

[32] He did not take this to be a definition, or at least not a satisfying one: "continuity is unbrokenness (whatever that may be)" (R 204, 7.535, n. 6, 1908).

[33] This is from the 1893 lecture parts of which are in R 860 and 955; see Chapter 3, Note 30.

[34] This book was posthumously titled *Grand Logic*, but according to de Waal, there is no evidence that Peirce himself ever called it that. See ILS 37, n. 26.

[35] This may be what Peirce had in mind when he wrote that "the *synechistic* philosophy ... carries along with it ... a logical realism of the most pronounced type" (6.163, W 8: 157, 1892).

[36] I take the date of this passage from Cornelis de Waal (personal correspondence).

than the actually existing individuals of which it is true, no matter how many such individuals there are. On the other hand, any non-actual particular would be "sunk" to the level of mere potentiality and therefore not really "there." At this point, before the move to strong modal realism in LOR, Peirce could conceive of the merely potential only in terms of the ignorance of someone in a given state of information. On the IR account, to assert that there are merely possible points on a line would amount to saying only that someone in a given state of information would not know that those points are not there. He proceeded to identify

> two propositions about time which, if they are acknowledged to be involved in the common-sense idea, determine the character of its continuity. One is, that there is in a sensible time room for any multitude, however great, of distinct instants. The other is, that the instants are so close together as to merge into one another, so that they are not distinct from one another . . . The former seems to express what there is that is true in Cantor's statement that a line includes *all* the points possible . . .
>
> According to that idea, then, the instants of a time are not a multitude. Each of the two propositions proves that. For, first, since any multitude whatever of instants exists among the instants of any given time, and since there is no maximum multitude, it follows that the instants of time do not in their totality form a multitude. In this sense, they may be said to be "more" than any multitude; that is, there is among them a multitude greater than any multitude which may be proposed. Second, [they] are not in themselves distinct from one another, as the units of any multitude are, even if they happen to be joined together. (OQ, NEM 3: 60–61, PM 162–163)

Matthew Moore notes that this reflects Peirce's discovery, made early in 1896, of Cantor's Theorem, and that

> [a] corollary of that theorem – that there is no greatest multitude – transformed his theory of the continuum. His quarrel with Cantor over "all the points" comes to take the form of a requirement of what he would eventually call *supermultitudinousness:* since a continuum must contain all the points it could contain, and since there is no greatest multitude, a continuum cannot be a collection of points with a definite multitude. Closely related to this is the idea that a continuum's points lack distinct identities. Both ideas are clearly present here, but Peirce does not yet use modality to connect them in a systematic way. (PM 159)

This failure to connect continuity and modality is reflected in the definition of continuity that Peirce accepted in OQ:

> [A] *continuum* is whatever has the following properties:

1st, it is a whole composed of parts. We must define this relation. The parts are a logical aggregate of mutually exclusive subjects having a common predicate; and that aggregate regarded as a single object is the whole.

2nd, these parts form a series. That is, there is a relation, *l*, such that, taking any two of the parts, if these are not identical one of them is in the relation, *l*, to everything to which the other is in that relation and to something else besides.

3rd, taking any multitude whatever, a collection of those parts can be found whose multitude is greater than the given multitude. Consequently, the indivisible parts, that is, parts such that none is a collective aggregate of objects one of which is in the relation, *l*, to everything to which another is in that relation and to more besides, – are not distinct. That is to say, the relation *l* cannot be fully defined, so that in any attempted specification of it, *l'*, any part which appears indivisible, becomes divisible into others, by means of a further specification, *l''*. (NEM 3: 62, PM 164)

The third clause requires that the parts of a continuum not be distinct one from the others. But that is inconsistent with the first and second clauses, each of which implies that the parts of a continuum *are* distinct ("mutually exclusive subjects"; "taking any two of the parts, if these are not identical").

This problem was not resolved in LOR, the article in which he first accepted strong modal realism. Therein he wrote that "a perfectly satisfactory logical account of the conception of continuity is required" for the further development of topology (or as he preferred, "mathematical topics") (3.526), but he offered no account of continuity in LOR. A new account did, however, come shortly thereafter. In "Multitude and Number" (MAN), a manuscript (R 25) written in 1897, he again identified continuity with generality ("continuity and generality are the same thing") and illustrated that claim in a way that reflected his new commitment to strong modal realism:

When we say that of all possible throws of a pair of dice one thirty-sixth part will show sixes, the collection of possible throws which have not been made is a collection of which the individual units have no distinct identity. It is impossible so to designate a single one of those possible throws that have not been thrown that the designation shall be applicable to only one definite possible throw; and this impossibility does not spring from any incapacity of ours, but from the fact that in their own nature those throws are not individually distinct. (4.172)

"[N]ot . . . from any incapacity of ours" – and so not from the ignorance of someone in a given state of information. Our inability to designate a merely possible throw of dice is due not to a lack of knowledge but to the fact that what is merely possible lacks existence as a distinct individual entity or event.

> The possible is necessarily general; and no amount of general specification can reduce a general class of possibilities to an individual case. It is only actuality, the force of existence, which bursts the fluidity of the general and produces a discrete unit ... Time and space are continuous because they embody conditions of possibility, and the possible is general, and continuity and generality are two names for the same absence of distinction of individuals. (MAN, 4.172)

This new understanding of continuity, as involving unactualized possibility, is reflected in his characterization of a line:

> [A]lthough it is true that a line is nothing but a collection of points of a particular mode of multiplicity, yet in it the individual identities of the units are completely merged, so that not a single one of them can be identified, even approximately, unless it happen to be a topically singular point, that is, either an extremity or a point of branching, in which case there is a defect of continuity at that point.
> ... [T]rue continuity is logically absolutely repugnant to the individual designation or even approximate individual designation of its units, except at points where the character of the continuity is itself not continuous. (MAN, 4.219–220)

In other words, a continuous line is a collection of *merely possible* points having no distinct identities. A merely possible point is not a concrete individual existing at a specific place and time. A collection of such points is like the collection of possible throws of a pair of dice, none of which has a distinct identity. It is the mere possibility of the points in a line that constitutes the line's continuity. Here for the first time, no more than a year after his rejection of the IR account of substantial modality in LOR, Peirce was conceiving of continuity as the absence of distinct, actual, individual units paired with the possibility that such units can be distinguished and thus made actual.[37] What's more, the mere possibility that characterizes a continuum is a kind of generality. *Point on this line* must be

---

[37] Peirce did not think of this conception of continuity as *entirely* new. As described earlier, before 1889 he had held continuity to be Kanticity, and between 1893 and 1897, he had taken Kanticity to be a necessary, but not sufficient condition of continuity. After his acceptance of the modal conception of continuity, he came to think that Kant's definition of continuity, and thus his own concept of Kanticity, had been muddled. In 1903, he wrote that his earlier definition of continuity as Kanticity plus Aristotelicity "involves a misunderstanding of Kant's definition which *he himself* likewise fell into. Namely he defines a continuum as that all of whose parts have parts of the same kind. He himself, and I after him, understood that to mean infinite divisibility, which plainly is not what constitutes continuity" (6.168, PM 138; see also NEM 2: 482, 1904). Having cleared up this

understood as a general, like *human*. But we cannot single out a merely possible point. To designate an individual point, one must actually construct that point and thereby disrupt the continuity of the line; prior to that construction, there is no actual point to designate. The "points" of which we speak are vagues, mere possibilities: "my opponents seem to think [that] the line is composed of actual determinate points. But in my view the unoccupied points of a line are mere possibilities of points, and as such are not subject to the law of contradiction, for what merely *can be* may also *not be*" (4.640, 1908; see also 6.182, ca. 1911).

So Peirce's recognition in 1896 of a sort of possibility that could not be explained in terms of ignorance enabled a revision of his conception of continuity and then, eventually, a revision of his conception of generality, which he had begun to identify with continuity in 1893. On this new way of thinking, unactualized possibility of the sort that cannot be explained in terms of ignorance is a necessary condition of generality. This was hinted at in MAN, in which the modal conception of continuity made its debut. It is more explicit in the work in which that conception next appeared, his 1898 Cambridge Conferences lectures:

> [A] continuum is a collection of so vast a multitude that in the whole universe of possibility there is not room for them to retain their distinct identities; but they become welded into one another. Thus the continuum is all that is possible, in whatever dimension it be continuous. But the general or universal of ordinary logic also comprises whatever of a certain description is possible. And thus the *continuum* is that which the logic of relatives shows the *true* universal to be. I say the *true* universal; for no realist is so foolish as to maintain that *no* universal is a fiction.
>
> Thus, the question of nominalism and realism has taken this shape: Are any continua real? (NEM 4: 343, RLT 160)[38]

---

confusion, he came to think that his new, modal conception was roughly the same as Kant's (NEM 3: 748, ca. 1901; see also 3.569, 1900). So his rejection of the IR account of substantial possibility did not result in a wholesale revision of his previous thinking about continuity. Rather, after he rejected the IR account, he reconceived Kanticity in modal terms, distinguishing it from infinite divisibility, and adopted this new, clarified concept of Kanticity as his account of continuity.

[38] For other statements of this modal conception of continuity, see 3.568, 1900; NEM 3: 388, 1903; 6.168, 1903. For a detailed analysis of the modal account of geometrical continuity that Peirce gave in these lectures, see Putnam (1995), a slightly different version of which was published as part of Ketner and Putnam's introduction to RLT. Potter and Shields (1977), Potter (1996), Myrvold (1995), and Havenel (2008) all maintain that Peirce adopted a new conception of continuity in 1908, but while Peirce did claim to have made important progress in his thinking about continuity in that year (4.642), he seems nonetheless to have retained the modal aspect of his 1897 conception of continuity: "I define a continuum as that which may be interrupted or cut at *any* multitude of places and the parts so produced will be of the same character. Perhaps this is the same as to say that it may be divided into any multitude of parts all like the whole in every definite respect & like each other

A real general is inexhaustible, in the sense that there is no limit to the number of individual things or events of which it might be truly predicable. And any general description defines limits within which any number of individual things or events whatsoever might be distinguished. In his 1903 Harvard lectures on pragmatism, he illustrated this point with the example of the general *sun*, the reality of which requires there to be merely possible suns:

> Take any two possible objects that might be called *suns* and however much alike they may be, any multitude whatsoever of intermediate suns are alternatively possible and therefore, as before, these intermediate possible suns transcend all multitude. In short, the idea of a general involves the idea of possible variations which no multitude of existent things could exhaust but would leave between any two not merely *many* possibilities, but possibilities absolutely beyond all multitude. (5.103, EP 2: 183)

To describe a general as that the expression of which suits merely many things is to describe "a very degenerate sort of generality" (ibid.) A general term is applicable, not just to many things, but to any number of objects whatsoever. A real general is predicable, not only of a multitude greater than that of the individuals existing at any given time, but also greater than that of all individuals that will *ever* exist.

According to Peirce, he came to believe that his strong modal realism is relevant to his pragmatism only as he prepared his 1903 Harvard lectures:

> The proposition that there is a man who if *he* goes bankrupt will commit suicide is false only in case, taking any man you please, he *will* go bankrupt, and *will not* suicide. That is, it is falsified only if every man goes bankrupt without suiciding. But this is the same as the state of things under which the other proposition is false; namely, that every man goes broke while no man suicides. This reasoning is irrefragable as long as a mere possibility is treated as an absolute nullity. Some years ago, however, when in consequence of an invitation to deliver a course of lectures in Harvard University upon Pragmatism, I was led to revise that doctrine, in which I had already found difficulties, I soon discovered, upon a critical analysis, that it was absolutely necessary to insist upon and bring to the front, the truth that a mere possibility may be quite real. (4.580, 1906)[39]

---

consequently. I say that a continuum cannot be Existential as such" (1601:5, ca. 1909) – that is, that a continuum cannot be composed of actual individual parts; "there would be no actually existent points in an existent continuum, and . . . if a point were placed in a continuum it would constitute a breach of the continuity. Of course, there is a possible, or potential, point-place wherever a point might be placed" (6.182, ca. 1911).

[39] Skagestad (1981: 109–110) analyzes this passage with attention to the suicide example and how it signals a change in Peirce's interpretation of conditionals generally speaking. But he does not

As we have already seen, Peirce had explicitly maintained that "a mere possibility may be quite real" prior to 1903. So it is likely that in this 1906 passage he had in mind that strong modal realism must be insisted upon in order to resolve a problem with his original explanation of pragmatism, viz. that its pragmatic clarifications covered only actual events and thus implied that whether, e.g., the untouched diamond was hard was merely a matter of language.[40] That problem was overcome by 1905, by which time his view was that to say of a stone that it is hard is not to say something about a collection of individual events or actions in the past, or even in the future. Rather, it is to make a general claim about what would happen in the future were specific conditions met. "[I]t is a real fact that it *would* resist pressure, which amounts to extreme scholastic realism," and that "would" is inexhaustible by any multitude of actual events, just as the continuous line is inexhaustible by any multitude of individual points. (8.208, ca. 1905)[41]

> The most insignificant of general ideas always involves conditional predictions or requires for its fulfillment that events should come to pass, and all that ever can have come to pass must fall short of completely fulfilling its requirements ... I say of a stone that it is *hard*. That means that so long as

---

recognize that Peirce had explicitly embraced realism about possibility in the years prior to the 1903 Harvard lectures.

[40] Although he did not emphasize his recently acquired strong modal realism in the 1903 Harvard lectures, there are a few passages therein in which he implied that pragmatism requires the reality of the merely possible, e.g., when he characterized the pragmatic maxim as the view that "the possible practical consequences of a concept constitute the sum total of the concept" (5.27, EP 2: 139), and when he asserted that pragmatism "allows any flight of imagination, provided this imagination ultimately alights upon a possible practical effect" (5.196, EP 2: 235). Note, too, his claim that "mere possibilities are not capable of being counted" (5.169, EP 2: 215).

[41] About two years later, Peirce described himself as a "scholastic realist of a somewhat extreme stripe" (5.470, 1907). Based on these late passages, in Lane (2004) I used the phrase "extreme scholastic realism" to refer to the later version of Peirce's theory, according to which there is both real generality and real possibility. However, I no longer think it historically accurate to restrict the phrase in that way, since Peirce considered himself an "extreme" scholastic realist *before* his scholastic realism became a form of realism about possibility. According to Fisch (1986: 193), he first called his realism about generals "extreme" in R 410 (1893). There he wanted to distinguish his realism both from nominalism and from "moderate" realism, according to which there are "real" laws the being of which consists in nothing but the being of their individual cases: "[T]he nominalists are imbued with the idea that nothing is quite real but individual cases; and they do not mean, I suppose, to deny the value of ... induction, but only to deny that the Law of nature which causes it has any independent existence such as they conceive an individual case to have. The majority of realists will admit that, though not the author of this volume. He believes the law to exist substantially in the same sense in which you or I exist. But that is extreme realism and not the usual realist opinion. Realists commonly say the law exists in that the individual cases exist, and exist in a not merely accidental way; but they admit that were a law without occasions in which it could produce any individual results, the distinction between its existing and not existing would vanish. The strength of the nominalistic opinion, and the weakness of the moderate realistic opinion, lies in this, that our sense of reality comes entirely from individual experiences" (R 410: 15).

the stone remains hard, every essay to scratch it by the moderate pressure of a knife will surely fail. To call the stone *hard* is to predict that no matter how often you try the experiment, it will fail every time. That innumerable series of conditional predictions is involved in the meaning of this lowly adjective. Whatever may have been done will not begin to exhaust its meaning. (1.615, 1903)

So the *would be's* conveyed by subjunctive mood clarifications must be accompanied by *can be's*. And the possibility embodied in a *can be* is not a matter of ignorance, even the ignorance of a hypothetical being, and thus cannot be accounted for by the IR account. But as with generals, these *can be's* are not abstract individual particulars or events. Just like the points in a continuous line, the possible future events to which a subjunctive conditional refers do not constitute a collection of distinct individuals.

No wonder that Peirce came to see the IR account of possibility as nominalistic (6.367, 1902) and why he came to think the same about the pragmatism of HTM (8.208, ca. 1905; 8.216, ILS 273, 1910). Nominalism implies that there is no real generality, so any conception of possibility on which it is non-general is a nominalistic conception, even if it is nonetheless consistent with the view that possibility is real. Peirce was an avowed realist about modality before he rejected the IR account of substantial possibility; but in hindsight he came to believe that his earlier view of modality had been nominalistic, since during that time he had not maintained that possibility was a form of generality. He came to see his adoption of strong modal realism in LOR as the first point in the development of his thought at which possibility *conceived as generality* could enter. Looking back from 1905, his tychism appeared to be only a "tentative" repudiation of the nominalistic view, in comparison with his later, "quite assertoric" insistence on the reality of possibility in LOR. And it was only after that "quite assertoric insistence" that he came to think of scholastic realism as implying that there is, besides real generality, also real possibility – hence his claim that the objectivity of possibility was "*implied*" in his 1871 defense of scholastic realism (5.527, 1905). Again, Peirce never rejected the IR account outright. In the years following LOR, he characterized it as "extremely helpful up to a certain point" since it was, on his view, adequate to explain a number of different types of possibility. But he nonetheless viewed it as "superficial" (6.367, 1902) because it was inadequate as an account of the "real possibility" relevant to continuity, generality, and pragmatism.

CHAPTER 7

"A Lacuna in the Completeness of Reality": *Deficit Indeterminacy*

7.1

In 1893, Peirce wrote that "there is an assumption involved in speaking of *the* actual state of things ... namely, the assumption that reality is so determinate as to verify or falsify every possible proposition ... I do not believe it is strictly true" (NEM 3: 759–760).[1] By that time, Peirce had come to believe that some propositions about real things are such that neither they nor their denials will ever be the contents of beliefs permanently fixed by investigation, and this is due, not to investigators' cognitive shortcomings or to the ineliminable indeterminacy of signs, but to the absence of facts for those propositions to represent. As he wrote in ca. 1900, "There may be a question that no amount of research can ever answer. If so, there is a *lacuna* in the completeness of reality" (8.156). This sort of indeterminacy is neither generality nor vagueness. I will call it *deficit indeterminacy*, since it is a matter of reality being deficient.

Putting the idea more precisely, we can say the following: it is deficit indeterminate whether S is P iff (i) S is real, (ii) it is possible for a real thing to be P, but (iii) there is no fact of the matter about whether S is P or not P. Given the representational aspect of Peirce's account of truth, that it is deficit indeterminate whether S is P implies that "S is P" is neither true nor false and thus that the principle of bivalence is false. And given Peirce's view that any proposition can be expressed in subject-predicate form (2.316–318, EP 2: 279–281, 1903), this formulation should be sufficient for expressing any example of deficit indeterminacy, i.e., any example of a proposition that predicates a real property of a real subject and yet does not represent "the real as it really is" (R 655: 30, 1910). This formulation also implies that if there is deficit indeterminacy, it is an aspect of the real world. It is indeterminate whether Harry Potter is a fan of the rock band Superchunk, but this is due, not to a lacuna in reality, but to the fact that J. K. Rowling did not specify, as

---

[1] I have edited this quotation to bring to the foreground one of its central ideas. The unexpurgated passage raises other issues with which I deal in what follows, including what Peirce meant at this time by "the principle of excluded middle."

part of the fictional world that she imagined, whether Harry Potter likes Superchunk. Peirce's idea of deficit indeterminacy anticipates the work of Terence Parsons, who has argued "that … [a] question can be completely coherent and well formed and yet lack an answer because of the way the world is (or because of the way the world is not). Not that there is an unknown answer, but rather that there is no answer at all" (2000: 4). Parsons' concern is with questions about numerical identity; he argues that for some values of x and y, the world does not provide an answer to the question whether $x = y$.[2] Deficit indeterminacy is also similar to the indeterminacy that is involved in what Bradley Skow (2010) calls the orthodox interpretation of quantum mechanics.

Peirce did not always believe that there is deficit indeterminacy. His eventual recognition of it followed a period in which he was committed to a strongly optimistic view of investigation and a concomitant metaphysical doctrine: there is a true answer, and thus a real fact, corresponding to every meaningful question about real things. We encountered his optimism about investigation in Chapter 2, in the context of his defense of the pragmatic clarification of the idea of reality against the buried secrets objection. Recall that in "How to Make Our Ideas Clear" (HTM), he considered the objection that there are "minute facts of history, forgotten never to be recovered … hopelessly beyond the reach of our knowledge" (5.409, W 3: 274) and, since investigation will never permanently settle beliefs corresponding to those facts, the pragmatic clarification of reality cannot be correct: reality cannot be exactly what will be represented in the permanently settled beliefs that we will have if we use investigation in our attempt to dispel doubt. Up to that point in HTM, the clarifications with which Peirce illustrated the pragmatic maxim, including the clarification of the idea of reality, were in the indicative mood. But in responding to the buried secrets objection, he shifted to a subjunctive-mood statement of the clarification of reality: "it is unphilosophical to suppose that, with regard to

---

[2] Parsons does not note Peirce's belief that there is deficit indeterminacy, but he does describe an aspect of his own methodology as Peircean: "I begin with ordinary beliefs, which I will reject only if some reason is found to challenge them. These are my tentative data: *ordinary* beliefs – such as the belief that I have exactly one wife [and] that there is exactly one dog in my back yard" (2000: 6). Here Parsons evokes both Peirce's early exhortation that we "not pretend to doubt in philosophy what we do not doubt in our hearts" (5.265, W 2: 212, 1868) and his late statement of critical common-sensism, according to which there are "indubitable propositions" (5.440, EP 2: 347, 1905). Parsons also notes that pragmatism, which he describes as "the idea that 'the world' is whatever is revealed by scientific investigation and theorizing," is one "reasonable conception[] of what the world is like that do[es] not preclude at least some indeterminacy" (2000: 12). In this regard Parsons cites not Peirce, but Quine.

any given question (which has any clear meaning), investigation would not bring forth a solution of it, if it were carried far enough" (5.409, W 3: 274, 1878). On the subjunctive-mood clarification, x is real exactly when it *would be* represented in the permanently settled beliefs that we would have as the result of investigation, and this is consistent with there being real things that *are in fact* never represented in any actual investigator's beliefs. As we saw in Chapter 6, it was not until 1896, almost twenty years after he wrote HTM, that Peirce became a strong modal realist, and it was not until 1903 that he began to think of subjunctive-mood pragmatic clarifications as covering merely possible events. But it seems as though he still had some sense, while authoring HTM, that the move to a subjunctive-mood clarification was necessary to avoid the problem of buried secrets.

The subjunctive-mood clarification does avoid one problem posed by buried secrets: purported reals that are not represented in actual beliefs because no investigation into them is ever conducted. But as we saw in Chapter 2, it still faces another: purported facts about the past all the evidence for which has completely disappeared. Try as we might to determine how many people occupied Placentia Palace on the day of Queen Elizabeth I's birth, the evidence is now gone forever, so that even if we were to investigate no holds barred, no belief about this would ever be permanently settled. Together with the subjunctive-mood clarification, this implies that there is no fact of the matter about how many people were in the palace on that day and thus that there is deficit indeterminacy.

We also saw previously that there are at least three possible responses to this aspect of the buried secrets objection. The first is to say, *contra* the objection, that for any past fact, investigation carried far enough *would* fix relevant beliefs about that fact, so that there are no permanently buried secrets. Peirce took this optimistic view during the 1870s, and during that time he also denied that there is deficit indeterminacy: "In the ideal final opinion which would perfectly represent the reality of things, all possible doubt would be resolved. It follows that the reality is something entirely definite" (W 3: 61, 1872–1873). This is echoed in "The Doctrine of Chances," which followed HTM in the *Illustrations* series:

> Having certain premises, a man draws a certain conclusion, and as far as this inference alone is concerned the only possible practical question is whether that conclusion is true or not, and between existence and non-existence there is no middle term. "Being only is and nothing is altogether not," said Parmenides; and this is in strict accordance with the analysis of the conception of reality given in [HTM, viz. the pragmatic clarification]. For we found that the distinction of reality and fiction depends on the supposition

that sufficient investigation would cause one opinion to be universally received and all others to be rejected. That presupposition involved in the very conceptions of reality and figment involves a complete sundering of the two. It is the heaven-and-hell idea in the domain of thought. (2.650, W 3: 280, 1878)

The second response is to revise the subjunctive-mood clarification so that the real includes what is represented in beliefs that would have been fixed by investigation had it been conducted at a time before the relevant evidence disappeared. As noted in Chapter 2, Peirce endorsed this view very late, in 1911 (EP 2: 457), after he had become an avowed realist about *would be's*, as described in Chapter 6. The third possible response is to grant that, as the objection maintains, there *are* questions that investigation would never answer and that there is therefore deficit indeterminacy. To my knowledge, Peirce never explicitly deployed this answer as a riposte to the buried secrets objection. But as I demonstrate in this chapter, it is nonetheless the position he took beginning in the 1880s – or, rather, it is *close* to the position he took. Here the distinction between questions that *would* never be answered and questions that *will* never be answered is crucial, as we will see.

Unfortunately, Peirce never developed a treatment of the subject of deficit indeterminacy of any significant length. His references to it are numerous, but they are brief and strewn across several different works; perhaps this is why most scholars of his thought have overlooked the subject.[3] What's more, his view of the subject is intertwined with his positions on several other issues, including the evolution of the universe, continuity, and the reality of the merely possible. To get clear on the historical development of this corner of Peirce's metaphysics requires understanding how his views on these matters shifted and intersected. Further complicating things is the fact that his reason for recognizing deficit indeterminacy changed over time. He began by seeing it as described earlier: a consequence of the conjunction of his pragmatic clarification of reality and a less than fully optimistic view about the power of investigation to settle all meaningful questions. But as I will argue, his understanding of these matters was clouded by his failure, described in Chapters 2 and 6, to see, before the early 1900s, that there is an important difference between indicative- and subjunctive-mood pragmatic clarifications. Once he overcame that problem, he was no longer motivated by the pragmatic clarification of reality to recognize deficit indeterminacy. But he continued to recognize it nonetheless. My account of Peirce's thinking

---

[3] I know of only two who have even briefly acknowledged it: Sandra Rosenthal (2004: 211) and Lesley Friedman (1997: 256, n. 8).

on these issues is not exhaustive. I do not attempt to trace every relevant thread, to incorporate every relevant claim, or to reconcile every tension there might be within the relevant works.[4] My goal in this concluding chapter is more modest: an interpretation of some of what Peirce had to say regarding unanswerable questions and reality.

As a preamble to this interpretation, I need to address Christopher Hookway's view that Peirce eventually distanced his account of reality from his account of truth and that he did so in order to maintain that there can be real facts about a subject even when investigation would never settle questions about it. If Hookway is correct, then my interpretation cannot be, since it is part of my view that Peirce was, from the 1880s until the early 1900s, driven to recognize deficit indeterminacy because he continued to think of the real as exactly what is represented in a true belief. In the following section, I show that Hookway is mistaken: Peirce continued closely associating the ideas of truth and reality into the last years of his life.

7.2

Hookway writes that "truth and reality were less intimately connected [in Peirce's writings] after 1880" (2012: 63) and that Peirce continued to accept what Hookway calls his "convergence thesis" about truth (roughly, what I have characterized as the investigative aspect of his dual-aspect account of truth), but no longer thought of the real as that which is represented in a true proposition.[5] But the textual evidence shows that Peirce repeatedly endorsed the pragmatic clarification of reality – according to which the real is what will be (or, on his considered view, what would be) represented in a true belief, i.e., a belief permanently settled by investigation – during and after the 1880s. For example, Peirce wrote in "Design and Chance" that the claim that *"real things exist . . .* comes to the same thing as [the claim] that every intelligible question whatever is susceptible in its own nature of receiving a definitive and satisfactory answer, if it be sufficiently investigated by observation and reasoning" (W 4: 545–546, 1883–1884). And in his review of Josiah Royce's *The Religious Aspect of Philosophy*, he said that

---

[4] In particular, I am setting aside Peirce's assertions that reality is a matter of degree. See 2.532, 1893; 7.569, EP 2: 2, 1893; R 955, 1.175, 1893; R 939: 27, 1905; R 1041: 15, 1905; R 498: 32, ca. 1906. He seems to have abandoned this view by 1909; see R 642: 10.

[5] As noted in Chapter 5, Misak agrees with Hookway on this point (1991/2004: 186). Atkin makes a similar claim (2016: 104ff.).

reality, the fact that there is such a thing as a true answer to a question, consists in this: that human inquiries, – human reasoning and observation, – tend toward the settlement of disputes and ultimate agreement in definite conclusions which are independent of the particular stand-points from which the different inquirers may have set out; so that the real is that which any man would believe in, and be ready to act upon, if his investigations were to be pushed sufficiently far. (8.41, W 5: 222, 1885)

There are many later passages in which he reiterated the connection between reality and truth:

> A fact is so much of the reality as is represented in a single *proposition*. If a proposition is true, that which it represents is a *fact*. (6.67, RLT 198, 1898)

> By a *reality*, I mean anything represented in a true proposition. (NEM 3: 773, 1900)

> [W]hat is that "object" which serves to define truth? Why it is the *reality*: it is of such a nature as to be independent of representations of it, so that, taking any individual sign or any individual collection of signs (such, for example, as all the ideas that ever enter into a given man's head) there is some character which that thing possesses, whether that sign or any of the signs of that collection represents the thing as possessing that character or not. (1.578, ca. 1902–1903)

> On pragmatistic principles *reality* can mean nothing except the *truth* of statements in which the real thing is asserted. (NEM 4: 162, PM 73, 1903)

> [T]he state of things which will be believed in th[e] ultimate opinion is real. (5.430, EP 2: 342–343, 1905)

> [*T*]*ruth* ... is obviously the character of a representation of the real as it really is. (R 655: 30, 1910)[6]

Hookway cites two passages in support of his view that Peirce eventually separated truth and reality. The first is from "A Syllabus of Certain Topics of Logic," which Peirce composed in 1903 as a companion to his Lowell lectures:[7]

> [E]very proposition is either *true* or *false*. It is false if any proposition could be legitimately deduced from it, without any aid from false propositions, which would conflict with a direct perceptual judgment, could such be had. A proposition is true, if it is not false. Hence, an entirely meaningless form

---

[6] For more examples, see 3.460, 1897; HP 1123–1124, ca. 1899; 6.173, 1902; 5.211, EP 2: 240, 1903; 5.432, EP 2: 343, 1905; R 290: 31–32, 1905; R 322: 21, 1907; 3.527, n. 1, 1908; R 681: 35–37, 1913.

[7] Selections 18–21 in EP 2 are drawn from this Syllabus. See the editorial introduction to selection 18 (EP 2: 258) for more information.

of proposition, if it be called a proposition, at all, is to be classed along with true propositions. (EP 2: 284–285)

Hookway says that although this passage

> is closely related to the truth as convergence thesis, it is formulated as a definition of falsity: truth is then defined as anything that cannot be refuted. Since Peirce would not want to conclude that the object of 'an entirely meaningless form of proposition' is real, his flirtation with this strategy – even if only briefly – suggests that he is questioning the idea that the object of any true proposition is real. Second, the definition is flawed. The qualifications introduced in his explanation of falsity suggest that he was aware that widespread ignorance or error in our background beliefs might prove a permanent obstacle to the convergence of opinion. But to try to repair his account by saying that our refuting (or failing to refute) some proposition must not depend upon any false propositions renders his explanation of *falsity* circular. (2012: 63)

But it is not obvious that Peirce intended his claims to be definitions of "falsity" and "truth." He may have been stating what he took to be facts about true and false propositions given his dual-aspect account of truth. Again, that account says, on the one hand, that a true proposition is one that represents the world as it really is, and on the other, that a true proposition is one that would be permanently believed as a result of investigation. Suppose that p implies q, either alone or in conjunction with other propositions none of which is false. Further suppose that q contradicts r, which is the content of a direct perceptual judgment. On the assumption that r is true, i.e., that r accurately represents the world and would be permanently believed as a result of investigation, and assuming that no proposition can be both true and false, then q, and therefore p, must be false, i.e., neither p nor q accurately represents reality, and neither would be permanently believed as a result of investigation. If I am right that Peirce was not defining "truth" and "falsity" in the quoted passage, then what he said about falsity need not rely in an objectionably circular way on the qualification about which Hookway complains.

The final sentence of the "Syllabus" passage is more compelling as evidence that Peirce was entertaining an account of truth that distances it from reality. A meaningless proposition would be one that failed to represent at all, and so it would not represent reality; what's more, it could not serve as the content of a belief – or, at least, it is unclear what it would be to believe a meaningless proposition. And so it is unclear how a meaningless proposition could live up to either aspect of Peirce's dual-aspect account of truth. But it is not just his account of truth that he seems to have abandoned here. Given his view that a proposition is a sign, it is not clear how he could countenance a *meaningless* proposition *at all*. Note, though, that Peirce wrote "*if* it be called a proposition." Given that he understood propositions to be signs, it is, I think, likely that he did not intend that condition to be fulfilled. And as Hookway himself notes, the passage "is taken from a manuscript and thus may not represent a lasting theme in Peirce's thought" (2012: 63).

Hookway finds what he believes to be "decisive evidence of [Peirce's] abandoning his analysis of reality," i.e., the pragmatic clarification of reality, in the Baldwin's *Dictionary* entry entitled "Truth and Falsity and Error." He says that therein,

> [t]ruth is still explained in terms of convergence: "Truth is that concordance of an abstract statement with the ideal limit towards which endless investigation would tend to bring scientific belief" (CP 5.565). Reality is now explained as "that mode of being by virtue of which the real thing is as it is, irrespectively of what any mind or definite collection of minds may represent it to be" (CP 5.565). (2012: 63)

The first quoted passage expresses the investigative aspect of Peirce's account of truth, and the second is a statement of his verbal definition of "reality." That he stated them both in this entry is no evidence that he had abandoned his pragmatic clarification of reality, which, as we saw in Chapter 2, he held to be consistent with his verbal definition of "reality." In fact, Peirce alluded to his pragmatic clarification in this same entry:

> The truth of the proposition that Caesar crossed the Rubicon consists in the fact that the further we push our archaeological and other studies, the more strongly will that conclusion force itself on our minds forever – or would do so, if study were to go on forever. An idealist metaphysician may hold that therein also lies the whole *reality* behind the proposition; for though men may for a time persuade themselves that Caesar did *not* cross the Rubicon, and may contrive to render this belief universal for any number of generations, yet ultimately research – if it be persisted in – must bring back the contrary belief. But in holding that doctrine, the idealist necessarily draws the distinction between truth and reality. (5.565, 1902)

As we saw in Chapter 3, the pragmatic clarification of reality implies Peirce's basic idealism, according to which anything real can be an object of belief. Hence, "an idealist metaphysician" may hold that the reality of an object amounts to its being represented in a true proposition. Peirce himself was such an idealist metaphysician.

Having established that, *contra* Hookway, Peirce did not distance his account of truth from his account of reality, I turn in the following section to the evidence that he acknowledged deficit indeterminacy. As we will see, the idea that there might be "a lacuna in the completeness of reality" emerged as he was first working out the details of his evolutionary cosmology.

7.3

Peirce's first, hesitant step toward recognizing deficit indeterminacy occurred in "Design and Chance" (DC):

> What I propose to do . . . is . . . to call in question the perfect accuracy of the fundamental axiom of logic.
> This axiom is that *real things exist* or in other words, what comes to the same thing, that every intelligible question whatever is susceptible in its own nature of receiving a definitive and satisfactory answer, if it be sufficiently investigated by observation and reasoning. (W 4: 545–546, 1883–1884)

Given his pragmatic clarification of reality, to say that "real things exist"[8] is to imply that there are things that would be represented in beliefs permanently settled by investigation – hence his equating the "axiom" with the claim that all meaningful questions can be settled by investigation. After commenting that "different logicians would state the axiom differently," he proceeded to question a "familiar" formulation of it, viz., that "*every event has a cause*" (DC, W 4: 546).[9] This is an early appearance of Peirce's tychism (although he did not yet call it by that name), according to which absolute chance is real and from which it follows that some events occur without having been caused to occur – or, at least, without having been caused to occur in a strictly lawful manner. Were it the case that every fact *had* been brought about in a lawful manner, then "every fact [would have] an explanation, a reason," including the particular fact that a given law obtains and "the general fact that there are laws" at all (DC, W 4: 547). But the general fact that there are laws cannot be explained by way of reference to anything that itself behaves in a completely lawful way, hence Peirce's conjecture that the universe's present lawfulness, its orderliness and generality, must have been preceded by a lesser degree of lawfulness and a greater degree of disorder.

> We ought to suppose that as we go back into the indefinite past not merely special laws but *law* itself is found to be less and less determinate. And how can that be if causation was always as rigidly necessary as it is now?

---

[8] Here Peirce was using "exist" in the looser, nontechnical way noted in previous chapters.

[9] "One, Two, Three," a manuscript written in the summer of 1886, opens with the same point about doubting axioms and raises as an example the axiom "that every thing that happens is completely determined by exact laws" (W 5: 293).

> . . . That very postulate of logic whose rigid accuracy I call in question,
> itself demands that every determinate fact shall have an explanation, and
> there is no reason in making any exception. Now among the determinate
> facts which ought thus to be explained is the very fact supposed in this
> postulate. This must also be explained, must be among the things which
> have been somehow brought about. How then can it be absolutely, rigidly
> & immoveably true? (DC, W 4: 548)

That is, how can it be explained that every meaningful question is capable of
being answered by investigation? How can it be explained that "real things
exist"? The implication is that these facts *cannot* be explained, not because
they have always obtained, but because, given the way the universe was
before they did obtain, there are simply no explanations of them. It is not
that the pertinent evidence is now lost to us; it is not that the answers are
buried secrets never to be unearthed. It is that there is not, and never was,
anything there to unearth. There is, in other words, deficit indeterminacy.[10]

But despite his avowed desire to call into question the axiom that "real
things exist," at this point Peirce pulled back from an explicit recognition
of deficit indeterminacy. Instead of saying outright that some facts are
completely inexplicable and that there are thus meaningful but unanswerable questions, he maintained that everything *is* explicable, albeit "not
absolutely" so.

> [T]he hypothesis of absolute chance is part and parcel of the hypothesis that
> everything is explicable, not absolutely, rigidly without the smallest inex-
> actitude or sporadic exception, for that is a self-contradictory supposition[,]
> but yet explicable in a general way. Explicability has no determinate &
> absolute limit. Everything being explicable, everything has been brought
> about; and consequently everything is subject to change and subject to
> chance. (DC, W 4: 549)

> Now I will suppose that all known laws are due to chance and repose upon
> others far less rigid themselves due to chance and so on in an infinite regress,
> the further we go back the more indefinite being the nature of the laws, and
> in this way we see the possibility of an indefinite approximation toward a
> complete explanation of nature. (DC, W 4: 551–552)

Because there is real absolute chance, not every event can be explained in a
completely determinate fashion; but for any given event, at least an approx-
imate explanation is possible. So Peirce's skepticism regarding the axiom that
"real things exist" did not immediately lead him to recognize deficit

---

[10] Hookway (2000: 178) offers an alternative account of Peirce's different formulations of the "fundamental axiom of logic."

indeterminacy. What's more, he wrote that "[a]s far as all ordinary and practical questions go I insist upon this axiom as much as ever, – as much as anybody can do" (DC, W 4: 546). We will see that, even when he came to explicitly recognize deficit indeterminacy, he insisted that that recognition should not affect our actual investigative practices.

7.4

That explicit recognition came in his 1885 review of Royce's *The Religious Aspect of Philosophy*. Therein he dramatically tempered the strong investigative optimism of HTM and other earlier works. He had maintained in HTM that "in no possible state of knowledge can any number be great enough to express the relation between the amount of what rests unknown to the amount of the known" (5.409, W 3: 274, 1878). While this excludes the possibility of a time at which *every* truth will have been discovered – as he had written a few years earlier, "we shall never know the true answer to every question" (W 3: 57, 1872) – it is consistent with the claim that for *any* given truth, belief in that truth will eventually be fixed. It is also consistent with his claim in the 1885 Royce review (RR) that we are justified, because of our past success in settling questions by way of investigation, in being optimistic about its power to fix beliefs that are actually or potentially "practical" (8.43, W 5: 227). What was new in this review was the idea that some questions will *in fact* never be answered:

> [T]he number of questions asked is constantly increasing, and the capacity for answering them is also on the increase . . . [T]he rate of the latter increase is greater than that of the former . . . In [this] case, there is but an infinitesimal proportion of questions which do not get answered, although the multitude of unanswered questions is forever on the increase . . . I will admit (if the reader thinks the admission has any meaning, and is not an empty proposition) that some finite number of questions, we can never know which ones, will escape getting answered forever. (RR, 8.43, W 5: 227)

When paired with the subjunctive-mood clarification of reality understood as including merely possible instances of investigation, this does not imply that there is deficit indeterminacy. But despite his intermittent use of the subjunctive mood during this time to state pragmatic clarifications, including that of reality, Peirce was not yet a strong modal realist and did not yet understand pragmatic clarifications, even when stated in the subjunctive mood, as covering unactualized possibilities. This, I believe, is why, at this time, he *did* believe that the claim that some questions *will* never be answered implies that there is deficit indeterminacy:

> Let us suppose . . . for the sake of argument, that some questions eventually
> get settled, and that some others, indistinguishable from the former by any
> marks, never do . . . [W]hile there is a real so far as a question that will get
> settled goes, there is none for a question that will never be settled. (RR, 8.43,
> W 5: 227–228)[11]

There are questions that investigation will never answer, and so there are
no facts that count as answers to those questions. Peirce went on to echo an
idea from DC, that if a question will never be settled by investigation, it is
due to an absence of lawfulness or generality.

> [I]f nothing is ever settled about [a given] matter, it will be because the
> phenomena do not consistently point to any theory; and in that case there is
> a want of that "uniformity of nature" (to use a popular but very loose
> expression) which constitutes reality, and makes it differ from a dream. In
> that way, if we think that some questions are never going to get settled, we
> ought to admit that our conception of nature as absolutely real is only
> partially correct. (RR, 8.43, W 5: 228)[12]

Misak quotes the first sentence of this passage and replaces the first "is" with
"would be" in order to represent Peirce's more considered view; as she
correctly notes, in 1885 "Peirce was not yet a committed realist about dispositions" (1991/2004: 155, n. 33). But the "is" that Misak replaces is important. A
proper diagnosis of his emerging commitment to deficit indeterminacy
requires that we keep in plain view the fact that at this time he did not yet
understand pragmatic clarifications as covering merely possible circumstances.
Again, I believe that this is why he took the fact that some questions will never
actually be settled by investigation to imply that there is deficit indeterminacy.
Had he understood the pragmatic clarification of reality as covering merely
possible instances of investigation, he could have taken his less optimistic view
about investigation without concluding that there are lacunae in reality.

---

[11] He went on to assert that this shows that "scepticism about the reality of things" – by which he
apparently meant the view that there are real things of which we can have no knowledge – is a defective
"conception of reality . . . for an unknowable reality is nonsense" (RR, 8.43, W 5: 227–228). Meyers
(1985: 228), Hookway (2000: 179), and Apel (2004: 3, n. 13) all mistakenly read this passage to mean that
if there are questions that inquiry will never settle, then Peirce's own conception of reality – what I have
called his pragmatic clarification – is defective.

[12] Meyers (2005: 336) misunderstands Peirce's statement about nature not being absolutely real: "[H]e
also retreats from his position that *every* question will be answered in the long run and admits that
some finite number of questions may remain unanswered. He says that if this is the case, 'we ought
to admit that our conception of nature as absolutely real is only partially correct,' although we will
'have to be governed by it practically.' But it is not clear why pragmatism is 'only partially correct'
and is not just false." *Contra* Meyers, it is not pragmatism that Peirce described as "only partially
correct," or even his pragmatic clarification of reality, but the claim that nature is "absolutely real."
And that idea is "only partially correct," not completely false, in that much of nature – aspects of
nature that correspond to true beliefs – *is* real.

Interestingly, in RR just as in DC, Peirce maintained that we should proceed as if there is a real answer to every meaningful question: "we shall have to be governed by it" – i.e., by the assumption that nature is absolutely real – "practically; because there is nothing to distinguish the unanswerable questions from the answerable ones, so that investigation will have to proceed as if all were answerable" (RR, 8.43, W 5: 228). The ratio of questions that will never get answered to those that will is "infinitesimal" – although, given the total number of meaningful questions, this is consistent with there being an enormous number of meaningful questions that will never get answered. Since there is no way to tell which sort of question is which, we should assume that investigation *will* eventually settle any question that we actually investigate.

Peirce's commitment to deficit indeterminacy seems to have weakened a bit between RR and "A Guess at the Riddle" (GAR, 1887–1888). Here he revisited the cosmogonical ideas of DC, arguing that the general fact that there is real lawfulness can be explained, "and since Law in general cannot be explained by any law in particular, the explanation must consist in showing how law is developed out of pure chance, irregularity, and indeterminacy" (1.407, W 6: 207). Our present concern, however, is not the explanation Peirce offered – his "guess at the riddle"[13] – but the evolution of his views about investigation and deficit indeterminacy. Here he maintained that the indeterminacy from which the orderly universe emerged is not something about which we can ask intelligible questions, because it is, quite literally, *not a thing*: "The original chaos, ... where there was no regularity, was in effect a state of mere indeterminacy, in which nothing existed or really happened" (GAR, 1.411, W 6: 209); it is "a point in the infinitely distant past when there was no law but mere indeterminacy" (GAR, 1.409, W 6: 208). But the lawful world that, on Peirce's account, sprang from that original nothing *is* something – it is real – and we can ask meaningful questions about it. Deficit indeterminacy obtains when there *is* something to ask a question about but the world affords no answer. In RR his view had been that there definitely are such questions; in GAR it was only that there "may be."

---

[13] In brief, his explanation was that there has always been a tendency of habit-taking in the world: "It is a generalizing tendency; it causes actions in the future to follow some generalization of past actions; and this tendency is itself something capable of similar generalization; and thus, it is self-generative. We have therefore only to suppose the smallest spur of it in the past, and that germ would have been bound to develop into a mighty and over-ruling principle, until it supersedes itself by strengthening habits into absolute laws regulating the action of all things in every respect in the indefinite future" (GAR, 1.409, W 6: 208).

But just as in RR, Peirce insisted in GAR that we must assume – or as he there began to put it, to "hope"[14] – that, with regard to any matter actually investigated, the questions we raise can in fact be settled:

> [E]very fact of a general or orderly nature calls for an explanation; and logic forbids us to assume in regard to any given fact of that sort that it is of its own nature absolutely inexplicable. This is what Kant calls a regulative principle, that is to say, an intellectual hope. The sole immediate purpose of thinking is to render things intelligible; and to think and yet in that very act to think a thing unintelligible is a self-stultification ... True, there may be facts that will never get explained; but that any given fact is of the number, is what experience can never give us reason to think; far less can it show that any fact is of its own nature unintelligible. We must therefore be guided by the rule of hope, and consequently we must reject every philosophy or general conception of the universe which could ever lead to the conclusion that any given general fact is an ultimate one. We must look forward to the explanation, not of all things, but of any given thing whatever. (GAR, 1.405, W 6: 206)

Peirce expressed this hope repeatedly during the 1890s. For example, he wrote in his "Reply to the Necessitarians" that

> [w]e cannot be quite sure that the community ever will settle down to an unalterable conclusion upon any given question. Even if they do so for the most part, we have no reason to think the unanimity will be quite complete, nor can we rationally presume any overwhelming *consensus* of opinion will be reached upon every question. All that we are entitled to assume is in the form of a *hope* that such conclusion may be substantially reached concerning the particular questions with which our inquiries are busied. (6.610, 1893)

That he understood this hope to be different from the strong optimism he had expressed in the 1870s is suggested by some of the revisions he made to HTM when he planned to include it in a book-length project: first *A Quest for a Method*, a.k.a. *A Search for a Method* (1893), and then *How to Reason*, a.k.a. *Grand Logic* (1894).[15] In 1893, he revised a portion of HTM (W 3: 273) as follows:

---

[14] Years earlier, Peirce had described a hope about the ultimate outcome of investigation, but it was not the assumption, made about a given question actually investigated, that that question might finally be settled. It was instead the hope that the community of all investigators will at some future time "arrive at a state of information greater than some definite finite information ... This infinite hope ... is something so august and momentous, that all reasoning in reference to it is a trifling impertinence" (5.357, W 2: 271–272, 1869).

[15] On the history of these two projects, see ILS 15–18.

[A]ll the followers of science are ~~fully persuaded~~ **animated by a cheerful hope** that the processes of investigation, if only pushed far enough, will give one certain solution to ~~every~~ **each** question to which they ~~can be applied~~ **apply it** ... No modification of the point of view taken, no selection of other facts for study, no natural bent of mind even, can enable a man to escape the predestinate opinion. This great ~~law~~ **hope** is embodied in the conception of truth and reality. The opinion which is fated to be ultimately agreed to by all who investigate, is what we mean by the truth, and the object represented in this opinion is the real. That is the way I would explain reality. (5.407)[16]

By the time Peirce wrote the passage with which this chapter began – a fragment from *A Quest for a Method* – he had apparently regained the confidence about deficit indeterminacy that he evinced in RR. A fuller quotation of that passage than the one given previously reveals that he connected deficit indeterminacy with what he then called "the principle of excluded middle":

[T]here is an assumption involved in speaking of *the* actual state of things ... namely, the assumption that reality is so determinate as to verify or falsify every possible proposition. This is called the *principle of excluded middle*. I do not believe it is strictly true ... But ... logic does not inquire into the truth of premises. It is convenient, not only in a practical but in a philosophical sense, to commence with the study of arguments which assume such an absolutely determinate state of things, without ourselves asserting that such a state is quite realized. (NEM 3: 759–760, 1893)[17]

---

[16] Perhaps it was this change that Peirce later described in *Minute Logic*: "[W]hen we discuss a vexed question, we *hope* that there is some ascertainable truth about it, and that the discussion is not to go on forever and to no purpose. A transcendentalist would claim that it is an indispensable 'presupposition' that there is an ascertainable true answer to every intelligible question. I used to talk like that, myself; for when I was a babe in philosophy my bottle was filled from the udders of Kant. But by this time I have come to want something more substantial" (2.113, ca. 1902).

[17] Peirce expressed similar views in an undated manuscript: "Logic requires us, with reference to each question we have in hand, to hope some definite answer to it may be true. That *hope* with reference to *each case* as it comes up is, by a *saltus*, stated by logicians as a *law* concerning *all cases*, namely, the law of excluded middle. This law amounts to saying that the [universe] has a perfect reality" (NEM 4: xiii). The transcription of this passage in NEM has "inverse" rather than "universe," but that does not make much sense, so I strongly suspect that the transcription is mistaken and that Peirce in fact wrote "universe." I have not been able to confirm this suspicion by checking what Peirce actually wrote. NEM indicates that the passage is from R 140, but that is incorrect; this passage does not occur in that manuscript, and I have not been able to identify its actual source. Hookway (2000: 153) quotes part of this passage, but his treatment of Peirce on bivalence and PEM is marred by a misunderstanding of what Peirce meant by "vagueness" and "excluded middle." He writes that "Peirce seems to insist that vagueness is a source of counterexamples to the law of excluded middle" (2000: 152), but as we saw in Chapter 6, Peirce held that PEM *does* apply to the vague (what it does not apply to is, on Peirce's view, the general).

Peirce had not yet begun to use "principle of excluded middle" to mean "the principle that no pair of mutually contradictory predicates are both false of any individual subject" (R 611: 13, 1908); so far as I am aware, he first used it in that sense in ca. 1896 (1.434). Before that time, what he called "the principle of excluded middle" is what we now call the principle of bivalence (PB), the principle that "[e]very proposition is either true or false" (W 4:241, NEM 3: 752, 1881).[18] Interestingly, in the just-quoted passage from *Quest*, Peirce used "principle of excluded middle" to mean, not simply PB, but the claim that "reality is so determinate as to verify or falsify every possible proposition," i.e., that there is no deficit indeterminacy. Reality is indeterminate such that there are meaningful questions that investigation will – or would?; Peirce is unclear – never settle and thus propositions that are neither true nor false.

From the 1880s into the 1900s, Peirce frequently stated that every proposition *is* either true or false.[19] This can be squared with his recognition of deficit indeterminacy and his claim that "the law of excluded middle" – PB – is not "strictly" true by noting that most of his statements in support of PB occurred in the context of his work in formal or informal logic and so can be read, not as evidence that he took PB to be universally true, but as statements of a principle provisionally assumed by classical logic. As he said in the recently quoted passage, the assumption of PB is both practically and philosophically "convenient." Before his first explicit commitment to deficit indeterminacy in 1885, he wrote that PB

> gives a very poor kind of logic, – one which is true indeed but which goes very little way. Because in all mathematical reasoning we do not merely distinguish the true & the false, lumping all that is not true in one indistinguishable mass as though it were equally valueless, but we recognize that though a proposition be false it may have a certain value if it is not *very* false, – and indeed wherever continuity comes in, and here alone the mathematical logic is fully developed, no real proposition is exactly true, – so that the question is *how* false a proposition is. This remark I repeat in season and out, that there may be no mistake about

---

[18] For other uses of "principle of excluded middle" or "law of excluded middle" to mean PB, see W 1: 170, 175, 1865; W 4: 256, 1881; W 4: 490, 1883; W 5: 355, 357–358, 1886; W 6: 4, 1886; NEM 3: 758, 1893; 2.352, ca. 1896. Peirce sometimes stated the principle, not in terms of propositions and their truth values, but in terms of the subject and predicate terms of propositions, e.g., "The law of excluded third is that *A* is either *B* or not-*B*" (W 1: 228, NEM 3:317, 1865). In still other works, he equated the two statements of the principle, writing, for example, that "the so-called *Principle of Excluded Middle* . . . is that every proposition is either true or false, (or *A* is either *B* or not-*B*)" (W 8: 74, NEM 3: 277, ca. 1890).

[19] For examples, see W 4: 264, 1881–1882; 3.365, W 5: 166, 1885; 6: 269, 1889; W 8: 65, ca. 1890; W 8: 71, ca. 1890; W 8: 210, 1891; EP 2: 284, 1903.

my view of the paucity of the old logic which however is absolutely true
as far as it pretends to go. (W 4: 490, 1883)

Later, in another fragment from *Quest*, he wrote that

[t]o speak of *the* actual state of things implies a great assumption,
namely that there is a perfectly definite body of propositions which, if
we could only find them out, are the truth, and that everything is really
either true or in positive conflict with the truth. This assumption, called
the principle of excluded middle, I consider utterly unwarranted, and do
not believe it. Still, I hold that there is reason for thinking it to be very
nearly true. (NEM 3: 758, 1893)

Why "very nearly true" but not "strictly true"? Perhaps because, as he had
insisted in RR, even though the number of questions that will never be
answered is enormous, the proportion of those questions to those that
investigation *will* settle is infinitesimal. This would warrant continuing to
assume PB in his work in both informal and formal logic. We will see later,
though, that in 1909 he was motivated to begin working on a formal logic
that allowed for a third truth value.

Peirce's thinking about indeterminacy and investigative hope took
another interesting turn in material written for *How to Reason*. There the
hope seems not to be just that any actual investigation will eventually result
in permanently settled beliefs; it seems to be, rather, that basic realism itself
is true.

The commodious and compact representation in our minds, or icon of our
hopes about beliefs[,] is that there is something fixed and not subject to our
wills called the *reality*, and that our beliefs come to shape themselves more
and more under experience in conformity to that reality. So far as they
accord with it we call them *true*. This is a handy ideal, – this of reality; – but
it represents nothing but a hope. We have no warrant for averring that belief
of all kinds will get more and more fixed, nor that belief of any kind will get
more and more fixed until its variations become indefinitely small. We
simply try to fix belief, and trying to do anything implies a hope that one
shall to some extent succeed. The pretence of some philosophers that there
is any justification for a broader "presupposition" than that is unfounded.
(R 408: 146–147, 1893)

Earlier, the hope that Peirce had urged was simply that an investigation
actually pursued will lead to a settled belief. That we cannot know for sure
that that will be the outcome of any specific course of investigation does
not justify doubt about there being real things, i.e., it does not warrant
skepticism about basic realism. So it is striking that Peirce came to think of
basic realism itself as something that we must hope to be true.

These intertwining ideas – that there is, or may be, deficit indetermi-nacy, and that we must assume either that investigation actually pursued will permanently settle belief or even that there are real things to be investigated at all – recur in other writings dating from the mid-1890s to the early 1900s. In 1893's "Immortality in the Light of Synechism," Peirce wrote that

> to say that a thing *is* is to say that in the upshot of intellectual progress it will attain a permanent status in the realm of ideas. Now, as no experiential question can be answered with absolute certainty, so we never can have reason to think that any given idea will either become unshakably estab-lished or be forever exploded. But to say that neither of these two events will come to pass definitively is to say that the object has an imperfect and qualified existence. (7.569, EP 2: 2)

In a manuscript of ca. 1895, he put the point in terms of the "compulsion" by which reality might steer the thinking of investigators toward true thoughts. If we attempt to fix our beliefs by way of investigation, the world will eventually force us away from some beliefs and toward others; our minds will be compelled by experience and reasoning toward a com-mon set of beliefs. But if our hope that we will eventually arrive at that "same result"

> is altogether vain, if there is no such compulsion, or externality, then there is no true knowledge at all and reasoning is altogether idle. If the hope is destined only partially to be realized, then there is an approximate reality and truth, which is not exact. (R 735: 3–4 alternative run of pages)

The language of approximation is echoed in 1896's "The Regenerated Logic":

> [A]s to an inquiry presupposing that there is some one truth, what can this possibly mean except it be that there is one destined upshot to inquiry with reference to the question in hand – one result, which when reached will never be overthrown? Undoubtedly, we hope that this, *or something approx-imating to this*, is so, or we should not trouble ourselves to make the inquiry. But we do not necessarily have much confidence that it *is* so. Still less need we think it is so about the *majority* of the questions with which we concern ourselves. (3.432)

Peirce once again characterized basic realism as a hope in the Cambridge Conferences lectures of 1898:

> What is reality? Perhaps there isn't any such thing at all. As I have repeatedly insisted, it is but a retroduction, a working hypothesis which we try, our one desperate forlorn hope of knowing anything. Again it may be, and it would seem very bold to hope for anything better, that the hypothesis of reality

though it answers pretty well, does not perfectly correspond to what is. (NEM 4: 343, RLT 161; see also 6.189, RLT 257)

This is consistent with his well-known exhortation from those same lectures: "**Do not block the way of inquiry** ... [T]o set up a philosophy which barricades the road of further advance toward the truth is the one unpardonable offense in reasoning" (1.135–136, EP 2: 48, RLT 178–179). One way to impede investigation is to assume that some fact or phenomenon is inexplicable. The only sort of inference that could possibly justify this is what he called a "retroduction," i.e., an inference to a possible explanation. "Now nothing justifies a retroductive inference except its affording an explanation of the facts. It is, however, no explanation at all of a fact to pronounce it *inexplicable*. That therefore is a conclusion which no reasoning can ever justify or excuse" (1.139, EP 2: 49, RLT 180). This injunction against positing the inexplicable is supposed to apply to any *specific* thing, state, or event. One can acknowledge that there are things about which investigation will not, or might not, ever settle belief, but this is an impermissible move with regard to any specific avenue of investigation. This reading is supported by the fact that in the years just following the Cambridge lectures, he continued to emphasize not only the investigative hope that a given question, actually pursued, will eventually be answered[20] but also the possibility that there is deficit indeterminacy:

> [E]very scientific research goes upon the assumption, the hope, that, in reference to its particular question, there is some true answer. That which that truth represents is a reality.
> ... [A]ccording to my notions there can be no mystery in the universe, in the sense of a real fact to which no approach to knowledge can ever be gained. For a reality is an idea that insists upon proclaiming itself, whether we like it or not. There may be a question that no amount of research can ever answer. If so, there is a *lacuna* in the completeness of reality. (8.153, 156, ca. 1900; see also 5.565, 1902)

7.5

So far as I have been able to discover, there is no textual evidence that Peirce continued to infer that there is deficit indeterminacy from his pragmatic clarification of reality after 1903. As mentioned previously, I suspect that this had to do with his evolving understanding of the pragmatic maxim.

---

[20] See R 1519, NEM 4: xii, undated but no earlier than 1900; 7.219, EP 2: 107, 1901; 5.609, 1901; 7.669, 1903; NEM 3: 1055, ca. 1903.

According to his own testimony (4.580, 1906), it was in the process of writing his 1903 Harvard lectures on pragmatism that he first clearly saw that the circumstances described in a pragmatic clarification should include not just actual, but also merely possible circumstances. By the time he saw this, he had adopted the strong modal realism that enabled him to understand the merely possible as something other than what someone in a given state of information would not know not to be true. His indicative-mood statement of the pragmatic clarification of reality in 1905's "What Pragmatism Is" – "the state of things which will be believed in [the] ultimate opinion is real" (5.430, EP 2: 342–343) – belies the fact that he had come to understand reality as including what would be represented in beliefs permanently fixed by investigation whether or not investigation actually does ever fix those beliefs. In the sequel to that article, "Issues of Pragmaticism" (IP), he explicitly committed to pragmatic clarifications that cover the non-actual: "Is it not a monstrous perversion of the word and concept *real* to say that the accident of the non-arrival of the corundum prevented the hardness of the diamond from having the *reality* which it otherwise, with little doubt, would have had?" (5.457, EP 2: 356–357). In understanding the pragmatic clarification of reality as covering what is represented in beliefs that would be fixed by investigation even if investigation never does in fact fix those beliefs, he no longer had reason to think that that clarification of reality committed him to deficit indeterminacy.

We saw previously that it may not be sufficient, as a response to the buried secrets objection, simply to say that reality includes what would be believed by investigators. This gets around the problem of questions never asked, but it does not obviously avoid the problem of past facts for which all evidence has now disappeared. One option for dealing with that sort of buried secret is to say that the real is what would have been believed had investigation been conducted before the relevant evidence disappeared, and as noted previously, Peirce took that position at least once, in 1911 (EP 2: 457). But a few years earlier, he instead denied the objection's presupposition that there can be past facts the evidence of which has completely disappeared. In a manuscript dated ca. 1904, he once again confronted the objection, but instead of agreeing that there are questions that will never be answered and positing deficit indeterminacy, he maintained that every past event has detectable consequences:

> "But what say you to the myriad details of Napoleon's life of which no vestige remains, – his having winked, let us suppose, one night when he was in absolute darkness. Did those events not occur?" So the questioner: to

which the Pragmaticist will reply, "You speak of a wink as if it were a small event. How many trillions of corpuscles are involved in the action, through how many million times their diameters they move, and during how many billions of their revolutions in their orbits the action endures, I will not undertake to calculate. But certainly you cannot yourself think that so vast an operation will have had no physical effects, or that they will cease for ages yet to come. Certainly, when you talk of an actual event leaving at a subsequent time absolutely no consequences whatever, I confess that I can attach no meaning at all to your words, and I believe that for you yourself it is simply a formula into which by some form of logic you have transformed a proposition that had a real meaning while overlooking the circumstance that the transformation has left no real meaning in it, unless one calls it a meaning that you continue vaguely to associate the memory-feeling with this empty form of words ... The intellectual meaning of a statement is precisely the same whether it refers to past or future time." (8.195, ca. 1904)[21]

At any future time at which investigation might be conducted, there will remain at least *some* evidence relevant to any given question about the past. There are no genuinely buried secrets, no past facts that would not, in the right circumstances, have some effect on how investigators might experience the world. In IP, he drove this line of thinking even further by characterizing claims about the distant and forgotten past, not as being neither true nor false, but as being covert claims about the future:

> [A]ccording to Pragmaticism, the conclusion of a Reasoning power must refer to the Future. For its meaning refers to conduct, and since it is a reasoned conclusion must refer to deliberate conduct, which is controllable conduct. But the only controllable conduct is Future conduct. As for that part of the Past that lies beyond memory, the Pragmaticist doctrine is that the meaning of its being believed to be in connection with the Past consists in the acceptance as truth of the conception that we ought to conduct ourselves according to it (like the meaning of any other belief). Thus, a belief that Christopher Columbus discovered America really refers to the Future. (5.461, EP 2: 358–359)

If there are questions about the past that would never be settled by investigation, "questions concerning which the pendulum of opinion never would cease to oscillate, however favorable circumstances may be," then they "are *ipso facto* not *real* questions, that is to say, are questions to which there is no true answer to be given" (5.461, EP 2: 358). Other works from about the same time demonstrate that he no longer explained unanswerable questions in

---

[21] In this same manuscript Peirce emphasized that the pragmatic maxim conveys only *intellectual* meaning and leaves aside an "ingredient" of "thereness" (8.195).

terms of deficit indeterminacy, but instead took such questions to be without meaning. For example:

> Now supposing we could look without limit into the conditional future, and could foresee what would be the [end] of indefinite research to which all hindrances should have been removed, then either this research would bring some decisive answer to the problems . . . or it would leave us after all utterly undecided . . . In the latter case, the conclusion would be that no action could reasonably be based on the affirmative proposition or its negative, and that, according to the principle of pragmatism, would be as much as to say that the question was nonsensical, and that consequently there was no truth in either side, the two sides being both equally unmeaning. It thus appears that where there is any truth, inquiry would, under favorable circumstances, ultimately reach it. (R 289: 14–16, LI 304, ca. 1905)

That there are questions that would never be answered no matter how far investigation were to be pushed does not indicate lacunae in reality. Such questions are simply meaningless.

Nonetheless, Peirce continued to believe that there is deficit indeterminacy. But before considering his reasons for doing so, I will examine Cheryl Misak's interpretation of Peirce's views on the hope that regulates investigation. Certain elements of my account call Misak's reading into question, and contrasting her interpretation with my own will, I hope, make my own interpretation clearer.

7.6

As is the norm in Peirce scholarship, Misak takes what I have called the investigative aspect of Peirce's account of truth to be the result of applying the pragmatic maxim to the idea of truth.[22] She analyzes Peirce's pragmatic clarification – or as she puts it, his "pragmatic elucidation" – of truth into two conditionals. One she calls the I-T (inquiry to truth) conditional: "*if*, if inquiry were to be pursued, then *H* [a hypothesis] would be believed, *then H* is true." The other she calls the T-I (truth to inquiry) conditional: "*if H* is true *then* if inquiry relevant to *H* were pursued as far as it could fruitfully go, *H* would be believed" (1994/2004: 43).[23] On Misak's reading, Peirce asserted the I-T conditional: he held that any belief that would result from sufficiently prolonged inquiry is true. But on her interpretation, he had a

---

[22] As I showed in Chapter 2, Peirce himself did not understand it that way during the 1870s and may not have begun understanding it that way until around 1905 (R 289: 13, LI 303).

[23] Misak does without this biconditional analysis in a later treatment of Peirce's account of truth (2013: 35–37).

different attitude toward the T-I conditional: he did not assert it, but held only that we must hope that it is true. The T-I conditional is, on Misak's reading, the regulative assumption that should govern the practices of actual inquirers. Peirce "does not straightforwardly assert the principle of bivalence. He does not assert that all genuine hypotheses are either true or false. We must merely assume that any hypothesis is" (1994/2004: 155). Still, she says, this attitude toward the T-I conditional does not justify a denial of, or even suspicions about, PB, and adopting this attitude should not lead us, and did not lead Peirce, to say about any specific proposition that it is neither true nor false. This is because Peirce considered the possibility that inquiry would never settle a given question

> *only as a (subjunctive) conditional statement.* That is, he says that *if* inquiry with respect to *H* were pursued as far as it could fruitfully go, and *if* belief were still to be unsettled about *H*, then *H* has no determinate truth-value. But since the antecedent of this conditional is about what would be the case if inquiry were pushed indefinitely far, we can never assert that it is fulfilled. (1994/2004: 156)

But as we have seen, Peirce did call PB into question, not with regard to any specific question asked by actual investigators, but as a general principle about all propositions, and he did so, at least from the mid-1800s until the early 1900s, for the reasons explained in the previous section.

Now this point alone does not undermine Misak's account of investigation's regulative assumptions: it is consistent to deny PB as a universal principle but to adopt as a regulative assumption the belief that any investigative activity in which one actually engages can succeed. On the other hand, it is important what we mean here by "succeed." I think it is a mistake to understand Peirce's pronouncements about the hopes of investigators as Misak suggests. In particular, I think it is wrong to include the concept of truth in the assumption that, on his view, investigators should make about the particular course of investigation in which they are involved. Some of his characterizations of that assumption suggest that he understood it to be, not what is conveyed by Misak's T-I conditional, but only what is stated in that conditional's consequent: if we continue to investigate, then we will eventually have a permanently settled belief. For example:

> Disputes undoubtedly occur among those who pursue a proper method of investigation. But these disputes come to an end. At least that is the assumption upon which we go in entering into the discussion at all for

unless investigation is to lead to settled opinion it is of no service to us whatever. (7.334, W 3: 43, 1872)

> We cannot be quite sure that the community ever will settle down to an unalterable conclusion upon any given question . . . All that we are entitled to assume is in the form of a *hope* that such conclusion may be substantially reached concerning the particular questions with which our inquiries are busied. (6.610, 1893)[24]

I will call this the I-B (investigation-to-belief) conditional. I prefer "investigation" to "inquiry" because, as we saw in Chapter 1, Peirce's view was that it is investigation in particular – the method of science, of experience and reasoning – that is best at permanently settling beliefs. Investigation is best because it is the only method that relies on our respective experiences of the external world and communal reasoning about those experiences and thereby guides its users toward beliefs that represent reality.

In my view, the I-B conditional captures better than the T-I conditional the success that investigators should hope for in their own investigative practices. This is because, on Peirce's view, investigators should not self-consciously aim at true beliefs. They aim at *permanently settled* beliefs. As he argued in "The Fixation of Belief," it is pointless to suggest to someone that she aim at having true beliefs, because

> as soon as a firm belief is reached we are entirely satisfied, whether the belief be true or false. And it is clear that nothing out of the sphere of our knowledge can be our object, for nothing which does not affect the mind can be the motive for a mental effort. The most that can be maintained is, that we seek for a belief that we shall *think* to be true. But we think each one of our beliefs to be true, and, indeed, it is mere tautology to say so. (5.375, W 3: 248, 1877)

When investigation succeeds in permanently settling beliefs, it does so because it results in beliefs that are true. This, I think, is why he sometimes expressed the hopeful assumption in terms, not just of settled belief, but of truth, e.g.:

> It is true we shall never know the true answer to every question, but in regard to any question concerning which there is a doubt, a struggle to rid ourselves from doubt, and an attempt at investigation, we go on the assumption that sufficient research – involving perhaps more experience and reasoning than our race will ever attain to – would produce this

---

[24] Peirce sometimes stated the hopeful assumption in terms of "success" or "solutions" to the question being asked; see 8.153, ca. 1900; R 1519, NEM 4: xii, undated but no earlier than 1900; 7.219, 1901.

state of true belief. (W 3: 57, 1872; see also R 735: 3 alternative run of pages, ca. 1895; 2.113, ca. 1902)

But given the investigative aspect of his account of truth, true beliefs *just are* what are already described in the I-B conditional: the permanently fixed beliefs that investigation is best at reaching. What any investigator must rationally assume is that her investigative activities are capable of settling belief. She must, in other words, assume the I-B conditional. What's more, the assumption must be that permanently settled beliefs are *actually* attainable – not just that investigation *would*, under some ideal but practically unattainable circumstances, lead to fixed beliefs.

So I agree with Misak that Peirce held that actual investigators must assume that their activities can be successful and that that assumption does not motivate any suspicions about PB. But we disagree about the exact content of that assumption – I do not think the hope for success that it embodies should be stated in terms of truth. And we disagree about whether Peirce did in fact deny PB. And as we will see, he was eventually motivated by the failure of PB to develop a family of operators for a three-valued system of logic. But by the time of that work in triadic logic, his doubts about PB were not driven by a confusion over the subjunctive-mood clarification of the idea of reality. They were driven instead by considerations of continuity and possibility.

7.7

We saw earlier that by 1905's "Issues of Pragmaticism" (IP), Peirce had come to believe that if there are questions about the past that would never be settled by investigation, they "are *ipso facto* not *real* questions" (5.461, EP 2: 358). Nevertheless, he still seemed to hold doubts about PB. Elsewhere in IP he wrote that "there are cases in which we can have an apparently definite idea of a border line between affirmation and negation. Thus, a point of a surface may be in a region of that surface, or out of it, or on its boundary" (5.450, EP 2: 353). Let p represent a point and s represent a surface. "p is on s" affirms the presence of p on s, and its negation, "p is not on s," denies the presence of p on s. But what if we were to say that p is on the boundary, b, between s and a neighboring surface? Peirce's suggestion is that p's being on b is something that we should neither affirm nor deny. It is not true that p is on b, nor is it false that p is on b. While both p and b are real, there is no fact of the matter as to whether p is on b.

By the time he wrote "The Bed-Rock Beneath Pragmaticism" (1908), a draft of what he intended to be the fourth in his series of *Monist* articles on pragmatism, he seems to have arrived at a view quite different than the one suggested in IP. He proposed that with regard to a question that would never be answered, there is an "indefinite" truth, by which he meant a proposition that is *both* true and false. He began by reminding readers of the position that he had defended in "The Fixation of Belief":

> "That the settlement of opinion is the sole end of inquiry is a very important proposition," etc. But the further exposition of my view [in "How to Make Our Ideas Clear"] shows that it was ... that the Truth is the opinion *which sufficient inquiry would establish* and fix forever. This I later modified [in IP] by adding that there is no reason whatsoever entitling us to any confidence that the pendulum of opinion will not, in regard to any given question you please, continue to oscillate back and forth forever, in which case, in regard to such question, there is no *real* truth, at all. (R 300: 7, LI 377)

As we saw earlier, he had said in IP that there is "no real truth" when it comes to such questions, not because there is deficit indeterminacy, but because unanswerable questions are not "real questions." But in "Bed-Rock" he modified this view in an important way:

> Today, however ... I say that in such a case (if such there be), the real truth would be of an *indefinite* nature, that is, would in some measure violate the principle of contradiction, being as much *pro* as *con*, somewhat the one and somewhat the other. This theory ... alone accords with the principle of Pragmatism. (R 300: 7–8, LI 377)

As we saw in Chapter 6, by this time Peirce had come to define the indefinite (i.e., the vague) as that to which the principle of contradiction (PC) does not apply. But he also held that the fact that PC "does not apply" to a proposition does not mean that that proposition is both true and false. To my knowledge, the quoted passage is the only one in which he considered the view that the indefinite *violates* PC. This is an unfortunate position for him to have taken. It is one thing to maintain that, no matter how far investigation were pushed, "the pendulum of opinion" would continue to swing and thus to think that there is deficit indeterminacy. It is quite another to maintain that "the real truth" is "as much *pro* as *con*." Given the investigative aspect of his account of truth, that p is both true and false amounts to saying that both the belief that p and the belief that not p would eventually be permanently settled in the minds of investigators.

Happily, he seems to have abandoned that view by February 1909, the date of the final major development in his thinking about PB and deficit indeterminacy. It was then that he created truth-table definitions for several truth-functional logical connectives – various analogues of negation, conjunction and disjunction – that yield three values: V (for *verum*), F (for *falsum*), and L. He described L as "the limit" between true and false. This work is recorded in his Logic Notebook (R 339).[25]

Peirce described the triadic logic that he envisioned as "not rejecting entirely the Principle of Excluded Middle" (PEM), but as "nevertheless recogniz[ing] that every proposition, S is P, is either true, or false, or else S has a lower mode of being such that it can neither be determinately P, nor determinately not-P, but is at the limit between P and not P" (R 339: 344 r, Feb. 23, 1909). In a letter to William James written three days later, he again expressed his desire to qualify PEM in some way:

> I have long felt that it is a serious defect in existing logic that it takes no heed of the *limit* between two realms. I do not say that the Principle of Excluded Middle is downright *false*; but I *do* say that in every field of thought whatsoever there is an intermediate ground between *positive assertion* and *positive negation* which is just as Real as they. Mathematicians always recognize this, and seek for that limit as the presumable lair of powerful concepts; while metaphysicians and oldfashioned logicians, – the sheep and goat separators, – never recognize this. The recognition does not involve any denial of existing logic but it involves a great addition to it to recognize such a mode of logic that it takes no heed of the *limit* between two realms. (NEM 3: 851, Feb. 26, 1909)

We saw in Chapter 6 that by this time, Peirce had come to use "principle of excluded middle" to mean, not PB, but "the principle that no pair of mutually contradictory predicates are both false of any individual subject" (R 611: 13, 1908). PEM implies that if there are substitution instances of "S is P" and "S is not P" neither of which is true, then S is not individual, i.e., it is general. Peirce's motive for working on a triadic logic was not propositions to which PEM does not apply; it was propositions to which PEM *does* apply and that *violate* PEM. Since the propositions that take L as

---

[25] Some of the pages of R 339 on which Peirce recorded this work are transcribed in Haack (2006: 217–220). Peirce's formal work in triadic logic was first described in Fisch and Turquette (1966), and since that paper's appearance Peirce has been recognized as the first to define connectives for a three-valued formal logic. Fisch and Turquette addressed what they took to be the philosophical motivations behind Peirce's introduction of that third value; in Lane (1999) I correct what I think are serious errors in their account. In subsequent papers, Turquette explored the formal aspects of Peirce's triadic operators; see Turquette (1967, 1969, 1972, 1976, 1978, 1981/4, and 1983). See also Parks (1971). Although his 1909 work was his first toward developing a formal logic of three values, earlier Peirce had considered the prospects for a logic that recognized more than two values. In 1883 (W 4: 490, 493), he had written that a formal logic that takes *true* and *false* as its only values is less useful than one that countenances degrees of falsehood. Propositions that come close to being true are sometimes of great worth despite their being, strictly speaking, false, and a formal logic that cannot account for this is of less practical value than one that can.

their value must be those to which PEM *does* apply, they must have individual subject-terms. His concern was individuals that, for some values of "P," "can neither be determinately P, nor determinately not-P."

So what sort of individual did he have in mind? The example he provided reveals that the answer has to do with continuity:

> Thus, a blot is made on a sheet. Then every point of the sheet is unblackened or is blackened. But there are points on the boundary line; and those points are insusceptible of being unblackened or of being blackened, since these predicates refer to the area about S [i.e., the area around the subject to which those predicates are being applied] and a line has no area about any point of it. (R 339: 344 r, Feb. 23, 1909)

Peirce was fond of such examples; he employed them as early as the cognition series, in which he considered "a piece of glass ... laid on a sheet of paper so as to cover half of it" and asked "is the line under the edge of the glass covered or not?" (5.336, W 2: 256, 1869).[26] But it was only after his move to strong modal realism that he could conceive of the possibility of, e.g., the points that compose a line in terms of something other than ignorance. Those points have "a lower mode of being" in that they are not *distinct* individuals. On his late, modal conception of continuity, merely possible objects – vagues – have no distinct identity, and a collection of mere possibilities is non-discrete, continuous.

As we saw in the previous chapter, vagues are not subject to the principle of contradiction (PC): "a pair of contradictory predicates, such as 'is P' and 'is not P' (or other than every P) are both true only of Nothing, and not of any definite [i.e., non-vague] subject" (R 611: 12–13, 1908). When Peirce wrote that "the unoccupied points of a line are mere possibilities of points, and as such are not subject to the law of contradiction, for what merely *can be* may also *not be*" (4.640, 1908), he was not implying that there are real objects of which inconsistent predicates are simultaneously true. If p is a merely possible point, it is true both that p may be black and that p may be non-black (6.182, ca. 1911). Given that he held that PC does not apply to the vague, my claim that he intended his third value, L, to be taken by propositions having merely possible individuals – vagues – as their subjects might seem inconsistent with the suggestion in his Logic Notebook that PC *does* apply to L propositions: "Of course it remains true, as far as the principle of contradiction is concerned[,] that the state of things represented by the proposition cannot be V and F" (R 339: 344 r, Feb. 23, 1909).

---

[26] See also W 2: 191, 1868; 4.127, 1893.

But there is no inconsistency here. To use Peirce's terms (R 678: 34, 1910), L propositions are not "assertions of possibility"; they are not of the form "S may be P." Were they of that form, then PC would not apply to them. Instead, L propositions are "simply assertory propositions" of the form "S is P" where the subject, S, is a *merely possible individual*. Where *p* is a merely possible point on the line between the black ink blot and the white surface, it is neither true nor false that *p* is black. This is because *p* has a "lower mode of being" such that there is no fact of the matter regarding whether it is black or non-black. It is deficit indeterminate whether *p* is black.

It is surprising, though, that Peirce took this view of propositions about merely possible individuals. In fact, it is surprising that he even considered that there might *be* such propositions. As we saw in Chapter 6, his view was that merely possible individuals are not, properly speaking, individuals at all, and no merely possible individual can be designated:

> When we say that of all possible throws of a pair of dice one thirty-sixth part will show sixes, the collection of possible throws which have not been made is a collection of which the individual units have no distinct identity. It is impossible so to designate a single one of those possible throws that have not been thrown that the designation shall be applicable to only one definite possible throw; and this impossibility does not spring from any incapacity of ours, but from the fact that in their own nature those throws are not individually distinct. (4.172, 1897)

If it is "impossible to designate" a merely possible individual, then it is impossible to formulate a proposition the subject term of which represents a merely possible individual. We ought not be able to predicate anything of a single unconstructed point on a line, a possible throw of a pair of dice, or any other merely possible individual thing or event. But perhaps that was what Peirce had in mind: such propositions fail to say anything either true or false about their subjects precisely because it is impossible to designate those subjects.

At any rate, despite his continued recognition of deficit indeterminacy and his skepticism about PB, Peirce never abandoned his verbal definition of "real," his pragmatic clarification of the idea of reality, or his view that investigation compels us toward beliefs in which the real is represented as it really is. It is fitting to close with one of his final statements on these matters (R 681: 35–36, 1913):

> . . . I was many years ago led to define "real" as meaning *being such as it is, no matter how you, or, I, or any man or definite collection of men may think it to be*; where I use the long and awkward phrase in order to avoid all appearance

of meaning *independently of human thought*. For obviously, nothing that I or anybody ever can mean can be independent of human thought. That is *real* which men *would* eventually and finally come to think to be absolutely necessary to be thought in order to understand the truth, supposing the existence and advance in knowledge of the human race to be continued without any limitation, though I cannot pretend that I have as distinct an idea of exactly what that means as I could wish. But, alas, there seems to be a principle as inexorable as that of action and reaction condeming [*sic*] those creatures who enjoy the privilege of perpetually learning to find their outlook forever confined within a sharply drawn horizon, a confinement the more exasperating for the fact that they have only to exert themselves sufficiently in order to enlarge it while leaving it still a prison-wall.

Bibliography

Almeder, R. (1980). *The Philosophy of Charles S. Peirce: A Critical Introduction.* Totowa, NJ: Rowman and Littlefield.

Almeder, R. (1985). Peirce's Thirteen Theories of Truth. *Transactions of the Charles S. Peirce Society*, 21(1), 77–94.

Altshuler, B. (1980). Peirce's Theory of Truth and His Early Idealism. *Transactions of the Charles S. Peirce Society*, 16(2), 118–140.

Apel, K.-O. (2004). Peirce's Theory of Reality and Truth. In J. de Groot, ed., *Nature in American Philosophy.* Washington, DC: The Catholic University of America Press, pp. 37–52.

Aristotle. (1984). *The Complete Works of Aristotle. The Revised Oxford Translation*, Vol. 2. J. Barnes, ed. Princeton, NJ: Princeton University Press.

Armstrong, D. (2004). How Do Particulars Stand to Universals? In D. Zimmerman, ed., *Oxford Studies in Metaphysics*, Vol. 1. Oxford: Oxford University Press, pp. 139–154.

Atkin, A. (2016). *Peirce.* New York: Routledge.

Austin, J. L. (1962). *Sense and Sensibilia.* Oxford: Clarendon Press.

Baldwin, J. M. and C. Ladd-Franklin (1902). Truth and Falsity and Error. In J. M. Baldwin, ed., *Dictionary of Philosophy and Psychology*, Vol. 2. New York: The Macmillan Company, p. 720.

Bergman, M. (2011). *Peirce's Philosophy of Communication.* New York: Continuum.

Berkeley, G. ([1710] 1874). *A Treatise Concerning the Principles of Human Knowledge.* C. P. Krauth, ed. Philadelphia, PA: J. B. Lippinoctt & Co.

Berkeley, G. ([1710] 1998). *A Treatise Concerning the Principles of Human Knowledge.* J. Dancy, ed. Oxford: Oxford University Press.

Boler, J. (1963). *Charles Peirce and Scholastic Realism: A Study of Peirce's Relation to John Duns Scotus.* Seattle: University of Washington Press.

Boler, J. (2004). Peirce and Medieval Thought. In C. Misak, ed., *The Cambridge Companion to Peirce.* Cambridge: Cambridge University Press, pp. 58–86.

Cooke, E. (2007). *Peirce's Pragmatic Theory of Inquiry: Fallibilism and Indeterminacy.* New York: Bloomsbury.

David, M. (2016). The Correspondence Theory of Truth. *The Stanford Encyclopedia of Philosophy*, fall 2013 edition, E. Zalta, ed. https://plato.stanford.edu/archives/fall2016/entries/truth-correspondence/.

DeGrazia, D. (2005). *Human Identity and Bioethics*. New York: Cambridge University Press.

Devitt, M. (1997). *Realism and Truth*, 2nd edn. Princeton, NJ: Princeton University Press.

Dummett, M. (1982). Realism. *Synthese*, 52(1), 55–112.

Englebretsen, G. (2006). *Bare Facts and Naked Truths: A New Correspondence Theory of Truth*. Burlington, VT: Ashgate.

Fisch, M. (1986). *Peirce, Semeiotic and Pragmatism: Essays by Max H. Fisch*. K. Ketner and C. Kloesel, eds. Bloomington: Indiana University Press.

Fisch, M. and A. Turquette. (1966). Peirce's Triadic Logic. *Transactions of the Charles S. Peirce Society*, 2(2), 71–85; reprinted in *Peirce, Semeiotic and Pragmatism: Essays by Max H. Fisch*. K. Ketner and C. Kloesel, eds. Bloomington: Indiana University Press, pp. 171–183.

Flew, A. (1984). *A Dictionary of Philosophy*, rev. 2nd edn. New York: St. Martin's Press.

Forster, P. (2011). *Peirce and the Threat of Nominalism*. New York: Cambridge University Press.

Friedman, L. (1997). Peirce's Reality and Berkeley's Blunders. *Journal of the History of Philosophy*, 35(2), 253–268.

Galluzzo, G. and M. Loux, eds. (2015). *The Problem of Universals in Contemporary Philosophy*. Cambridge: Cambridge University Press.

Glanzberg, M. (2014). Truth. *The Stanford Encyclopedia of Philosophy*, fall 2014 edition, E. Zalta, ed. http://plato.stanford.edu/archives/fall2014/entries/truth/.

Guyer, P. and R.-P. Horstmann (2015). Idealism. *The Stanford Encyclopedia of Philosophy*, fall 2015 edition, E. Zalta, ed. http://plato.stanford.edu/archives/fall2015/entries/idealism/.

Haack, S. (1976). The Pragmatist Theory of Truth. *British Journal for the Philosophy of Science*, 27(3), 231–249.

Haack, S. (1978). *Philosophy of Logics*. New York: Cambridge University Press.

Haack, S. (1992). Extreme Scholastic Realism: Its Relevance to Philosophy of Science Today. *Transactions of the Charles S. Peirce Society*, 28(1), 19–50.

Haack, S. (1994). How the Critical Common-sensist Sees Things. *Histoire Épistémologie Langage*, 16(1), 9–34.

Haack, S. (1997). The First Rule of Reason. In J. Brunning and P. Forster, eds., *The Rule of Reason*. Toronto: University of Toronto Press, pp. 241–261.

Haack, S. (2003). *Defending Science – Within Reason: Between Scientism and Cynicism*. Amherst, NY: Prometheus Books.

Haack, S., ed. (2006). *Pragmatism, Old and New*. Amherst, NY: Prometheus Books.

Haack, S. (2013). The Real, the Fictional and the Fake. *Spazio Filosofico* (8), 209–217.

Haack, S. (2016). The World According to Innocent Realism. In J. Göhner and E.-M. Jung, eds., *Susan Haack: Reintegrating Philosophy*. Cham, Switzerland: Springer International Publishing, pp. 33–55.

Hausman, C. R. (1993). *Charles S. Peirce's Evolutionary Philosophy*. New York: Cambridge University Press.

Havenel, J. (2008). Peirce's Clarifications of Continuity. *Transactions of the Charles S. Peirce Society*, 44(1), 86–133.

Hirst, R. J. (1967). Realism. In P. Edwards, ed., *The Encyclopedia of Philosophy*, Vol. 7. New York: Macmillan Publishing Co. and the Free Press, pp. 77–83.

Hookway, C. (1985). *Peirce*. New York: Routledge.

Hookway, C. (2000). *Truth, Rationality and Pragmatism*. Oxford: Oxford University Press.

Hookway, C. (2012). *The Pragmatic Maxim: Essays on Peirce and Pragmatism*, Oxford: Oxford University Press.

Jardine, N. (1986). *The Fortunes of Inquiry*. Oxford: Clarendon Press.

Kant, I. ([1783] 2004). *Prolegomena to Any Future Metaphysics*. G. Zöller, ed. Oxford: Oxford University Press.

Kant, I. ([1787] 1998). *Critique of Pure Reason*. P. Guyer and A. Wood, eds. New York: Cambridge University Press.

Khlentzos, D. (2004). *Naturalistic Realism and the Antirealist Challenge*. Cambridge, MA: MIT Press.

Khlentzos, D. (2016). Challenges to Metaphysical Realism. *The Stanford Encyclopedia of Philosophy*, winter 2016 edition, E. Zalta, ed. https://plato.stanford.edu/archives/win2016/entries/realism-sem-challenge/.

Lane, R. (1997). Peirce's "Entanglement" with the Principles of Excluded Middle and Contradiction. *Transactions of the Charles S. Peirce Society*, 33(3), 680–703.

Lane, R. (1999). Peirce's Triadic Logic Revisited. *Transactions of the Charles S. Peirce Society*, 35(2), 284–311.

Lane, R. (2004). On Peirce's Early Realism. *Transactions of the Charles S. Peirce Society*, 40(4), 575–605.

Lane, R. (2007a). Peirception: Haack's Critical Common-sensism about Perception. In C. de Waal, ed., *Susan Haack: A Lady of Distinctions – The Philosopher Responds to Her Critics*. Amherst, NY: Prometheus Books, pp. 109–122.

Lane, R. (2007b). Peirce's Modal Shift: From Set Theory to Pragmaticism. *Journal of the History of Philosophy*, 45(4), 551–576.

Lane, R. (2009). Persons, Signs, Animals: A Peircean Account of Personhood. *Transactions of the Charles S. Peirce Society*, 45(1), 1–26.

Lane, R. (2011a). The Final Incapacity: Peirce on Intuition and the Continuity of Mind and Matter, Part I. *Cognitio*, 12(1), 105–119.

Lane, R. (2011b). The Final Incapacity: Peirce on Intuition and the Continuity of Mind and Matter, Part II. *Cognitio*, 12(2), 237–256.

Legg, C. (2014). Charles Peirce's Limit Concept of Truth. *Philosophy Compass*, 9(3), 204–213.

Loux, M. (2001). Realism and Anti-Realism. In M. Loux, ed., *Metaphysics: Contemporary Readings*. New York: Routledge, pp. 449–458.

Mayorga, R. M. (2007). *From Realism to "Realicism": The Metaphysics of Charles Sanders Peirce*. Lanham, MD: Lexington Books.

Mayorga, R. M. (2012). Peirce's Moral "Realicism." In C. de Waal and K. Skowronski, eds., *The Normative Thought of Charles S. Peirce*. New York: Fordham University Press, pp. 101–124.

Meyers, R. (1985). Peirce's Doubts about Idealism. *Transactions of the Charles S. Peirce Society*, 21(2), 223–239.

Meyers, R. (2005). Peirce's "Cheerful Hope" and the Varieties of Realism. *Transactions of the Charles S. Peirce Society*, 41(2), 321–341.

Michael, F. (1988). Two Forms of Scholastic Realism in Peirce's Philosophy. *Transactions of the Charles S. Peirce Society*, 24(3), 317–348.

Migotti, M. (1998). Peirce's Double Aspect Theory of Truth. In C. Misak, ed., *Canadian Journal of Philosophy, Supplementary Volume 24: Pragmatism*, pp. 75–108.

Misak, C. (1991/2004). *Truth and the End of Inquiry: A Peircean Account of Truth*, expanded paperback edn. Oxford: Oxford University Press.

Misak, C. (2013). *The American Pragmatists*. Oxford: Oxford University Press.

Moore, M. (2010). Peirce's Cantor. In M. Moore, ed., *New Essays on Peirce's Mathematical Philosophy*. Chicago and La Salle, IL: Open Court, pp. 323–362.

Morgan, C. (1979). Modality, Analogy, and Ideal Experiments According to C. S. Peirce. *Synthese*, 41(1), 65–83.

Morgan, C. (1981). Peirce-Semantics for Modal Logics. In K. Ketner, J. Ransdell, C. Eisele, M. Fisch, and C. Hardwick, eds., *Proceedings of the C. S. Peirce Bicentennial International Congress*. Lubbock: Texas Tech Press, pp. 207–215.

Murphey, M. (1961). *The Development of Peirce's Philosophy*. Cambridge, MA: Harvard University Press.

Murphey, M. (1968). Kant's Children the Cambridge Pragmatists. *Transactions of the Charles S. Peirce Society*, 4(1), 3–33.

Myrvold, W. (1995). Peirce on Cantor's Paradox and the Continuum. *Transactions of the Charles S. Peirce Society*, 31(3), 508–541.

Ney, A. (2014). *Metaphysics: An Introduction*. New York: Routledge.

Noble, B. (1989). Peirce's Definitions of Continuity and the Concept of Possibility. *Transactions of the Charles S. Peirce Society*, 25(2), 149–174.

Parks, R. Z. (1971). The Mystery of Phi and Psi. *Transactions of the Charles S. Peirce Society*, 7(3), 176–177.

Parsons, T. (2000). *Indeterminate Identity: Metaphysics and Semantics*. New York: Oxford University Press.

Peirce Edition Project (2001). "Scientific Fallibilism": Peirce's Forgotten Lecture of 1893. *Peirce Project Newsletter*, 4(1). www.iupui.edu/~peirce/news/4_1/4.1.htm.

Potter, V. (1996). Peirce on Continuity. In V. Potter and V. Colapietro, eds., *Peirce's Philosophical Perspectives*. New York: Fordham University Press, pp. 117–123.

Potter, V. and P. Shields (1977). Peirce's Definitions of Continuity. *Transactions of the Charles S. Peirce Society*, 13(1), 20–34.

Price, H. (2003). Truth as Convenient Friction. *Journal of Philosophy*, 100(4), 167–190.

Putnam, H. (1981). *Reason, Truth and History.* New York: Cambridge University Press.

Putnam, H. (1995). Peirce's Continuum. In K. Ketner, ed., *Peirce and Contemporary Thought: Philosophical Inquiries.* New York: Fordham University Press, pp. 1–22.

Riley, G. (1974). Peirce's Theory of Individuals. *Transactions of the Charles S. Peirce Society,* 10(3), 135–165.

Robin, R. (1967). *Annotated Catalogue of the Papers of Charles S. Peirce.* Amherst: University of Massachusetts Press.

Robin, R. (1971). The Peirce Papers: A Supplementary Catalogue. *Transactions of the Charles S. Peirce Society,* 7(1): 37–57.

Rosenthal, S. (2004). Peirce's Pragmatic Account of Perception: Issues and Implications. In C. Misak, ed., *The Cambridge Companion to Peirce.* Cambridge: Cambridge University Press, pp. 193–213.

Savan, D. (1995). Peirce and Idealism. In K. Ketner, ed., *Peirce and Contemporary Thought.* New York: Fordham University Press, pp. 315–328.

Scheffler, I. ([1974] 2011). *Four Pragmatists: A Critical Introduction to Peirce, James, Mead and Dewey.* New York: Routledge.

Sfendoni-Mentzou, D. (1995). Reply to Savan. In K. Ketner, ed., *Peirce and Contemporary Thought.* New York: Fordham University Press, pp. 329–337.

Short, T. L. (1996). Review Essay. *Synthese,* 106(3), 409–430.

Short, T. L. (2000). Peirce on the Aim of Inquiry: Another Reading of "Fixation." *Transactions of the Charles S. Peirce Society,* 31(1), 1–23.

Short, T. L. (2007a). *Peirce's Theory of Signs.* New York: Cambridge University Press.

Short, T. L. (2007b). Response [part of a symposium on Short 2007a]. *Transactions of the Charles S. Peirce Society,* 43(4), 663–693.

Short, T. L. (2010). Did Peirce Have a Cosmology? *Transactions of the Charles S. Peirce Society,* 46(4), 521–543.

Short, T. L. (2015). Empiricism Expanded. *Transactions of the Charles S. Peirce Society,* 51(1), 1–33.

Skagestad, P. (1981). *The Road of Inquiry.* New York: Columbia University Press.

Skow, B. (2010). Deep Metaphysical Indeterminacy. *Philosophical Quarterly,* 60(240), 851–858.

Smart, J. (1986). Realism v. Idealism. *Philosophy,* 61(237), 295–312.

Thompson, M. (1953). *The Pragmatic Philosophy of C. S. Peirce.* Chicago: University of Chicago Press.

Turquette, A. (1967). Peirce's Phi and Psi Operators for Triadic Logic. *Transactions of the Charles S. Peirce Society,* 3(2), 66–73.

Turquette, A. (1969). Peirce's Complete Systems of Triadic Logic. *Transactions of the Charles S. Peirce Society,* 5(4), 199–210.

Turquette, A. (1972). Dualism and Trimorphism in Peirce's Triadic Logic. *Transactions of the Charles S. Peirce Society,* 8(3), 131–140.

Turquette, A. (1976). Minimal Axioms for Peirce's Triadic Logic. *Zeitschrift für mathematische Logik und Grundlagen der Mathematik,* 22(1), 169–176.

Turquette, A. (1978). Alternative Axioms for Peirce's Triadic Logic. *Zeitschrift für mathematische Logik und Grundlagen der Mathematik*, 24(25–30), 443–444.

Turquette, A. (1981/4). Quantification for Peirce's Preferred System of Triadic Logic. *Studia Logica*, 40(4), 373–382.

Turquette, A. (1983). Defining Peirce's Verum. In V. Cauchy, ed., *Philosophy and Culture: Actes du XVIIe Con'gres mondial de Philosophie*, Vol. 2. Montreal: Editions Montmorency, pp. 842–845.

Whately, R. (1848). *Easy Lessons on Reasoning*, 5th revised edn. London: John W. Parker.

Wiggins, D. (2004). Reflections on Inquiry and Truth Arising from Peirce's Method for the Fixation of Belief. In C. Misak, ed., *The Cambridge Companion to Peirce*. Cambridge: Cambridge University Press, pp. 87–126.

Wilkinson, P. R. (2013). *Concise Thesaurus of Traditional English Metaphors*. London and New York: Routledge.

Williams, B. (1990). *Descartes: The Project of Pure Inquiry*. New York: Penguin Books.

Wilson, A. (2012). The Perception of Generals. *Transactions of the Charles S. Peirce Society*, 48(2), 169–190.

Index

a priori method, 13, 17–19, 20, 40n5
Abbott, Francis Ellingwood, 59
Absolute, the, 74, *See also* idealism, absolute
abstract terms, 132
abstraction, 10, 127, 128, *See also* hypostatic abstraction; prescission
agapasm, 81n36
Almeder, Robert, 3n2, 4n4, 24n22, 44n13, 61, 66n13, 79n33, 85n2, 106n3, 143n12
Altshuler, Bruce, 60
anancasm, 81
anti-realism, 32, 38n1, 43n9
  about artifacts, 1
  about minds, 1, 5, 7
  about modality, 148, 153
  about truths, 14
Apel, Karl-Otto, 176n11
Aristotelicity, 156, 160n37
Aristotle, 10, 16, 22, 72n25, 146, 156
Armstrong, David, 112n16
Atkin, Albert, 169n5
Austin, J. L., 5n5
authority, method of, 13, 16–17, 18–19, 33, 40n5

Bain, Alexander, 42
Baldwin, James Mark, 26n27
basic realism. *See* realism, basic
belief. *See also* doubt; methods of fixing belief
  as having no place in science, 23–24
  as sensible effect of real things, 42
  contrasted with doubt, 26–27, 28, 42, 45–46
  pragmatic clarification of the idea of, 45–46, 130n48
Bergman, Mats, 46n15
Berkeley, George, 10, 36, 43, 54, 60n3, 68, 68n19, 70, 79, 87n4, 88n5, 91n9, 97n15, 106, 112n15, 113, 114, 115n23, 116n26, 117, 120, 122, 147
Bernard of Chartres, 112n15

bivalence, principle of (PB), 11, 165, 180–181, 187, 189–193
Boler, John, 61, 106n3, 113n17, 130n48, 134n58
buried secrets, 8, 51–56, 145n14, 166–168, 174, 184–186

can be's, 144–145, 164
Cantor, Georg, 156, 157, 158
Cantor's Theorem, 158
cardinal comparability theorem, 154
Carus, Paul, 36n40, 106n2
chance. *See* tychism
clear and distinct ideas, 40–41
coenoscopic science, 27
cognition(s)
  as continuous, 89–91, 94, 96, 103
  real vs. unreal, 97
cognitionism, 97n15
conceptualism, 109–110
concrete individuals. *See* individuals, concrete
continuity, 11, 77, 90, 124, 134n58, 148, 152, 153n23, 155–164, 168, 180, 189, 192, *See also* synechism
  and generality, 157, 159, 160–161
  and possibility, 156–157, 158, 160–161
contradiction, principle of (PC), 139–142, 144–145, 161, 190, 192–193
Cooke, Elizabeth, 24n22
cosmogony, 71–75, 81, 177
cosmology, 60, 173
critical common-sensism, 64, 166n2

David, Marian, 21n18
de Waal, Cornelis, 35n37, 154n24, 157n34
"definite" and "indefinite," Peirce's uses of, 140n9
"determinate" and "determined," Peirce's definitions of, 123
deficit indeterminacy, 11–12, 56, 165–194
DeGrazia, David, 112n14

Descartes, René, 34, 69, 74n29, 91n9
determinacy, absolute, 108, 121, 123, 124, *See also*
　　individuals, strict
determinism, 72–73, 150
Devitt, Michael, 6
diamond example, 53, 55, 142–146, 163, 184
Dinge an sich. See things-in-themselves
doubt, 8, 17, 19, 32–33, *See also* belief
dreams
　　as internal, 79
　　as real, 86
　　contents of, as figments, 86
Dummett, Michael, 113n19

"Elegy Written in a Country Churchyard"
　　(Thomas Gray), 55n23, 86
emotions, as internal, 4, 79
Englebretsen, George, 24n22
ens, 96, 113
entities, 112–113
excluded middle, principle of (PEM), 110,
　　139–140, 144, 165n1, 179–181, 191–192
"existence," Peirce's use of, 71n23, 121n31,
　　128n45, 131n52, 173n8
existence, 10, 110–112, 116
　　unintelligibility of, 111–112
existential graphs, 148
external, the, 3–4, 5, 6, 7, 9, 19, 20, 29, 30, 31, 34,
　　47, 50n17, 64–65, 66, 70, 76, 77n31, 79,
　　105n22, 114n20, 119, 182, *See also* realism,
　　about the external
　　as cognizable, 94–95, 100, 121
　　as continuous with the internal, 89–92
　　as external to individual minds, 79–81
　　causes of sensation, 115, 117–121

feeling, unpersonalized, 71–72, 73, 75
　　vs. individual minds, 81–82
feelings, as external, 82–83
fictional, the, 3, 4n4, 50n17, 86, 96, 101, 110, 114,
　　142, 151, 165–166, 167–168
fictive, the. *See* fictional, the
figments. *See* fictional, the
final (ultimate) opinion, 43, 57, 58, 84, 85, 98, 116,
　　117–118, 122, 137, 167, 184
Firstness, 66
Fisch, Max, 97n15, 107, 153n23, 156n30,
　　163n41, 191n25
Flew, Anthony, 68n18
Forster, Paul, 20n14, 24n22
Fraser, Alexander Campbell, 10, 43, 87n4, 106
Friedman, Lesley, 65n11, 168n3

Galluzzo, Gabriele, 112n16
general concepts, 10, 122, 127, 128, 157

and hypostatic abstraction, 131–135
and prescission, 130–131
general facts, 178
general signs, 122–126, 129, 138, 139–140
　　and the reality of generals, 129–130
　　same as indeterminate signs on Peirce's early
　　　view, 123
general thoughts, 109
general words, 107–108
generality, 11, 111, 113, 115, 152, 163n41, 164, 165,
　　176, 179n17
　　and continuity. *See* continuity, and generality
　　and possibility, 148, 155, 160–162, 164
generals, 9–10, 11, 19n11, 43n10, 106–113, 121–122,
　　128–130, 133, 142–143, 157, 162
　　as external, 83, 107, 114n21, 121, 127–128
　　not entities, 112–113, 129, 132, 133, 134, 135
　　not existents, 110
　　that correspond to hypostatically abstracted
　　　concepts, 134
genuine, the, 5
Glanzberg, Michael, 24n22
Guyer, Paul, 68n18

Haack, Susan, 5, 13n2, 21n16, 24n22, 25n24,
　　36n39, 92n11, 112n16, 116n25, 122n33, 143n12,
　　191n25
haecceity, 112, 116, 128, 129
Harris, William T., 87n4
Hausman, Carl, 57n25, 76–77
Havenel, Jérôme, 156n28, 161n38
Hegel, Georg, 66, 70, 74, 123n35
hic et nunc, 112, 134
Hirst, R. J., 6, 60
Hookway, Christopher, 2, 4, 11, 14, 23n20, 24n21,
　　65n10, 114n22, 125n40, 136, 153n23, 174n10,
　　176n11, 179n17
　　on whether Peirce separated truth and reality,
　　　169–172
hope and investigation, 11–12, 23, 56, 178–179,
　　181–183, 186–189, *See also* optimism about
　　investigation
Horstmann, Rolf-Peter, 68n18
Hume, David, 106n2
hylopathy, 71
hypostatic abstraction, 65n9, 131–135

icons, 126
ideal world, 155n27
idealism, 7, 9, 58, 135, 172
　　definitions of, 60n3
　　Flew's statement of, 68n18
　　Hirst's statement of, 6, 60
　　Peirce's definition of, 65n11
idealism, absolute, 66–67, 70, 74

idealism, actual (Kant), 63, 64, 68
idealism, basic, 9, 59–60, 62–70, 77–78, 84, 85, 87, 90, 111, 124, 125n39, 128, 172
idealism, conceptual, 85n1, 125n39
idealism, conditional, 67, 68n19, 76
idealism, critical (Kant), 63n6
idealism, dogmatic (Kant), 91n9
idealism, empirical (Kant), 91n9
idealism, epistemological, 61
idealism, material (Kant), 90–91
idealism, mystical and visionary (Kant), 91n9
idealism, objective, 9, 60, 61, 62, 66n13, 68n18, 70–83
idealism, ontological, 6, 68–69, 70, 79, 85, 97n15
    Guyer and Horstmann's statement of, 68n18
idealism, pragmatistic, 68n17
idealism, problematic (Kant), 91n9
idealism, realistic, 66
idealism, semiotic, 85n1, 125n39
idealism, transcendental (Kant), 62–64, 70, 91n9, 179n16
idealistic theory of reality. *See* real, the (reality), idealistic theory of
identity, 166
idioscopic science, 27
indices (indexical signs), 112n13, 126–127
"individual," meaning of, 108
individualism, 108, 112n15, 129
individuals, 10, 108, 157–158, 162
    concrete, 108–109, 110–112, 116, 122, 124, 125–126, 127, 134n58, 138, 139
    strict, 108–109, 111n12, 112, 124–125, 127, 134n58, 138, 139
induction, 87
Information-Relative (IR) account of modality. *See* modality, Information-Relative (IR) account of
inkstand example, 66
inquiry. *See* methods of fixing belief
internal, the, 3n2, 4, 5, 7, 9, 20n14, 66, 79, 88, 114n20, *See also* realism, about the internal
    as continuous with the external, 89–92
    as internal to some individual mind, 79–81, 88, 107, 115, 152
interpretants, 103, 104
introspection, 88
intuition, 89, 90
investigation. *See* science, method of (investigation)

James, William, 36, 39n2, 68n17, 116n26, 191
Jardine, Nicholas, 56n24

Kant, Immanuel, 5, 46, 48, 62–64, 68, 70, 89n6, 91, 156, 160n37, 178, 179n16
Kanticity, 156, 160n37
Ketner, Kenneth, 161n38
Khlentzos, Drew, 7
Krauth, Charles, 60n3
Kripke, Saul, 112n14, 126n43

Ladd-Franklin, Christine, 26n27
laws, 19n11, 173–174, 176, 177, *See also* generals
    natural, 106, 108n5, 138n3, 148, 150, 163n41
    of perception, 29–30
    psychical vs. physical, 72–74, 75–76, 77
Legg, Catherine, 46n15
Leibniz, Gottfried, 108n7
Locke, John, 61
Loux, Michael, 1, 5, 112n16

material objects. *See* physical objects
materialism, 68–69, 73, 75, 77
mathematics, 136
matter. *See* mind(s), and matter
may be's, 140n9
Mayorga, Rosa Maria, 44n13, 53n20, 60, 66n12, 106n3, 108n5, 112n14
methods of fixing belief, 7, 13, 14–21, 24–25, 35, *See also a priori* method; authority, method of; science, method of (investigation); tenacity, method of
Meyers, Robert, 176n11
Michael, Fred, 129n46
Migotti, Mark, 24n22, 26n26, 31n33, 39n5, 46n15
Mill, John Stuart, 130n47
"mind," Peirce's use of in the cosmological series, 71
mind(s), 1, 3, 4, 5, *See also* feeling, unpersonalized
    and matter, 72, 73–76, 77, 81, *See also* idealism, objective
    universal, 61–62
mind-independence, 1, 4, 5, 6, 7, 47–48, 76, 194
Misak, Cheryl, 4, 8, 12, 14, 47n16, 50n17, 56n24, 113n17, 118n30, 136, 169n5, 176
    on bivalence and investigative hope, 186–189
    on whether Peirce accepted a correspondence account of truth, 47–50, 65n10
modal realism. *See* realism, modal
modality, 9, 10, *See also* necessity; possibility
    essential (or logical), 149
    Information-Relative (IR) account of, 11, 147–155, 156n28, 158, 160, 164, 184
    mathematical, 149
    metaphysical, 149
    physical, 149, 152

modality (cont.)
  practical, 149
  subjective, 149, 151, 153n23
  substantial, 149–153, 154–155, 160, 164
monism, 71, 73, 76
Moore, Matthew, 156n28, 158
Morgan, Charles, 148n19, 153n23
Murphey, Murray, 61, 85n1, 113n17, 130n48
Myrvold, Wayne, 154, 156n28, 161n38

necessitarianism. *See* determinism
necessity, 10, 141
neutralism, 73
Ney, Alyssa, 112n16
Noble, Brian, 153n23, 156n28
nominalism, 83, 106n2, 107–108, 114, 117n26, 127,
  128, 129, 133n54, 145, 146, 161,
  163n41, 164
nominalistic conception of reality. *See* real, the
  (reality), nominalistic conception of
nominalistic element of Peirce's theory of
  cognition, 129
nominalistic Platonism, 112, 117, 132, 134
normative sciences, 40, 135
noumena, 119

objectivity, 4, 5, 6, 7, 59n2
Ockham (Occam), William of, 128
Ockham's razor, 73n27
ontological idealism. *See* idealism, ontological
opium example, 118–119, 133–134
optimism about investigation, 54–55, 56,
  166–167, 168, 175, 176–177, 178–179

panpsychism, 61
Parks, R. Z., 191n25
Parmenides, 167
Parsons, Terence, 166
Pearson, Karl, 66, 87n4
Peirce Edition Project, 59n1, 77n30
percepts, 87n4, 92
perceptual judgments, 92n11
percipuum, the, 92n11
phenomenalism, 92
Philip of Macedon example, 123–127, 139
physical objects, 6, 20n13, 79, 83
Plato, 113n17
Plutarch, 124n37
Porter, Noah, 112n13
possibility, 10, 11, 12, 28n28, 141–144, 163n41, 168,
  189, 192, *See also* vagueness; vagues
  and continuity. *See* continuity, and possibility
  and generality. *See* generality, and possibility
  logical, 154–155
  positive and negative, 153–154

substantial. *See* modality, substantial
Potter, Vincent, 156n28, 161n38
powers, 118–119
pragmatic clarifications, 62n5, 163
  as general, 138
  do not supersede first- and second-degree
    clarifications, 44–45, 121
  indicative mood vs. subjunctive mood, 53, 58,
    95n12, 117n27, 142–143, 144, 148, 166–167,
    168, 175, 176, 184
pragmatic maxim, 8, 10, 26n26, 37, 38–41, 43, 44,
  45, 101, 102, 122n32, 130n48, 138, 145, 163n40,
  166, 183
pragmaticism, 39, 142, 143, 146–147,
  155, 185
pragmatism, 7, 35n37, 64, 67, 101, 102, 117n26,
  119, 133, 134, 143n12, 146, 148, 152, 153n23,
  162, 163, 164, 166n2, 176n12, 186, 190
prescission, 127n44, 130–131
Price, Huw, 47
probability, 148n20
propositions, 29, 126–127, 165
protoplasm, 75
psychology, 27–28
Putnam, Hilary, 30, 161n38

quantum mechanics, 166
Quine, W. V. O., 166n2

"real"
  Peirce's definition of, 5–6, 98, 114, 137, 144,
    151, 172
  Peirce's use of as synonymous with "true,"
    97–99
real, the (reality)
  absolute conception of (Williams), 65n10
  and hope, 181–183
  as a matter of degree, 169n4
  as consensus, 84–85, 93–94, 99, 101
  as ideal, 105n22
  clarification of the idea of to the first and
    second degrees, 41
  idealistic theory of, 9, 66n13, 83, 84–85, 93–105,
    116, 121
  nominalistic conception of, 113, 115–116,
    117–120, 121
  pragmatic clarification of the idea of, 3n2, 8, 9,
    10, 11, 14, 37, 38–58, 62, 67–68, 70, 76, 101,
    102, 116, 134, 135, 136, 137–138, 145n14, 146,
    147, 166–168, 169–170, 172, 173, 175,
    176n12, 179, 183–184, 189, 193
  realist conception of, 10, 43, 113, 116–120,
    121–122
  social theory of, 97
realis, 2n1

realism
  about artifacts, 5
  about minds, 5, 83, 85, 87, 88, 89, 109
  about the external, 3–4, 9, 62, 65–66, 69,
    70n21, 79, 82, 84, 85, 89, 92–94, 99,
    105n22, 119
  about the internal, 4, 70n21
  about the physical, 20n13, 83
  about truths, 14
  Devitt's statement of, 6
  Hirst's statement of, 6, 60
  Khlentzos's statement of, 7
  Loux's statement of, 1, 5
realism, basic, 2–3, 5–6, 7, 9, 20, 29, 30–34, 45, 58,
    60, 62, 65, 68, 70, 78, 84–85, 87–88, 93–94,
    96, 99, 100, 105n22, 106n2, 119, 181–182
realism, epistemological, 3n2, 79n33
realism, logical, 157n35
realism, modal, 56, 137–164
  strong, 11, 53, 95n12, 148, 153, 155, 158, 159, 162,
    163, 167, 175, 184, 192
  weak, 148, 152–153, 155
realism, scholastic, 7, 9–11, 30n30, 43n10, 65n9,
    76, 83, 106–136, 137, 142, 143, 147, 148,
    153n23, 157, 161, 163, 164, See also generals
  Early Argument for, 10, 122, 126, 127, 129, 138
  Late Argument for, 10, 137–138, 143
realism, scientific, 3n2
realist conception of reality. See real, the (reality),
  realist conception of
reality. See real, the (reality)
retroduction, 182–183
Riley, Gresham, 123n35
Robin, Richard, 25n24
Rosenthal, Sandra, 168n3
Royce, Josiah, 66–67, 70, 74, 169, 175

Savan, David, 60
Scheffler, Israel, 24n21
Schelling, Friedrich, 78
Schiller, Ferdinand Canning Scott, 36, 39n2
scholastic realism. See realism, scholastic
Schröder, Ernst, 147
science, method of (investigation), 7, 8, 9, 11–12,
    13, 14, 19–21, 24, 26, 29–31, 32, 33, 34, 35, 39,
    42–43, 44, 51–56, 57–58, 62, 84, 94, 97, 100,
    102, 117, 118, 120, 121, 122, 125–126, 127, 135,
    138, 143, 145–146, 165, 166–168, 169–170, 173,
    174, 175, 176, 182, 185, 187–189, See also hope
    and investigation; optimism about
    investigation
  and the reality of generals, 128–130, 134, 135, 136
  vs. the activities of professional scientists, 24
Scotus, Duns, 2n1, 106, 107, 108n7, 112, 113, 127,
    128, 129

Secondness, 66, 110n10
semiotic, 29, 102, See also signs; thought-signs
semiotic indeterminacy, 10, 23, 165, See also
  general signs; vague signs
  as underspecificity, 123–124
sense experience, 20, 29–30, 31
  and generals, 115–116
sentiment, 18
Sfendoni-Mentzou, Demetra, 60
Shields, Paul, 156n28, 161n38
Short, T. L., 3n2, 13n1, 15n5, 19n10, 25n23, 43n11,
    53n19, 71n22, 72, 73n26,
    74n29, 85n1, 112n13, 116n25, 123, 125n39,
    126n43, 127, 129n46, 133n55
signs, 49, 50, 86, 90, 92, 98, 103
"singular," meaning of, 108
singular signs, 139
Skagestad, Peter, 23n20, 24n22, 50n18,
    70n21, 113n17, 122n32, 130n48,
    131n50, 143n12, 162n39
skepticism, 34
Skow, Bradley, 166
Smart, J. J. C., 38n1
social impulse, 15, 17, 19, 35
sorites paradoxes, 139n4, 141n10
speculative grammar, 27
Spinoza, Baruch, 69, 123n35
strict individuals. See individuals, strict
subjectivity, 5
supermultitudinousness, 158
symbols (symbolic signs), 21, 126–127
synechism, 44n13, 77, 147n16, 157n35,
    See also continuity

Tarski, Alfred, 47
tenacity, method of, 13, 14–15, 18n9, 24n22, 40n5
things-in-themselves, 49, 59n2, 62, 63, 64–65,
    95, 119
thinking vs. thought, 58n26, 61, 109–110, 122
Thirdness, 66
Thompson, Manley, 153n23
thought-signs, 89–90, 92, 94, 98, 109, 124
  virtual meaning of, 103–105
time, continuity of, 158, 160
"transcendental"
  Kant on, 63n6
  Peirce's definition of, 63n6
triadic logic, 12, 181, 189
truth, 7, 116
  and the a priori method, 18
  and the external, 19
  and the method of authority, 16
  and the method of tenacity, 15
  as convergence, 169, 171, 172
  as indeterminate, 136

truth (cont.)
  as property of propositions, 23, 26, 28, 48–49
  as satisfaction, 8, 34–37
  Berkeleyan conception of, 36
  clarification of the idea of to the first and
      second degrees, 46–47,
  coherence theory of, 47
  correspondence theory of, 14, 21, 24n22,
      26n27, 46n15, 47–49
  deflationist theory of, 47
  genealogy of the idea of, 7–8, 13, 20, 24–29,
      38–39
  impersonal nature of, 17, 18, 19, 30
  indefinite, 190
  investigative aspect of Peirce's account of, 8, 13,
      14, 25–26, 28, 29, 30, 34, 37, 39, 42–44, 48,
      49, 51, 56, 68, 98, 117, 125, 138, 143, 145, 169,
      171, 172, 179, 186, 189, 190
  Peirce's pragmatic theory of, 8, 14, 38, 47,
      56n24
  pragmatic clarification of the idea of, 46–51,
      68, 186
  public nature of, 15–16, 17, 18, 19, 30
  representationalist aspect of Peirce's account
      of, 8, 13, 14, 21–23, 24, 25–26, 28, 30, 34,
      37, 38, 42, 48, 51, 65, 95–96, 98, 136, 143,
      165, 171

"Truth and Falsity and Error," 23, 26,
      135–136
Turquette, Atwell, 191n25
tychasm, 81n36
tychism, 72–73, 147n16, 148, 150–151, 152, 164,
      173–174

ultimate opinion. *See* final (ultimate) opinion
universals. *See* generals

vague signs, 123n36, 137, 138–141
vagueness, 10, 11, 165, 179n17, 190, *See also*
      possibility
vagues, 10, 11, 136, 137, 142, 161, 192–193, *See also*
      possibility
Venn, John, 23n19

Watson, John, 70
Welt an sich. See things-in-themselves
Whately, Richard, 108n6
Wiggins, David, 18n9, 20n13, 25n24,
      35n37, 44n13
Williams, Bernard, 65n10
Wilson, Aaron, 116n25
would be's, 19n11, 52–53, 140n9, 144–145, 164,
      168
would have been's, 55, 145